—The Great British—
CHEESE
—Book—

The Great British CHEESE Book

Patrick Rance

M

MACMILLAN LONDON

To Janet
who has stayed married to me throughout
the writing of this book, despite
three years of my antisocial hours, moods and habits;
three years of keeping things going between house and shop;
three years of reading a succession of messy drafts, unravelling their knotty ambiguities,
lightening their dark corners,
and always managing to make me feel
that the agony was worth while.

Illustrations by Chris and Hilary Evans

Copyright © Patrick Rance 1982

ISBN 0 333 28840 8

First published 1982 by
Macmillan London Limited
London and Basingstoke

Associated companies in Auckland, Dallas,
Delhi, Dublin, Hong Kong, Johannesburg,
Lagos, Manzini, Melbourne, Nairobi,
New York, Singapore, Tokyo, Washington
and Zaria

Printed in Great Britain by
Butler & Tanner Ltd, Frome and London

Contents

Preface

If human perfection truly springs from the happy coincidence of duty with pleasure, then good cheese can make momentary paragons of us all. Cheese is economical and healthy in its concentration of rich natural nourishment, and has the quality, unique among palatable foodstuffs, of actually protecting the teeth. By playing endless variations on the themes of texture, flavour and aroma it also has the versatility to cater for almost every palate. These virtues, combined in no other single form of food, make the eating of cheese a dietetic duty of incomparable delight.

The hard cheeses of England and her firm-crusted blues are the finest in the world. Apart from Stilton they are also the least known. Even our most generous original gift to humanity, Cheddar, is really known to comparatively few people. Most meet it in name alone. What they eat is some hard-pressed rectangular substitute, often foreign, usually emasculated in character and chilled into irredeemable immaturity.

I can still remember my mid-morning treat on sunny days in the 1920s as I played in the East End vicarage garden of my early childhood. Through the kitchen window a fond hand would reach out bearing a buttery crust crowned with hunks of nutty-flavoured Cheddar. From the 1930s, I can recall a pub garden of Rupert Brooke's Grantchester and my first pint of hoppy beer, set off to perfection by a tangy descendant of my childhood Cheddar. I relished it then as I have relished it ever since.

For the last twenty-seven years I have sought out, lived with and worked with every surviving variety of British cheese, alongside the rarest and finest of the foreign. If you offered me a desert island with just one kind of food, a farmhouse Cheddar would be my unhesitating choice: its mouthwatering texture and flavour could never bore, but only change for the better through all the months of eating.

My aim in sharing my private satisfaction with you is to stimulate the demand for real British cheeses: cheeses deserving of their name by being made, clothed and matured in the traditional way. The successful fight to save Real Ale, and its successor, the battle for Real Bread, proved that public clamour is necessary to preserve any rich heritage which does not conform to the convenience of mass manufacturers and sellers. Your clamorous protests alone can save our Real Cheese from being lost for ever in the rising flood of plastic-smothered insipidity. I want to revive England's pride and pleasure in her great dairy tradition, and in the tranquil countryside from which it stems.

Cheese hunting is a heart- and stomach-warming sport. It takes you to our loveliest and least spoilt regions, and into their remotest by-ways. It takes you into the dairy, on to the farm and into the farmhouse, and introduces you to some of the hardest working, healthiest and happiest people you will find anywhere.

Acknowledgements

My first and greatest debt of gratitude must go to Dr J. G. Davis. His work, *Cheese*, is not only an almost inexhaustible well of knowledge and experience, but an engaging fount of affection for his subject.

My next debt is to Caroline Gillies, who commissioned from me in 1973 an article on English cheese for the English Tourist Board. The results of my research disturbed me so much that from then on this book was struggling to be born. I thank my patient but firm editor, Angela Dyer, for acting as midwife during the last stages of an elephantine literary pregnancy, and for dealing with an infant manuscript of correspondingly excessive dimensions.

I was spurred on to accept the task by admiration for our cheesemakers: this book is my grateful attempt to help preserve their craft in a machine-dominated world, and to encourage its renaissance.

Among the many people who have helped me generally in my research I should like to thank the following: Dr George Cooke of the Agricultural Research Council; Sir William (Gregor) Henderson; P. J. Boyle, Director, Commonwealth Bureau of Pastures and Field Crops at the Grassland Research Institute; Dr Gordon Cheeseman and Dr Donald Manning of the National Institute for Research in Dairying, and the Librarian and staff at NIRD; Dr Jeffrey Harborne; Dr Bruno Reiter; Professor E. L. Crossley; Roy Cornwell of the English Country Cheese Council; Raymond Duveen. Creamery managers for the Board and Express Dairies and many farmers have keenly responded to my enquiries.

Many people have assisted me on specific subjects: *ewes' and goats' milk cheese*, Olivia Mills and the Goat Keepers' Federation and its journal; *traditional Cheddar today*, Guy Churchouse, Kay Maddever, Stan Thorp, secretary of the Farmhouse Cheddar Cheesemakers' Federation, and its members; *Devon cheesemaking*, Christopher Murray of Dartington Hall; *Blue Vinney*, Joan Ward; *Gloucestershire*, Miss Lilla Smith, Charles and Monica Martell, the staff of Gloucester Public Library; *Stilton*, Anna Cox of NIRD Library, R. H. Watson; *Derby*, Mrs D. V. S. Gibson and Mrs Janet Arthur; *Cheshire*, Verity Frampton, David and Mrs Hutchinson Smith, Oulton and David Wade, Ruth Harrison, Mark Beavan, Mr Lloyd, Tom and Ted Hassall; *Lancashire*, Mr and Mrs Butler; *Northern cheeses*, Kit Calvert, Elizabeth Steele, Kate Mason, Marie Hartley, Joan Ingilby, Mrs Longstaff, Mr and Mrs Alderson, Mr and Mrs Alwyn Cross, David Coulton; *Wales*, Leon and Joan Downey, Dougal Campbell, Joanna Gilpin; *Scotland*, the *Scotsman*, *Scots Magazine*, the staff of Edinburgh Public Library, John Godsell of Fife Creamery, Mr Gilmore of McLelland's, Dr Crawford and Miss Janet Galloway of the West of Scotland Agricultural College, Leslie Auld.

Notable restaurateurs who have given me advice include Patrick and Sonia Stevenson, Paul and Kay Henderson, Nevill and Elizabeth Ambler, Charles

Spackman, Tony Hampton, Dick Ainsworth and Gregory Ward.

I thank all the editors of journals and periodicals who found space for mention of my project, and those of their readers who responded with information. I tried to answer them all by return of post, but where I failed (as I must have sometimes) I offer my apologies and my belated thanks.

Now I come to the most vital 'without whoms' of all, those who took on an extra burden of work so that I should have time and peace for writing: my family, and my shop staff, Jenny Lawrence, Jean Harris, Betty Price, Sue Hookway, Susan Bailey, Frances Taylor and Yasmin Cade.

Finally I must reveal that no one could ever read what I have written but for the miraculous ability of Sue Stayte to decipher my manuscript. Her imperturbable cheerfulness in the face of one appalling chapter after another qualifies her for employment as a decoder of undeciphered scripts.

I have gone to great trouble to trace facts, and to check and recheck them, but if errors have crept in the fault is mine, not that of my helpers. Opinions not otherwise qualified are, of course, my own; but strong though they are, the body of technical and scientific evidence to support them has grown in the course of my writing.

My relief at finishing the book, many months past the deadline, is qualified by the inevitable regret that I could not spend as much time on it as the subject deserves. The decisive factor in my acceptance of this shortcoming is that the perfect book would never have got written, and British cheese needs urgent attention.

Part One
THE CHEESES OF BRITAIN

N

Llanllyfni
CLWYD
GWYNEDD
SALOP
Nebo
HEREFORD &
WORCESTER
Capel-Betws-Lleuco
HEREFORD
DYFED
Bredwardine
Dymock
Charlt
Esgerdawe
POWYS
Bromsberrow
King
FISHGUARD
Heath
GLOUCEST
Castle
CARMARTHEN
GLOUCESTE
Morris
GLOUCESTERSHI
PEMBROKE
GWENT
TENBY
SWANSEA
Caldy Island
GLAMORGAN
BRISTOL
CARDIFF
AVON
WILTS
WELLS
SHEPTON
MALLET
BRIDGWATER
Stoke Rivers
SOMERSET
SHAFTESBURY
BARNSTAPLE
Warkleigh
TAUNTON
SHERBORNE
Chittlehamholt
YEOVIL
Langtree
Morchard Bishop
DORSET
Newton St Cyres
EXETER
Ashwater
DEVON
DORCHESTER
HONITON
Bridford
Buckland-in
-the-Moor
CORNWALL
Harbourneford
Shinners Bridge
Withiel
Harbertonford
Ashprington
Valley
BODMIN
Loddiswell
PLYMOUTH

KEY

Farmhouse
or small dairy

Creamery

Main road

2

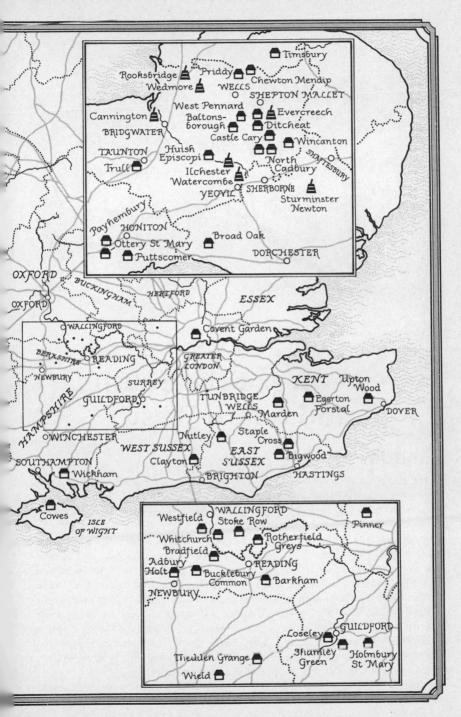

1
Cheeses of the South and South West

Cheddar

During the reign of the first Queen Elizabeth Thomas Fuller could describe cheeses made at Cheddar in Somerset as 'the best and biggest in England'. 'Their worst fault', he said, was that they were 'so few and so dear, hardly to be met with, save at some great man's table'.

Nearly four hundred years later, in the reign of Queen Elizabeth II, the same could be said. In an age when more of the world's cheese is sold as Cheddar than by any other name, Somerset's traditional cheese is still 'the best and biggest in England'. Indeed, it is the best on earth; but it has again become so rare that there is only enough of it to put on two British tables out of every three hundred where 'Cheddar' is served. As for the village of Cheddar, some of its residents had so little pride in its name in 1980 that they opposed the resumption of cheesemaking there because a dairy might smell. I am glad to report that their objections were overruled, and hope that by the time you read these lines Cheddar-made Cheddar will be on the market once more.

Somerset has always been the heart of the Cheddar country, with East Devon, Dorset and, later, Wiltshire as its satellites. Places throughout the rest of Devon and Cornwall have traditionally starred in the dairy world for their remarkable creams and butter, although Billingsley reported to the Department of Agriculture in 1794 that in North Devon 'little attention was paid to cheese or butter'. (These reports on the state of agriculture were commissioned in the late eighteenth and early nineteenth centuries from various sources, some of the writers being local and little known, as Billingsley, others of national repute such as William Marshall.

Up to 1940 Cornish pastures were largely grazed by Guernsey cows, hence her naturally golden yellow cream. Of even that splendid product, however, there could sometimes be a surplus. This was kept for up to seven days, occasionally even longer, before being bagged in muslin and left to drain on a flat surface, either on its own or under a weight. It was then ladled into muslin-lined rectangular moulds, the muslin being later folded over the curd. The eventual creamy cheese weighed about 4 ounces and contained up to 60 per cent fat.

Cheddar from the sixteenth to the eighteenth century

No doubt sheep had preceded cattle here, as elsewhere in the South of England, but Cheddar made from cows' milk must have been established in Tudor times or earlier. By the Elizabethan period village dairies were making cheeses in co-operative fashion for those local farmers whose daily milk yields were too small for farmhouse cheesemaking. This led to the unhandy habit of making very large cheeses, from 90 to 120 lb in weight, which took from two to five years to mature. Fuller noted this combination of farms at the start of the seventeenth century, and Defoe remarked on communal cheesemaking over one hundred and twenty years later. Cows grazed common land, and each man's milk was measured, so that he would profit in due proportion from the sale of the cheese, the size of which depended on the yield of milk. It can only be assumed that cheeses varied in height rather than diameter, or that smaller cheeses were made when the big mould would not take all the curd. There must have been some limit to the variety of moulds kept in the dairy. One of the biggest was needed to shape the cheese made early in the eighteenth century for Lord Weymouth (perhaps for his coming of age at Longleat): it was 'big enough to hold a girl of 13'. Big cheeses explain the need for long maturing, but their keeping quality (only approached in recent years by the top-grade Canadian cheeses we used to enjoy) suggests fine, close texture and a very high finish. Defoe wrote at this time: 'without all dispute, it is the best cheese that England affords, if not that the whole world affords.'

The parish of Cheddar was still being reported in the 1790s, along with Meare (six miles south west of Cheddar), as outstanding among cheesemaking villages; but it was the geological wonders of the Gorge that had always brought travellers from afar. The local Somerset cheeses tasted at the inns and taverns were good enough to encourage visitors to take some home to share with family and friends, to all of whom it was 'cheese from Cheddar'. By the name of the village where it was bought, it became nationally famous, as was later to be the case with Stilton (marketed but never made in Stilton). All the Somerset makers came to accept Cheddar's name and fame with good grace. If Cheddar was what people asked for, Cheddar their cheese should be called. There is a sad aspect, however, to England's casual way with names. The honourable name of Cheddar has been given away to all the world, and is now equated in its home country with mouse-trap fodder by those who only know it through eating cheese which never should have borne its name.

In the seventeenth and eighteenth centuries Cheddar was a luxury, fetching in London two to three times the price of respectable Cheshire. By the last decade of the eighteenth century, however, when Gloucester prices had collapsed, Cheddar prices were rising again, up to 6*d* a pound wholesale in 1797 for six-month-old cheeses. Many of them, and some Dorset cheeses, were sold to buyers from the London Market at Bridgwater Fair, others at Weyhill Fair in Hampshire and St Giles' Hill Fair, Winchester. Billingsley had it that they were sold in London as Bridgwater cheeses or as Double Gloucester. It can only be supposed that merchants were still trading on the peak of fame and favour attained by Gloucester cheese in the early 1780s, despite the unrivalled reputation of Cheddar by its own name, and on the special reputation for flavour won by cheeses made between Bridgwater and Cross.

The notable technical advance of the closing century was the invention of the cheese mill. This device saved labour and made the final breaking down of the curd before it went into the mould more uniform, thus contributing to more even packing of the mould and to a better Cheddar texture. Cheddar cheesemaking was plainly successful and profitable; but Billingsley, who spoke highly of Cheddar and Meare cheeses in particular, reported scathingly to the Department of Agriculture in 1794 about north Somerset herdsmanship (the Cheddar area lay mainly astride or north of the line Axbridge, Glastonbury, Shepton Mallet, south of which was said to be predominantly butter dairy). There was 'shameful inattention to the management of the milk and the wintering of cattle', which were kept out with no shelter all the year round: 'Servants must be sent to milk cows in detached and distant' enclosures. This meant a later start for cheesemaking and unsteady temperatures in the milk (and, as we now know, more risk of contamination of milk than when it is produced close to the dairy). The Dairy Shorthorn was the preferred breed, for its milk was well suited to cheesemaking and it had a long working life. Between six and twelve years of age was considered the cow's best period, and some stayed good milkers past twenty. The basic principles of Cheddar making, including the two scaldings of the curd, were well and long established by this time. One report, however, shows that external salting (see p. 8) was then practised, and sometimes repeated daily over a period of fourteen days, reminiscent of old Cheshire methods.

Wiltshire

A contemporary report by Thomas Davis, steward to Lord Bath at Longleat, paints a remarkable picture of dairy farming in north-west Wiltshire, with its rich pastures on the Lower Avon and the Thames, 'so famous for the feeding of cattle, and still more so for the production of one of the most excellent kinds of cheese this island can boast'.

There had been a recent change in grassland management with the building of winter cover, used from December or November ('sooner if need be') to avoid the poaching of the lower wetlands. Stall dung was carted to the fields as soon as cows went out, and spread as soon as the first hay was in. Quality of hay was put before quantity, with early mowing before the ear was formed, a practice whose virtue has been recently rediscovered by some (though never forgotten by others, see p. 124). The cattle were commonly fattened on extra hay alone. Newly sited farm buildings stood at the heart of the farm. The cows were brought in for milking, and the milk came fresh to the adjacent dairy where the early start made cheesemaking possible twice a day.

The old Gloucester cow, the original source of milk in this area, was by 1794 'almost extinct' and replaced by the Longhorn from the North, notable for appearance and fatter calves rather than for her dairy virtues. Marshall, who deeply loved the Gloucester, would have preferred another breed 'immediately fit for the pail'. He conceded, however, that Wiltshire's management of the dairy was 'a source of so much profit as well as credit to the county that it must in principle be right'.

The cheese had formerly been sold in London under the name of Gloucester, which it imitated, but was now well known as North Wiltshire and thought equal or superior to the cheese from the favourite Hundred of Berkeley. The rivalry had stimulated improvement; good cheese was being produced on varying soils and situations, the resultant difficulties being overcome by experienced dairywomen. The quantity of cheese now exceeded that produced by the Vales of Berkeley and Gloucester.

Up to 1914 large Wiltshire cheeses were still being made either like Gloucester in wheels, or in cylinders; but the two-scald Cheddar system was used, so regardless of shape the cheeses were distinct from Gloucesters in texture and flavour, and closer to Cheddar. Smaller cheeses, however, despite their high 'truckle' appearance, were closer to Gloucester in character. They stood 9 inches high and were called Wiltshire loaves.

Cheddar making in the nineteenth century

The nineteenth century produced three great Cheddar makers, Joseph Harding, T. C. Candy and Henry Cannon, and at the close of the century the great codifier and scientific innovator, F. J. Lloyd. Harding was born in 1805. In 1859 he published his account of cheesemaking at the Marksbury farm where his wife made Cheddar from the milk of her herd of seventy-three cows. He advocated methodical training of cheesemakers, and careful attention both to hygiene and to temperature control during making and maturing. The following year he reported his further conclusions: first, that quicker scalding of the curd to 100°F while it was still 'pulpy', immediately followed by draining of whey, milking and salting, produced a finer cheese; secondly, that a maturing temperature of 50–70°F in a dry atmosphere achieved within three months a rich standard of mellow ripeness which had sometimes earlier been difficult to obtain in eight or nine months at a lower temperature in damper conditions. Harding's system was adopted in the Lowlands of Scotland, and he was consulted by the Danes in 1866 and the Americans in 1886. Although his system excluded starter (use of starter was first mentioned by A. McArden of Kilmarnock in 1861) he was to welcome the advent of standardised rennet in 1874.

Later in the century Candy, of Cattistock in Dorset, stressed the need to keep up the temperature of the evening milk for effective ripening and was against the use of sour whey as starter. He approved of scalding, but did not follow Harding's 1860 shortening of the making process (from scald to milling). Nor did Cannon; but Cannon did recommend using starter from the previous day's whey, and varied his advice at every stage of making according to acidity. Acidity was still judged by instinct and the hot iron test. It was Lloyd who introduced a simple scientific way of measuring acidity, recorded the work of these three great Cheddar men and enriched it with new scientific reasoning and discoveries, for example, on lactic acid fermentation, inhibitory organisms and taints.

By the 1890s Lloyd found many cheesemakers using Harding's system with modifications of their own, but he was able to show how good results could be obtained from general adherence to any of the three systems, provided the essentials of hygiene, temperature control and acidity recording were observed. In 1890 the Bath and West and Southern Counties Society founded a school, appointing Cannon's daughter to teach his method of Cheddar making. This remained very much the standard until 1950, but the use of starter shortened the old process by two hours.

The twentieth century

Up to 1914 the farms were the backbone of Cheddar, but some village dairies still survived. Miss Haggett of Godney, north of Glastonbury, in the old Meare–Cheddar area, was buying most of the milk of the parish farms to make Cheddar.

The *Grocers' Handbook* of about 1910 records that 'the dairies are not sufficiently large to make cheese of a uniform size', so that Cheddars came in 14 lb tall cylindrical loaves (harder pressed and popular), and cheeses weighing 18–22 lb, 60–70 lb, and up to 1½ cwt. Among the less conventional methods mentioned by this book were the encouragement of rind formation in Cheddar by brine-soaking, or external salt-rubbing; some survivals from pre-Cheddar times, or perhaps introduced by a cheesemaker from another region. As we have seen, Wiltshire Cheddars, except for the Gloucester-type truckles, were Cheddars in varied shapes, with the new addition in the 1900s of a rectangular, wooden-boxed 'Little Wilts', about a pound in weight. I have been told that some small Wiltshire cheeses were made in the form of dolphins or other animals.

After 1918 times were hard for the farming world. Creamery manufacture of Cheddar increased, but this was still mainly unpasteurised, clothbound cheese. Many farms had gone out of cheesemaking during the First World War, and many dairy farmers were only rescued by the advent of the Milk Marketing Board in 1933, which bought all their milk with a reliable monthly cheque, and sold it back to them on the farm at a lower price if they wished to make cheese from it. In the South West 514 farms were registered as cheesemaking in 1939, the last year before the Ministry of Food centralised hard cheesemaking in factories for the duration of the war and some years after. Of those farms, 333 were making Cheddar, over one-fifth of the 117,000 tons produced in England; and it has to be remembered that all this was made in the traditional way. In 1948 the Board had only 57 Cheddar farms on its register, and by 1974 this had dwindled to 33: 2 farms in Devon, 2 in Dorset and 29 in Somerset. This was the year in which significant distaste for prepacked cheese and demand for 'fresh cut' was publicised in a market research report. At this stage few farms had gone over to factory-scale production of block cheese, but some esteemed makers had retired because of the rigid grading practice followed since the Second World War.

The varied character of Cheddar

The characteristics of good Cheddar have always varied from farm to farm, season to season, and cheesemaker to cheesemaker. Sweet and sharp, moist and hard, provided that they have keeping quality, all are part of the variety needed to suit different tastes. Unfortunately the wartime austerity demanded by the Ministry of Food left its mark in the preference among graders for 'safe cheeses', which meant cheeses of the drier, harder, more uniform type. The more interesting and individual traditional artistry which also produced looser, moister cheeses tended to be eliminated and wasted on the cheese processing factories. One of the finest Cheddar farmers whose cheeses I have matured, eaten with relish and sold to happy customers, retired prematurely because he could not, or would not, bend his methods to the grading fashion. I mourn the loss of his rich dewy cheeses. It was and still is important that the earlier flexibility of grading practice should be restored, allowing cheeses about which graders have reservations a second chance to prove their virtue after two months or so of maturity. Block Cheddar produced at Express Dairies' new Devon factory in 1974 was graded at two months so I can see no reason why a farmer should accept less latitude for his more valuable produce. Apart from its virtues of flavour and texture, moist cheese will ripen faster than hard cheese, a financial advantage of great importance.

It is as unintelligent to grade all cheeses in infancy as it was to price all meat on the hoof, rather than on how it cuts up. The loss to the quality cheese market is uneconomic and inexcusable. The love and long labour that goes into the making of these cheeses, backed by a combination of chemistry and intuition, is akin to the work and devotion of the winemaker. And the months of a good Cheddar are like the years of a good wine. Some mature in a few months, some need fifteen to twenty-four.

Dr J. G. Davis, in the preface to Volume III of his book _Cheese_, writes: 'English _real_ Farmhouse Cheddar, English factory Cheddar, New Zealand Cheddar and Canadian matured Cheddar may differ more among themselves than do the common French unripened soft cheeses which bear distinctive names.'

The introduction of 'block' cheese

If this was true of the cylindrical cheeses Dr Davis was writing about, the gap between farmhouse traditional cheese and farmhouse block, let alone factory block, has become a chasm. The Milk Marketing Board itself demonstrated in June 1978 that a large number of assorted guests, tasting 'blind' two anonymous identical-looking pieces of nine-month old farmhouse Cheddar, unanimously preferred the flavour of the piece which, it transpired, had been cut from the heart of a traditional clothbound cheese. The other had been made as block. The Cheddar farms have been so swept along with the tide of the Board's block policy that in 1978-9 77 per cent of their production was in this form. Of all the

Cheddar made by English farm and creamery put together, only 2.4 per cent is the traditional kind which the tasters preferred.

If good creamery traditional Cheddar were made in quantity the customer might find some consolation; but now, when public taste has demonstrated effectively in the realms of beer and bread and many other aspects of food that it wants more variety and better quality, the Milk Marketing Board and Express Dairies have shut their ears and emitted almost nothing but streams of plastic-coated extruded curd. This they call Cheddar. The *Daily Telegraph*'s food writer, Paula Davies, wrote in November 1979 that it was hard to buy really mature Cheddar because supermarkets were only interested in quick turnover. She said she would rather pay more than have to buy 'an immature cheese masquerading as mature'. Nearly a third of the public is known to share this view. Disappointment leads many of them to buy foreign cheese instead.

The only gesture towards cheese-shaped cheese is the production at the Board's Watercombe and Sturminster Newton creameries of cylindrical, waxed cheeses. These are not made for very long keeping, but unfortunately they were released much too young in 1978, when one of the largest farm producers of traditional Cheddar went over to block. This provoked strong reaction among Keymarkets' customers. Having been used to this particular farmhouse cheese at one year's maturity, they blenched at the two-month-old substitute, and turned instead to other more expensive cheeses. Thus do mass production and fallen standards of maturing lose sales.

A return to traditionally made Cheddar?

Two big London cheesefactors with national trade, Anthony Rowcliffe and John Adamson and Son, told me in 1980 that their demand for traditional cheese had been growing over the previous eighteen months, on both the home and the export market. Anthony Rowcliffe himself, who has been selling less and less block, reminded me that the big farm change to block had come in the middle of a traditional cheese publicity campaign, sponsored by the Milk Marketing Board and featuring John Arlott. J. T. P. Williams and K. C. Plowman, who run the only Board creameries making traditional Cheddar (and almost no block), have found a steady demand, with a suggestion of growth since 1979. Express Dairies had wind of the traditional trend in that year, and I was told that winter by one of their research scientists that they were considering going into traditional truckles again in the South West. Some of the best hard truckles I have ever had came years ago from the Bladen creamery at Milborne Port. Even when converted by Express Dairies to block, Bladen cheese remained for some years an exceptionally agreeable example of the species. Then the cheeses were not only let out at eight weeks (frankly admitted on their dated wraps), but obviously stored at much too low a temperature. When opened they collapsed into a sweaty stodge of unpleasant flavour and I had to give them up. My letter of complaint was not answered.

Duncan Reekie, managing director of Matthews and Skailes, old-established factors, complained in 1974 that the reputation of English Cheddar was being threatened by 'some suppliers and retailers' who were releasing cheese too young because of a shortage of matured cheese. Express Dairies said that three months was the minimum and that it was 'not in anyone's interest to take it out carlier'. They had certainly proved their point with me over Bladen. Unigate said: 'There is no deliberate policy to cut the age of cheese. Ours is going out at around 12 weeks. It is true that with the supply position being so tight mature cheese – which needs seven months upwards for maturing – is not around. But we would restrict sales rather than send out immature cheese just to meet demand.' Mr Reekie was right, of course.

Unigate was then producing about half Britain's total output. Express Dairies' production, with no traditional output (even after those 1979 thoughts), is just under a quarter of the whole; Co-operative Wholesale Society produces 10 per cent (all block), and the Board, now swollen by the acquisition of Unigate Creameries, produces about 60 per cent. This is not a healthy position for a country asking for better Cheddar; and it is exacerbated by the folly of putting farms to block making. Even after the virtual elimination (through the EEC) of our old Canadian and New Zealand Cheddar imports, nearly a third of our Cheddar consumption was met by imported block 'Cheddar' in 1978. Increased supplies of traditional Cheddar properly matured could reduce the impact of European 'Cheddar' on our market. This is particularly important now that Commonwealth cheese is returning in increasing quantity.

In 1980 the Board told me that 23 farms in Avon, Somerset, Dorset and Devon were still making Cheddar. Only 11 of these make it in traditional form, and all but 3 of the 11 pasteurise their milk, inexcusable for farm cheesemakers. These are the reasons given to me. Some were told (by unscrupulous machinery salesmen?) that EEC regulations would enforce pasteurisation in a few years' time; I cannot see French farmers or dairymen bowing to such effrontery, any more than our own North Country dairymen-farmers have. Most farms rely for half or more of their milk on 'co-operators'. In earlier days farmhouse cheese had to be made on the farm, of milk of that farm. The restriction was then loosened to allow the farmer to get up to 50 per cent of his milk from another (co-operator) farm. There are now 160 co-operators shared among at the most nineteen farms making cheese with milk from outside. As some of the nineteen only have from one to four co-operators, these figures expose the mockery of applying the label 'Farmhouse Cheddar' to the factory-scale product of the biggest makers, whose milk may come from up to twenty farms. This lack of immediate control over herdsmanship and the milking operation is the biggest reason for pasteurisation of milk (see Chapter 8).

Hope for the future of Cheddar

In the cause of fuller and more varied flavours and of quicker ripening, it is to be hoped that at least some block cheesemakers will go back to traditional production, and that the traditional farm cheesemakers will overcome the obstacles to making their cheeses of unpasteurised milk. Fortunately, outside the Board's registered farms, an increasing number of other farmers are going into cheesemaking. All that I know of are given in the list which follows overleaf. A notable new feature is the South Hams area of Devon, where Dartington Farms (themselves cheesemakers) are encouraging four farms and a small dairy in cheese production and helping to sell it in their shop at Shinners Bridge. This should be a spur to other potential cheesemakers. Any farmer with fewer than twenty cows need have no dealings with the Board. The only formality (if sale to the public is contemplated) is to get the help of the Agricultural Development Advisory Service, Great Westminster House, Horseferry Road, London S.W.1, in becoming licensed to sell your dairy products.

Sources of traditional Cheddar and other cheeses in the South West

CORNWALL

WITHIEL VALLEY DAIRY, Withiel Valley (*5 miles W. of Bodmin*)
Visitors welcome
1   Cornish Hard
Natural crust; loose
Cheddar type, but distinctive flavour
2   Cornish Cream
With garlic, herbs and black pepper; no crust; small
3   Goat
Plain or with herbs
All UNpasteurised, vegetarian (no animal rennet)
Jersey herd
Where to buy: At dairy; Truro: Real Ale and Cheese Shop, 9 New Bridge Street

DEVON

THE OLD RECTORY, Ashwater (*about 8 miles N.N.E. of Launceston or S.S.E. of Holsworthy, E. off A388*)
Visitors welcome
Hard Goat Cheese
Rindless; about 1 lb round
Farmer, cheesemaker: Paulien Veltman
Toggenberg, British Saanen, British Alpine goats
Where to buy: On farm; Tavistock: Creber Delicatessen and Health Store

STAPLETON FARM, Langtree (*3 miles S.W. of Great Torrington*)
Cottage Cheese
No crust
Farmer: P. Duncan
Where to buy: On farm; Bovey Tracey: W. Mann and Son

BUTLER'S FARM, Chittlehamholt (*11 miles S.E. of Barnstaple*)
1   Cheddar
Natural, clothbound; 3–10 lb
2   Cheshire Type Herb Cheese
Rindless; herbs are home-grown
3   Cream Cheese
All UNpasteurised

Farmer: Sally Oakley; *cheesemaker:* Bisi Vernon
Channel Island and Friesian herd; permanent pasture and leys, partly organic
Where to buy: On farm; South Molton Pannier Market

PARK FARM, Warkleigh (*9 miles S. of Barnstaple via Umberleigh and 2 miles N.E. of Chittlehamholt*)
Visitors welcome
1   Plain or Herb Goat Cheese (Vegetarian)
3–4 lb drums
2   Chittlehamholt White
Cheshire type: plain or with herbs; 8 lb truckles
3   Devon Garland
Pressed with centre layer of herbs; 8 lb wheels
All natural, clothbound; UNpasteurised
Moist summer cheeses mature in 6 weeks; firmer cheeses need 3 months
Farmer: Peter Charnley; *cheesemaker:* Hilary Charnley
Anglo-Nubian and Toggenberg goats; Jersey cows; permanent pastures (half water meadows)
Where to buy: On farm; Barnstaple Market: own stall; Bideford: Whole and Hearty; Cambridge: Arjuna; London: Paxton and Whitfield, Jermyn Street, S.W.1; Totnes: Dartington Cider Press Centre, Shinners Bridge

SUE LUGG'S SMALLHOLDING, Stoke Rivers (*E. of Barnstaple via Goodleigh or via A39 to N.E., turning right after 2½ miles*)
Visitors welcome
Soft Goat Cheese
Plain or with garlic, parsley and chives, or walnut and winter savory; UNpasteurised; no crust; 4 oz cartons
Young unripened cheeses
Farmer, cheesemaker: Sue Lugg
Toggenberg goats
Where to buy: At house; Barnstaple Pannier Market

LITTLE CHILLATON FARM, Loddiswell
(_5 miles N. of Kingsbridge_)
Cheddar
UNpasteurised; natural crust
Farmer, cheesemaker: Dr Delia Elliott

BEENLEIGH MANOR FARM, Harbertonford (_3 miles S. of Totnes on A381_)
Visitors welcome in the afternoon
Beenleigh Blue
Made from UNpasteurised ewes' milk; natural crust; 4 lb drums
Farmer, cheesemaker: Robin Congdon
East Friesland sheep; river meadows (including water meadow); permanent pastures on Devon Red Sandstone
Where to buy: On farm (wholesale or retail); Totnes: Dartington Cider Press Centre, Shinners Bridge; Streatley: Wells Stores

SHARPHAM FARM, Ashprington (_2 miles S. of Totnes_)
Visitors tel. Harbertonford (080 423) 216
Cheddar
UNpasteurised; natural, clothbound; 2 lb truckles
Farmer: Maurice Ash; _manager:_ Garth Bromley
Jersey cows, Mule and Border-Leicester sheep
Where to buy: On farm; Totnes: Dartington Cider Press Centre, Shinners Bridge
It is hoped to milk the ewes in 1982 to provide extra milk for Beenleigh cheesemaking

DARTINGTON HALL HOME FARM, Dartington Cider Press Centre, Shinners Bridge (_2 miles N.W. of Totnes_)
Visitors welcome; cheesemaking to view through dairy windows
1 Dartington Truckle
Cheddar: plain, herb or smoked; natural clothbound; 2 lb cylindrical; made salt-free to order
2 Dartington Soft Cheese
Natural crust; 8–10 oz
Both UNpasteurised
Cheesemaker: Charlotte Crawford
Friesian herd; permanent pastures on medium loam
Where to buy: Dartington Cider Press Centre (also by post and wholesale); London; Paxton and Whitfield, Jermyn Street, S.W.1
This enterprise encourages cheesemaking on Devon farms, selling their produce as

well as small-scale cheesemaking equipment, including moulds to order

MOORLANDS, Harbourneford, South Brent (_on old Buckfastleigh/Plymouth road_)
Visitors welcome
Goat Cheeses
Various types, all UNpasteurised
Farmer, cheesemaker: Judy Hewitt
British Alpine, British Saanen, Anglo-Nubian goats
Where to buy: At house; through Mrs Hewitt's catering business, tel. South Brent (036 47) 3225

THE GARDEN, Buckland-in-the-Moor (_2 miles N.W. of Ashburton_)
Visitors tel. Ashburton (0364) 53169
Coulommiers
Made from UNpasteurised goats' milk; natural crust
Farmers, cheesemakers: Charles and Mary Staniland
British Toggenberg goats
Where to buy: At house
Charles Staniland learned cheesemaking in the Pyrenees

STONEMILL FARM, Bridford (_4 miles E. of Moretonhampstead_)
Visitors welcome, casual or tel. Christow (0647) 52195
1 Soft Feta Type
No crust; 4 in. cubes stored in brine and whey
2 Hard Goat Cheese
Natural crust; 3–5 lb cylindrical
Both made from heat-treated goats' milk
Cheesemaker: Mrs Mary Pinnington
British Saanen, Anglo-Nubian goats
Where to buy: On farm (will post hard cheese); local shops; Plymouth: El Greco Restaurant, Barbican
Mrs Pinnington teaches cows' and goats' milk cheesemaking

LYDCOTT, Frost, Morchard Bishop (_7 miles N.W. of Crediton_)
Visitors welcome
1 Soft Goat Cheese
UNpasteurised; no crust; 100 g. round
2 Coulommiers Type
UNpasteurised; natural crust; 8 oz round
Cheesemaker: David Evans
British Toggenberg goats, Ayrshire cows

Where to buy: At house; Crediton: Food Fayre; Newton St Cyres: Home Farm Shop (see below); Topsham: Saturday morning market

HOME FARM, Newton House, Newton St Cyres (*5 miles N.W. of Exeter on A377*)
Visitors tel. Newton St Cyres (039 285) 222
1 Traditional Cheddar
Natural crust; 5 lb, 60 lb cylindrical
2 Double Gloucester
Clothbound; 40 lb cylindrical
Close-textured, warm-flavoured cheeses. Most sold at 5–6 months, but cheeses of 9 months or more available
Farmers: J. B. Quicke family and partners; *cheesemaker:* Barry Rowe
Pedigree Friesian herd
Where to buy: At farm shop (retail, wholesale); London: Paxton and Whitfield, Jermyn Street, S.W.1
This farm also has a herd of Friesland/Dorset sheep which are not yet milked for cheesemaking

LITTLE BURCOMBE, Ottery St Mary (*10 miles E. of Exeter*)
Soft Garlic Cheese
Small; no crust
Cheesemaker: Mrs D. Lea
Where to buy: On farm

MILTON FURZE, Payhembury (*3½ miles N. of Ottery St Mary, 2 miles S. of A373*)
Visitors tel. Broadhembury (040 484) 300
1 Hard Colby
Natural crust; 1½–2 lb cylindrical
2 Feta
Made from UNpasteurised goats' milk; no crust
Farmer: Dr D. A. Whitehead
Saanen goats; permanent pastures on loamy clay
Season: March to December
Where to buy: On farm

HIGHER WISCOMBE FARM AND WINERY, Puttscomer (*between Sidmouth and Seaton, turn off A3052 on to B3174; turn E. for 2½ miles at Hare and Hounds*)
Visitors always welcome
1 Coulommiers Type
Natural crust; 11 oz, 1¾ lb
2 Lactic Cream Cheese
No crust; 110 g. pots
Both UNpasteurised
Farmer, cheesemaker: Mrs Helen Downs

British Toggenberg goats; mainly permanent pastures, plus herbal leys, lucerne, kale and root rotation, woodland and orchard; slightly acid soil
Season: All year, but telephone first in winter, Farway (040 487) 360
Where to buy: On farm; Honiton: Davey's; Seaton: Golden Hamper
Mrs Downs will teach cheesemaking to groups of five or under

DORSET (SOUTH-WEST)

DENHAY, Broad Oak (*3 miles N.W. of Bridport*)
Only trade visitors to cheese house, tel. Bridport (0308) 22717
Traditional Cheddar
Pasteurised; natural, clothbound; 56 lb cylindrical
A Cheddar of gentle flavour
Farmers: Streatfeild Hood; *cheesemaker:* Ken Corben
Friesian herd; clay loam
Where to buy: On farm, Monday and Thursday only

SOMERSET

HAMWOOD FARM, Trull (*1 mile S. of Taunton, N. of M5*)
Visitors welcome; parties please telephone well in advance, Blagdon Hill (082 342) 248
Traditional Cheddar
UNpasteurised; natural, clothbound; 56 lb cylindrical
Farmers: H. and E. J. Grant
Where to buy: On farm
Real traditional methods used here, with upright presses and hand-rolling of butter in the dairy adjoining old farmhouse

CANNINGTON CREAMERY (*2 miles N.W. of Bridgwater*)
Lymeswold
Soft blue, mild, pasteurised; 2¼ lb flat, round
Dairy Crest's latest addition, perversely named for Somerset cheese

CRACKNELL FARM, Huish Episcopi (*1 mile E. of Langport, off A372*)
Visitors tel. Langport (0458) 250731
Goat Cheese
Where to buy: On farm

WEST TOWN HOUSE, Baltonsborough
(*3 miles S.E. of Street, S. of Glastonbury*)
Visitors tel. Baltonsborough (045 85)
50260
Traditional Cheddar
Pasteurised; natural, clothbound; 60 lb
cylindrical
Farmers: R. L. Clapp and son
Where to buy: On farm

ROOKS BRIDGE DAIRY, Rooks Bridge
(*between Burnham-on-Sea and Wells on
A38, 1 mile E. of M5*)
1   Traditional Cheddar
Natural, clothbound; 4 lb, 9 lb truckles
These excellent cheeses mature to an
agreeable flavour in 6 months, though
larger truckles can be matured for up to a
year for greater strength; the smaller
cheeses are thinner, more tubular than
most small truckles, and liable to over-
harden if kept too long
2   Block Cheddar
Rindless; 10 lb, 40 lb rectangular
All pasteurised
Where to buy: Through most good cheese
factors (wholesale); many shops

WALNUT TREE FARM, Heath House,
Wedmore (*7 miles W. of Wells, S. of
B3139, B3151 crossing*)
Traditional Caerphilly
UNpasteurised; natural crust; 5 lb, 8 lb
Can be kept longer than creamery Caer-
philly and develops a rich flavour
Farmer: R. Duckett
Where to buy: On farm; Chewton Mendip:
Priory Farm Shop; Streatley: Wells Stores

NEWTON FARM, West Pennard (*3 miles
E. of Glastonbury*)
Visitors tel. Glastonbury (0458) 32952
Traditional Cheddar
Pasteurised; natural, clothbound; 60 lb
cylindrical
Farmer: John Green; *cheesemaker:* David
Higdon
Friesian herd; permanent pastures on clay
and peat
Where to buy: On farm

UNIGATE CREAMERY, Evercreech
(*3 miles S.E. of Shepton Mallet on
B3081*)
Cream and Cottage Cheeses
With chopped ham, vegetables, fruit, nuts,
etc.; no crust; tubs
Where to buy: Evercreech: Top Shop

DITCHEAT HILL FARM, Ditcheat, near
Shepton Mallet
Visitors tel. Ditcheat (074 986) 213
(though not necessary)
Traditional Cheddar
Pasteurised; natural, clothbound; 60 lb
cylindrical
Farmer, cheesemaker: John K. Longman
Ayrshire, Friesian herd; medium loam,
good fertile grassland
Where to buy: On farm
*This is the fourth or fifth generation of
cheesemaking by the Longman family on
their 1000 acres of farmland. The dairy,
with cheese store above, was added to the
existing farmhouse 200 years ago*

MARYLAND FARM, ABBEY FARM,
MANOR FARM, Ditcheat
1   Traditional Caerphilly
Pasteurised; unbound; 9 lb millstone
**2   Block Cheddar, Leicester, Double
Gloucester**
Pasteurised; rindless
Farmers: A. J. and R. G. Barber
Where to buy: Maryland Farm (Caerphilly,
wholesale); North Cadbury: North Leaze
Farm (wholesale); Streatley: Wells Stores
(Caerphilly)

MANOR FARM, Castle Cary
Visitors tel. Castle Cary (0963) 50286
Traditional Cheddar
Pasteurised; natural, clothbound; 4 lb, 6 lb,
9 lb truckles, 60 lb, all cylindrical
After a year acquires a firm but creamy con-
sistency and a rich, not sharp, flavour
Farmers: Guy and E. C. Churchouse, W. J.
and R. E. H. Longman; *cheesemaker:* Roy
Cronie
Friesian herd; light stone brash to medium
loam
Where to buy: At farm shop; North Cad-
bury: North Leaze Farm (wholesale or re-
tail); Streatley: Wells Stores

MILK MARKETING BOARD CREAMERY,
Bunford Lane, Watercombe, near Yeovil
Visitors by appointment, tel. Yeovil (0935)
23071
1   Traditional Cheddar
Clothbound, waxed; 14 lb truckles, 56 lb
cylindrical
Kept for 4–8 months before sale
2   Double Gloucester
Clothbound; 30 lb wheels
3   Leicester
Clothbound; 30 lb

Manager: J. J. P. Williams; *cheesemaker:*
Ron Groom
Local milk
Where to buy: Crewe: Embertons; Wells:
Crump Way

ILCHESTER CHEESE COMPANY, Free
Street, Ilchester
1   Ilchester
Cheddar with beer and garlic
2   Applewood
Paprika-coated smoked Cheddar
3   Cheddar
With port, sage or pickle
4   Double Gloucester
With onion and chives, or mustard pickle
All rindless; 10 lb drums
Where to buy: At dairy (wholesale); London: Crowson (also at Cheltenham
branch)
*In the early 1960s a hotelier, Ken Seaton,
played about with leftovers of Cheddar,
garlic and Worthington E and invented
Ilchester cheese, first sold in pots. Others
followed, including a Stilton with port;
only the large cheeses are made now*

NORTH LEAZE FARM, North Cadbury (*8
miles E. of Ilchester, N. of A303*)
Visitors tel. North Cadbury (0963) 40285
1   Block Cheddar
Rindless; 40 lb rectangular
2   Traditional Double Gloucester
Coloured and white; natural crust; 17–
20 lb wheels
3   Leicester
Clothbound; 17–20 lb wheels
All pasteurised
Traditionals are tasty and quick maturing
Farmers: Longman brothers; *cheesemaker:*
Martin Biggs
Friesian herd; low-lying clay and sandy
loams
Where to buy: At farm shop; Castle Cary:
Manor Farm Shop; Galhampton: Longman
Farmhouse Fare, Fir Tree (wholesale);
Streatley: Wells Stores (Double Glouces-
ter)

MANOR FARM, North Cadbury
Visitors tel. North Cadbury (0963) 40243
Traditional Cheddar
UNpasteurised; natural, clothbound; 8 lb,
55–60 lb truckles, cylindrical
Noted for its individual character and full
flavour, as good as any I have tasted
Farmers: J. A. and N. E. F. Montgomery
Ayrshire/Friesian crosses, with Holstein

blood through AI; parkland, permanent
pastures and leys, medium loam soil
Where to buy: On farm

MOORHAYES FARM, Wincanton
Visitors, small numbers only, tel. Wincanton (0963) 32286
Traditional Cheddar
UNpasteurised; natural, clothbound; 60 lb
cylindrical
Farmers: G. H. and D. M. Keen and sons;
cheesemaker: Victor Parsons
Friesian herd; valley clay and higher sandstone
Where to buy: On farm
*Cheddar has been made on this farm for as
long as anyone can remember. The Friesians achieve a butterfat level of 4.1 per
cent*

DORSET

MILK MARKETING BOARD CREAMERY,
Sturminster Newton (*E. of Blackmoor
Vale, 12 miles S. of Wincanton*)
Visitors by appointment, tel. Sturminster
(0258) 72617
1   Traditional Cheddar
Clothbound, waxed; 60 lb cylindrical
2   Top Hat Truckle Cheddar
Red waxed; 14 lb cylindrical
Matured for 3–4 months
3   Traditional Double Gloucester
Clothbound, waxed; 28 lb wheels
4   Caerphilly
Natural crust; 8 lb wheels
Manager: K. C. Plowman; *cheesemaker:*
Derek Hall
Where to buy: Sturminster market, Mon-
days 8 a.m.–4.30 p.m.
*Avis Colnett taught Double Gloucester
cheesemaking at this creamery in the early
1950s (see p. 30, 31)*

SOMERSET

PRIORY FARM, Chewton Mendip (*5
miles N.E. of Wells on B3114*)
Visitors welcome, 8 a.m.–5 p.m. Monday
to Friday; closed for lunch Saturday and
Sunday; tel. Chewton Mendip (076 121)
560
Traditional Cheddar
Pasteurised; natural, clothbound; 5 lb,
6½ lb, 8 lb, 60 lb truckles
Farmer: Lord Chewton; *cheesemaker:*
Peppy D'Ovidio
Friesian, Ayrshire herd; carboniferous
limestone-based medium loam

Where to buy: On farm (wholesale or retail; will post also); Streatley: Wells Stores _Cheese is made here with milk from this and three neighbouring farms on Earl Waldegrave's estate. Cheesemaking can be seen every morning, and butter-making by hand two or three afternoons a week_

WELLINGTON FARM, Priddy (_5 miles N. of Wells via Wookey Hole_)
Visitors welcome
Soft Goat Cheese
Plain or with garlic, chives, spring onions, herbs, or coated (poppy seeds, dill seeds, etc.); no crust; 4 oz rounds (occasionally larger), tubs
Farmer, cheesemaker: Mrs Sue Humber
British Saanen, British Toggenberg goats; permanent pastures
Where to buy: On farm

AVON

SLEIGHT FARM, Timsbury (_8 miles S.W. of Bath on B3115_)
Visitors welcome (but dairy not always manned), tel. Timsbury (0761) 70620

1   Soft Goat Cheese.
Unripened; with oregano and garlic, pepper or rosemary; no crust (but acquires natural mould with keeping); small, cylindrical
2   Pickled Goat Cheese
No crust (sealed in brine in bags); 5–8 oz pieces
3   Hard Goat Cheese
Waxed or olive oil rubbed rind; 8 lb cylindrical
All UNpasteurised
Farmer, cheesemaker: Mary Holbrook
British Alpine, British Saanen, British Toggenberg, Anglo-Nubian goats, East Friesland, Dorset Horn sheep; old permanent pastures on clay
Season: March to November
Where to buy: On farm; Bath: Abbey Delicatessen, Harvest, La Bottega; Frome: Waites; London: Harrods; Saltford:, The Cake Shop; Timsbury: V.G. Foodstores; Wells: Good Earth
In 1982 it is planned to use mixed goats' and ewes' milk

The South

For many years cheesemaking was almost unheard of in the Southern Counties. Indeed, two regional officials of the Milk Marketing Board in Reading seriously discouraged the idea of its revival in Sussex. Fortunately a number of enterprising farmers and smallholders have got going despite the Board, and those minded to join them should contact the Agricultural Development Advisory Service.

Most of the southern cheese farming is isolated, and individual in character, but there is one pocket of hard cheese making around Dorking in Surrey which deserves mention. At least four farms are making there, using Cheddar and traditional Welsh recipes, some with herbs and some smoked. So far as I know their enterprise benefits only these farming families and their 'privileged friends' (to quote one of them); but I earnestly exhort them to expand production enough to allow the sale of their cheeses to wandering cheese lovers, and perhaps to the local public in certain shops in their district.

My tour through the South of England begins in the Isle of Wight, crosses to Hampshire, with the splendid Dutch cheesemaker Albert Van Dieyen at Wickham, the Bicknell Jersey cheeses of Thedden Grange and Olivia Mills' ewes' milk banons. It meets goats in Berkshire, ewes and goats in Oxfordshire, and a variety of enterprises in Middlesex, Surrey, Sussex and Kent. Not all farms can receive visitors, but the exceptions sell their cheeses locally, or will advise other cheesemakers.

Sources of cheese in the South

ISLE OF WIGHT

DOTTENS FARM, Baring Road, Cowes (*N. of Round House*)
Visitors welcome all year, 9 a.m.–1 p.m., 2–5.30 p.m. Monday to Saturday; talks on cheesemaking (small fee) 11.30 a.m. and 2.30 p.m. Easter to September
1 **Smallholder Cheddar**
Natural, clothbound; 2½–3 lb
Kept for 6–8 weeks before sale
2 **Isle of Wight Cheese**
No crust; ½ lb (I.o.W. shape), 1½ lb (rectangular)
York/Cambridge type with green layer
3 **Lactic Curd**
Plain, or with herbs and garlic, hazelnuts, ham, chives or ginger; skimmed pasteurised milk; no crust
All low-fat, hand-made
Farmer, cheesemaker: Mrs Jane M. Ross
Channel Island herd; permanent pastures on clay
Where to buy: At farm shop

HAMPSHIRE

MAYLES FARM, Mayles Lane, Wickham
Stop press: Cheesemaking as below ceased in Nov. 1981, when the Van Dieyens returned to Holland to buy a larger farm
Gouda
Hard plastic crust; 22–38 lb flat, rounded edges
Made twice daily from UNpasteurised milk; salted in brine bath for 4½ days; matured for 3 months to a year
Farmers: Van Dieyen brothers; *cheesemaker:* Albert Van Dieyen
Friesian herd from Dutch bloodline; leys on clay and loam
Where to buy (while stocks last): Wells: Crump Way (wholesale); Streatley: Wells Stores

WIELD WOOD FARM, Alresford (*1 mile N.W. of Upper Wield off B3046*)
Visitors tel. Alton (0420) 63151
1 **Petit Friese**
Yoghurt curd, plain or with chives; UNpasteurised; no crust; 4 oz rounded disc
2 **Quarg Type**
Ewes' milk; no crust
Cheesemaker: Mrs Olivia Mills
Friesland dairy sheep; chalk
Where to buy: On farm; Petersfield: The Bran Tub; Streatley: Wells Stores

THEDDEN GRANGE DAIRY (*2 miles W. of Alton*)
Visitors tel. Alton (0420) 86564
1 **York Type**
With orange slice; no crust
2 **Coulommiers**
Firm; natural crust
3 **Soft Cheese**
With chives only, or chives, parsley and garlic; no crust
4 **Fresh Curd Cheese**
With herbs
All UNpasteurised, vegetarian, organic
Cheesemaker: Lawrence Bicknell
Jersey herd; organic pasture
Where to buy: On farm

BERKSHIRE

FIRSTONES, Adbury Holt (*N. of Newbury New Town*)
For information on cheesemaking, tel. Newbury (0635) 42742
Goat Cheese
Various types, including blue
Cheesemaker: Mrs Pam Stevenson
British Alpine, British Toggenberg goats
Where to buy: Not making for sale, but happy to advise actual and potential cheesemakers

HILLIER'S LODGE, Bucklebury Common (*3 miles N. of Woolhampton*)
Visitors tel. Woolhampton (073) 521 3601
Creamy Lactic Goat Cheese
UNpasteurised; no crust; 4 oz rounded disc
Sold at 1 or 2 days old, or from stock deep-frozen at that age
Cheesemaker: Mrs F. J. Suthill
British Toggenberg, British Alpine goats
Where to buy: At house

QUARRY LODGE, Bradfield (*3 miles S.W. of Pangbourne*)
No casual visitors, tel. Reading (0734) 744228
The Admiral Cheese
UNpasteurised goats' milk; natural, waxed
Mild and refreshing at 6 weeks, reminiscent in consistency and shape of Cotherstone
Farmer: R. M. Beavis; *cheesemaker:* G. M. Beavis
British Saanen goats
Where to buy: On farm

BAILIFF'S COTTAGE, Barkham (*2 miles W.S.W. of Wokingham on B3349*)
Visitors weekdays 9 a.m.–6.30 p.m., tel. Wokingham (0734) 787400
1 Crowdie
Soft; no crust; 5 oz tubs
2 Colwick
Soft; soft crust; 2½ lb
3 Smallholder
Hard-pressed; natural crust; 2½ lb
All made from UNpasteurised goats' milk
Farmer, cheesemaker: Mrs Janet Firth
British Alpine goats; permanent rough pastures on clay, hedges for foraging
Where to buy: On farm (summer and autumn)

OXFORDSHIRE

KINGSTANDING HILL FARM, Westfield (*1 mile N. of Streatley on A417*)
Visitors welcome
1 Gramons Soft Goat Cheese
Full-cream
2 Gramons Cottage Goat Cheese
Skimmed milk
No crust; 4 oz, 4 lb tubs
Cheesemaker: Jean Tymons
Saanen, British Saanen, British Toggenberg, Anglo-Nubian goats
Where to buy: On farm; Abingdon: Frugal Foods; Calne: Elizabeth Synden (wholesale); Oxford: Palm's, 84 Covered Market; Watlington: Ronaldo's

HARTSLOCK FARM, Whitchurch (*N. of Whitchurch on Thames beyond Coombe Park*)
Hartslock
Ewes' milk cheese, semi-soft, UNpasteurised; natural firm crust; 2 lb
Farmer, cheesemakers: Julian and June George (for Child Beale Trust)
Friesland sheep; permanent pastures on rich loam
Open textured, tasty and refreshing after only 3 weeks

SKOMER, Stoke Row (*3 miles S. of Nettlebed, off B481*)
No visitors; for advice on goat farming (by appointment only), tel. Goring (0491) 680591 or Reading (0734) 55449
1 Labna
Soft; 4 oz
2 Chiltern
Pressed, waxed; 5 oz, 3½ lb
Yoghurt-started, vegetable renneted, pasteurised goats' milk cheeses

Labnas are drained in 12 hours by vibration in linen bags, then transferred to nylon
Farmer, cheesemaker: George Lovering; *assistant:* Raymond Gomm
Saanen, British Saanen, British Alpine, Anglo-Nubian, Toggenberg goats
Where to buy: Amersham: Holland and Barrett (also at Maidenhead, Slough, Windsor branches); Henley: The High; Reading: County Delicacies, 14 Kings Road; The High, Market Place; Wallingford: The Health Food Stores

ROSE FARM, Rotherfield Greys (*1½ miles W. of Henley*)
Visitors tel. Rotherfield Greys (049 17) 348
1 Tuma
Plain or with black peppercorns; natural crust; 4 lb tubby millstones, or 8 lb
Tuma is the firm young cheese which becomes Pecorino after 3 months of maturity. Methods used here, including use of lamb-rennet and stirring with a fig branch, date back to classical times
2 Pecorino (*see Tuma, above*)
3 Ricotta
No crust; 2½–4 lb, basket-moulded
Unlike most Ricottas, the ewes' milk variety contains 22–36% fat
Season: spring and summer
All made from UNpasteurised ewes' milk
Farmer: Aldo Bevacqua; *cheesemaker:* Geraldine Bevacqua
East Friesland sheep; permanent pastures on thin loam over flint–chalk
Where to buy: On farm; Streatley: Wells Stores
Mrs Bevacqua was taught cheesemaking by a Sicilian shepherd

MIDDLESEX

PINNER PARK FARM (Rivendell Dairies), Pinner (*on N.E. side of George V Avenue*)
Visitors tel. 01-863 1078
1 Soft Full-Fat Cheese
Pasteurised; no crust; small rectangular, 4 oz pots, 5 lb bags
2 Goat Cheese
Pasteurised; 4 or 8 oz pots, 5 lb bags
Farmer: Charles Hall; *cheesemaker:* Miss Charlton
Friesian herd

LONDON

NEAL'S YARD DAIRY, Covent Garden, W.C.2 (*approachable from Monmouth Street or Shorts Gardens, which form a' triangle with Neal Street*)

For advice on cheesemaking (by appointment only), tel. 01-379 7646
1 **Coulommiers**
a) Cows' milk: plain or with black pepper and garlic or parsley and garlic
b) Ewes' milk: plain or with chives
All natural crusts
2 **Colwick**
Full-fat; unsalted; natural crust (*see also p. 54*)
3 **Curd**
a) Cows' milk: full-fat; no crust; 6 oz
b) Ewes' milk: full-fat
Both without crusts
4 **Pressed Curd**
Ewes' milk; flavoured with chives; no crust; 2 oz
5 **Crowdie**
Low-fat; no crust; 6 oz
6 **Cottager's**
Full-fat lactic; no crust; 6 oz
7 **Single Cream**
35% fat content; no crust; 6 oz
8 **Double Cream**
Plain, oatmeal-coated or walnut-coated; 67% fat content; no crust; 4 oz
9 **Lancashire Cream Slice**
Plain; no crust; 8 oz round
10 **Fromage Frais**
Skimmed milk lactic; no crust; 6 oz tubs
11 **Yoghurt Cheese**
Plain or with dates; no crust; 6 oz
12 **Spiced Cheese**
With parsley, onion, wine, garlic, salt, black pepper; no crust; 6 oz
13 **Chèvre**
White, goats' milk; 1½ in. diameter, 1½ in. deep
14 **Pyramid**
White, goats' milk; 6 oz
All UNpasteurised, vegetarian; many other farmhouse cheeses available
Cheesemakers: Clare Ash, Isabella Carroll, Simon Cunliffe, Randolph Hodgson
Where to buy: At dairy, 10.30 a.m.–5.30 p.m. Monday to Saturday (closes 3.30 p.m. Wednesday)

SURREY

LOSELEY PARK (*1½ miles S.W. of Guildford, 1 mile from Compton on B3000*)
Soft Cheeses
Farmer: Major More-Molyneux

WILLINGHURST, Shamley Green (*2½ miles S.S.E. of Guildford on B2128*)
Visitors tel. Cranleigh (048 66) 2828

Willinghurst Goat Cheese
Plain or with herbs; lactic, sea-salted, UNpasteurised; no crust; 5 oz sealed tubs (14 days' shelf life)
Cheesemaker: Ann Syms
Mixed herd of goats
Where to buy: Camberley: Holland and Barrett (also at Dorking branch); Cobham: Whole Foods; Cranleigh: Nuts; Godalming: Health Food Store; Guildford: Cranks (also at London branch); Kingston: Bentalls

UPFOLDS FARM, Holmbury St Mary (*7 miles S.W. of Dorking on B2126*)
No casual visitors, but cheesemaking will be taught
Hard Cheese
Plain or with garlic or herbs, or smoked; natural pale to dark yellow, clothbound; 3–8 lb tubby barrels (old Welsh farm recipe)
Matured for 3 months
Cheesemaker: Jane Biggins
Jersey herd; old permanent pastures and reseeded leys
Cheeses made only for family and friends
Upfolds Farm is one of four farms in this area making cheese that I can vouch for

WEST SUSSEX

HOLT VALLEY FARM, Underhill Lane, Clayton (*1 mile S. of Hassocks*)
Visitors tel. Hassocks (079 18) 5158
1 **Feta**
Hard, white; no crust; 2–3 lb but can be ordered to any size
2 **Cottage**
Mild curd, unpressed; no crust
3 **Ripened Soft Cheese**
Waxed
All made from skimmed UNpasteurised goats' milk, without starter, only rennet added
Mostly made to order
Farmer, cheesemaker: Mrs W. Byars Thomson
British Saanen goats
Where to buy: On farm

EAST SUSSEX

HUMPHREYS FARM, Nutley (*6 miles S.E. of East Grinstead on A22*)
Visitors tel. Nutley (082 571) 2432
Willow Down Goats' Milk Cheese
Soft, unripened, medium-fat, UNpasteurised; no crust; 4 oz cylindrical
Made from warm milk (strained) immediately after milking, with the addition only

of a small amount of lactic acid and rennet
Cheesemaker: Mrs Margaret Willcock
British Saanen goats
Season: April to November, but cheese is
made in winter from frozen curd
Where to buy: On farm; Forest Row: Red-
mile Gordon, The Square, and Seasons,
Hartfield Road

STOCKLANDS FARM, Staple Cross (*8
miles N. of Hastings on B2165*)
No visitors
1   Miracle Goat Cheeses
a) Hard, lightly pressed; 8 lb truckles
b) Soft; 2 lb
Both UNpasteurised; natural crust
2   Miracle Cheddar
UNpasteurised; lightly pressed, natural
crust; 8 lb truckles
Cheesemakers: Mr and Mrs J. F. Douglas
British Saanen goats, British Friesian, Ayr-
shire cows
Where to buy: London: G. Baldwin, 173
Walworth Road, S.E.17; Nutrition Centre,
Chalk Farm, N.W.1; Sesame, 128 Regent's
Park Road, N.W.1; Whole Foods, 112
Baker Street, W.1

VOCOT, Bigwood (½ *mile N. of Battle on
A2100*)
Visitors tel. Battle (042 46) 3827
Bigwood Labna
Plain or with garlic, chives or thyme; UN-
pasteurised ewes' milk; no crust; 4 oz
rounded disc
A yoghurt-based cheese of Middle-East-
ern origin
Farmer, cheesemaker: Sarah Warren
East Friesland sheep; newly established
permanent pastures

Where to buy: On farm; Brighton: Infinity
Foods, North Street

KENT

PRIESTLAND GOAT FARM, Marden (*7
miles S. of Maidstone*)
Mrs Anne May *(cheesemaker) is not now
producing commercially, but gives one-
day courses in goats' and cows' milk
cheesemaking. Write for details*

WATERSHEET, Egerton Forstal (*9 miles
S.E. of Maidstone*)
Visitors tel. Egerton (023 376) 226
Egerton
Pont L'Eveque type interior; natural crust;
4 oz pots (locally made earthenware); 2½ lb
boxed
Farmer: A. C. B. Lamport; *cheesemaker:*
Mrs Lamport
Ayrshire herd
Where to buy: On farm; Cranbrook: Perfect
Partners; Egerton: P.O. Stores; Pluckley:
Heasman's

UPTONWOOD FARM, Upton Wood, near
Coldred (*5 miles N.W. of Dover on A2*)
Visitors tel. Shepherdswell (0304) 830263
Lactic Cheese
Plain or with chives; wholemilk, soft,
medium-fat; no crust; 4 oz tubs
Farmer: J. H. Rolfe; *cheesemaker:* D. V.
Rolfe
Saanen goats; permanent pastures and
herbal leys on medium heavy loam
Where to buy: On farm; health shops and
delicatessens in Canterbury and several
coastal towns

South Wales

Caerphilly

Caerphilly, the one cheese associated by outsiders with Wales, was widely
available for Welsh miners from the farms of Glamorgan and Monmouth
between the early 1800s and 1914. Judging by the number of my Welsh
customers whose mothers, aunts or grandmothers made cheese, small-scale
cheesemaking on farms must still have been fairly common up to 1940, when it was
stopped by the Ministry of Food. None of my Welsh informants can tell me of any
Welsh Caerphilly making now, but I shall be delighted if this negative report
is contradicted. Meanwhile the farm cheese must be regarded as an émigré natur-
alised by long residence in Somerset, where it has been made for many years.

With the exception of some Somerset farm cheese, Caerphilly made today is generally whiter and more acid than its firmer, slower-ripening Welsh predecessor. The best of these came from Carmarthenshire, then renowned as the finest dairying county in the Principality.

Caerphilly is now made at Dairy Crest creameries at Four Crosses (Powys) and Newcastle Emlyn (Dyfed). Up to twice the traditional quantity of salt is used in factory cheeses today, according to Dr Davis, and the machinery is identical to that used for Cheddar.

The Eppynt

Inland from Glamorgan and Gwent in the south west of Powys lies the Eppynt, another traditional cheesemaking area, never famous outside Wales. This beautiful range of hills and moorlands runs north west from Brecon to Llanwrtyd Wells with Builth Wells its north-eastern tip and Llandovery its westernmost point. Until the Second World War it was a sheep- and pony-raising area, with horses, cows and pigs on the fifty farms. The locals produced butter and cheese, killed their own pigs, made their own candles and cut peat for their fires

At one of these farms, Gwybedog, the family made a cheese from one skimmed and one whole cows' milking mixed with a gallon of ewes' milk 'for body'. Half a pint was a good yield from a ewe, so it was 'an awful fiddling job', as Mrs Ceinwen Davies described it. Any cheese and butter surplus to family needs was sold in Llanwrtyd, except for August cheese which they kept to sell at the November Fair in Brecon. Mrs Davies says, 'There was a tremendous amount of cheese sold in Brecon in those days.' They kept their cheese for at least two months, but preferred its 'much nicer flavour' and much harder crust at six months. Eppynt cheeses were of Caerphilly shape and the type was probably common in South Wales before the quick-selling Caerphilly developed in the early nineteenth century.

The nearest cheesemaking I know of now is on a farm near Talybont (seven miles south east of Brecon). It is on so small a scale that I do not think there is likely to be any to spare for casual travellers.

Dyfed

Recently two farms in Dyfed have started making individual types of cheese, of which details are given below.

Caldey Island

The monks of the Abbey on Caldey Island used to make a Saint Paulin type of cheese, but found it uneconomic. They now make soft lactic chive cheese and sell it to visitors.

Clwyd

One of the oldest and most considerable cheesemaking areas of Wales was the Vale of Clwyd, where one farm on the Shropshire border still makes Cheshire. As this formed part of the Cheshire Cheese Federation region I have dealt with it in the Cheshire section of the chapter on the North West (see p. 55).

Sources of cheese in Wales

DYFED

TY'N GRUG, Esgerdawe, Llandeilo
Visitors welcome
Ty'n Grug Farmhouse Cheese
Hard, UNpasteurised; washed natural crust, yellow; 20–30 lb cylindrical
Normally cellar-matured for 6–8 months, sometimes up to a year (there is occasional blueing)
Farmer, cheesemaker: Dougal Campbell
Jersey herd; permanent pastures on heavy clay
Season: April to December
Where to buy: On farm
Dougal Campbell learned from an old Swiss cheesemaker, and is willing to teach others

ABBEY OF OUR LADY AND SAINT SAMPSON, Caldey Island (off Tenby)
Caldey Island
Soft, lactic cheese, pasteurised, with chives
Dairy manager: John Cattini
Where to buy: At the Abbey

LLANGLOFFAN FARM, Ty Uchaf, Castle Morris, near Haverfordwest
Visitors welcome (can stay on farm as paying guests), tel. St Nicholas (034 85) 241
Llangloffan
Semi-hard, full-cream, UNpasteurised; firm golden, clothbound, natural surface mould; 6–15 lb mill-wheels made in wooden hoops
A rich, fresh, open-textured cheese, of appetising creamy appearance when cut
Farmers, cheesemakers: Leon and Joan Downey
Jersey herd; permanent pastures
Season: April to November
Where to buy (in season and into December): On farm; local shops; Streatley: Wells Stores

CLEDAN, Nebo, Llanon, Ceredigion
Haminiog
Smallholder goat cheese, pressed; natural crust, 8–10 lb

Farmer, cheesemaker: Mrs P. D. Grisedale
Dairy goats; mixed pastures
Where to buy: On farm; sometimes in local shops; at agricultural shows in Wales and Borders; deliveries fortnightly to Manchester, Irby, Wirral, Wrexham

PORTHRHIW, Capel Betws Lleucu, Llwyngroes, Tregaron (_about 12 miles S. of Aberystwyth, 10 miles N. of Lampeter; 1 mile along B4342 road takes sharp bend left and uphill; turn right off road, through Penclwc farm gate_)
Visitors welcome; please tie dogs at gate
1   Soft Smooth Cheese
Neufchatel type
2   Cottage Cheese
Both sold in 4 or 8 oz tubs or loose
3   Porthrhiw
Semi-hard; natural crust; 1 lb, 12 oz cylindrical, cut to order
All made from UNpasteurised goats' milk
Smallholders: Mark and Gill Tennant
British and British Saanen goats; reseeded ley and permanent pastures, loam and clay on limestone
Season: Porthrhiw all year; soft cheeses April to autumn fresh, then frozen
Where to buy: On farm

GWYNEDD

MAES MAWR, Llanllyfni (_7 miles S. of Caernarfon on A487; along Lonty Gwyn Lane by chapel, past school, and over fields at end_)
Visitors tel. Nantlie (028 689) 809
1   Smallholder
Semi-soft, creamy, rich; natural crust; 1–2 lb
2   Lactic
Soft, mild; 5 oz cartons
Both made from UNpasteurised goats' milk
Smallholder, cheesemaker: Mrs Jean Rickford
Anglo-Nubian, British Alpine goats; unimproved pastures, with marginal acid land
Where to buy: At house

Gloucestershire

Gloucestershire has been a shire since at least the tenth century, and featured in the *Anglo-Saxon Chronicle* in 1016. Regional cheese was exported in the eighth century, and its importance gave rise to the ancient annual custom of rolling cheeses down Cotswold slopes (with the interesting implications that Gloucester cheeses were always wheel-shaped and tough-crusted). Some examples of this tradition are still to be seen: four cheeses are rolled and chased down Cooper's Hill, on the edge of the Cotswolds between Gloucester and Cheltenham, every Whit Monday. At Randwick, two miles north west of Stroud, the custom, which was originally associated with May Day, became part of the celebration of Rogation Sunday, on which it has been observed again since 1971. A 1911 account describes how three litters each holding a cheese decked with flowers were carried into the church accompanied by 'shout, song and music'. In the churchyard, after the decorations have been removed, the cheeses are rolled three times round the church anti-clockwise. They are then dressed up again and taken back into Randwick, where one is cut up and distributed to the parishioners. The other two are kept for Wap Fair, the following Saturday, when they are rolled down the hill.

Gloucestershire's three biggest natural divisions are the Vale of Gloucester, or Upper Vale, stretching from the Cotswolds round the city northward to the Vale of Evesham and north westward to the Forest of Dean, with Hereford beyond; the Vale of Berkeley, or Lower Vale, bordering the Severn mouth on its south side towards Bristol; and finally the Cotswolds covering half the county east and south east of a diagonal running from Broadway in Worcestershire through Cheltenham to Dursley in the south west. From early on the three districts' cheesemaking customs were distinct; but the greatest then and the only important one later for cheese was the Vale of Berkeley, with its pastures on the clays of the Lower Lias. The Cotswolds always put sheep first, and the Vale of Gloucester by the 1900s had become more noted for corn and turnips than for cheese. Nevertheless, 350 tall farmhouses, with their curious blank look below the roof, where third-storey windows might be expected, still bear witness to past cheesemaking in all three regions. Those unfenestrated floors under the eaves were the old cheese rooms, where generations of Double and Single Gloucesters matured until the factors were ready to receive and market them.

The native cattle, the Gloucesters, were an ancient breed, resembling in marking and profile the wild ox illustrated in the caves of Lascaux in prehistoric times, from which they may well be descended. Bones of this animal, *bos taurus primigenus*, have been found in Gloucestershire. The Gloucesters could also have descended through the finch-backed Norwegian breed, introduced into Normandy by the Vikings in the tenth century and imported into England by Robert Fitzhamon, who owned half of Gloucestershire around 1100. He later ruled over Glamorgan, which boasted a closely related breed now extinct (the last survivor was traced in 1926).

The old Gloucester breed is of striking beauty. Legs and head are black, the strong, chiselled profile being set off by long, upswept horns of white, tipped with black again. The deep mahogany of the body glows a rich chestnut red when the sun lights up its flank. The final glory is a brilliant fine white V starting at a point in the small of the back. Scarcely more than a stripe at first, it widens over the tail and spreads down and round the udders, to cover the belly and the ribs between the forelegs. In size the Gloucester is larger than the Guernsey and smaller than the Ayrshire, whose cheesemaking virtues it shares: a good percentage of fat of small globulin size in the milk. The breed and the rich soil of the Vales shared the credit for Gloucester's cheese fame until its climax in the mid-eighteenth century. Disease then hit the herds, which were reinforced with Bakewell's improved Longhorns from the Midlands, and virtually supplanted by them within fifty years.

Gloucestershire in the Middle Ages was noted more for sheep than for cattle, and the sheep were valued mainly for their fleeces. Records of the Cotswold manor of Minchinhampton in 1307 and 1330 show that in both years they kept seventeen milch cows and made cheese; but only through a note of 16s 8d payment to a cooper for five days' work making pails '_pro ovium lacte_' do we know that some of their 442 ewes were milked for cheesemaking too. It was an old habit in Wales and other parts of England to put extra bite into cows' milk cheese by adding some ewes' milk, long after cows had generally supplanted ewes in the dairy (see p. 22 and 127).

The summer cheeses were usually of 8-10 lb. The 'rewayn' or aftermath cheeses (cf. French _regain_) were often under 2 lb. Of 445 cheeses made in 1307, 307 went to the nuns at Caen whose abbey owned Minchinhampton. Although some of the remainder probably fed living-in help and a 4 lb cheese was put aside for the 'lads' taking the cheeses to the ship, cheese was not the common man's fare other than as part of his wage. His whole day's pay would have bought only one pound in the market.

Gloucester cheese from the sixteenth century

Gloucester cheese is mentioned by name as early as 1594, which suggests that it was already travelling outside the county borders. Architecture and documentary records preserve evidence of widespread and large-scale cheesemaking from the sixteenth century onwards. A sixteenth-century listed building, Apperley Hall, at Deerhurst in the Upper Vale, has a first-floor room with an original floor-level window on one side and a ventilator on the other, plainly designed from the start as a cheese chamber. Allcocks Farm on the Forthampton Estate in the Upper Vale, a listed building of the sixteenth or seventeenth century, was recorded in 1802 as having a dairy, and a cheese room over the bedrooms. In the western Cotswolds, Street Farm, Nympsfield, dated 1613, has an original cheese room over the kitchen. In the Vale of Berkeley, New Hall Farm, Wickwar, dated 1691, has cheese rooms in its original structure.

Seventeenth-century sales documents and inventories include such revealing items as cheese rings (today called hoops, i.e. moulds). On 16 June 1688, 39 cheeses were in stock on one farm, 43 on another and 200 in the upper loft at Baynham Court. The farms identified with cheesemaking were well spread over the Upper Vale, and down from Gloucester through the Vale of Berkeley, with a sprinkling in the western Cotswolds.

Single and Double Gloucester

In the sixteenth and seventeenth centuries the full-cream cheeses were usually

A Gloucestershire farmhouse, showing the distinctive wooden dormer vents of the cheese chamber.

'single meal', that is, made fresh from one milking, and they were coloured. They were called 'best making' or just 'best' until the mid-nineteenth century. 'Two-meal' cheeses were normally made from skimmed evening milk, ripened overnight to start the full-cream morning milk. These cheeses, uncoloured, continued to be made, mainly in the Upper Vale and the Cotswolds, for as long as the farms made cheese. Termed Single Gloucester, because they used the cream of only one milking, they were normally kept for two months. Some farms made them only during the spring flush for haymaking time.

The full-cream cheeses, however, were also later made from two meals, either of cream from the overnight milking added to the whole morning milk, or of the whole overnight milking ripened to start the whole morning milk when added to it. This was the cheese which became known by 1772 as Double Gloucester. The purist view is that it was so called because it used two full-cream milkings. The other view, shared by William Fream in *Encyclopaedia Britannica* (1911 edition) and by many other writers, is that the double-milking cheese's extra size earned it the name. The Single Gloucester, having had its fat and solids reduced by the skimming of the overnight milk, was of course a smaller cheese than the Double. This lent logical support to the claim that the size dictated the description, but now that both cheeses are being made again I contend that the vital point for the consumer is the distinction between one type of cheese and another; size can be judged by eye alone.

It should not be thought, however, that Single Gloucesters are poor cheeses. Even when the farmers took a little morning cream off as well, the fraud was not always detectable. The best Single Gloucesters in the eighteenth century were said by William Marshall to equal whole-milk cheeses from counties with poorer soil and less admirable cattle. They were made with lower acidities and lower temperatures than the Doubles, and left four to five days in the press. Sage cheeses were made too, but probably for harvest or Christmas eating on the farm rather than for sale. A recipe from William Marshall is given on p. 28.

The eighteenth century

Although the Gloucester breed was declining in numbers in the latter half of the eighteenth century, there were 50,000 milkers in the mixed Gloucester and Longhorn herds of the Vales, newly reinforced by the first Shorthorns (developed from the Durhams of Teesdale). They were estimated by Samuel Rudder in 1779 to be producing 7500 tons of cheese a season, with a further 500 tons coming from the Cotswolds. William Marshall's calculation in 1783 that each milker was producing 3–4 cwt of cheese in a six to seven month season confirmed Rudder's broad figures. The cheese was fetching about 3*d* a pound in 1779.

While most herds had twenty to twenty-five milkers, there were a number of larger herds up to a hundred strong, which explains the size of many of the cheese rooms. One of these hundred-strong herds belonged to Ralph Bigland of Frocester Court, south west of Stroud in the Vale of Berkeley. He not only farmed and made cheese, but was one of the largest cheese factors. A man of varied achievements, he was county historian, became Garter King of Arms and invented a way of turning his cheeses by water power. Park Farm, Alderley, to the east of the Vale (now on the Avon border), also has such machinery.

There were cheese fairs at Berkeley, Lechlade and Stow on the Wold and the crucial Barton Fair at Gloucester (see below). This was probably the height of Gloucestershire's fame and prosperity as a cheese producer. The farms of the Upper Vale delivered their cheese to market at Michaelmas (the end of September) and in the spring. The larger farms also sold cheeses in July. Cheese factors dealt with the same farms year after year, often buying unseen cheeses down to the age of six weeks. Marshall commented on the great trust between farmer and factor, a trust uncommon in the cheese world and almost unheard of in any other. The general standard must have been very high, and the demand constant. Naturally beginners or those showing signs of uncertain standards were circumspectly treated. Gloucester crusts were meant to be almost indestructible and their interiors close textured and firm. These requirements were put to the test by factors, who would actually jump on doubtful cheeses, breaking only the weak or the 'hoven' (those blown out with gas).

In 1783 at the annual Michaelmas Barton Fair (held in Barton Street, Gloucester) there were twenty waggon-loads and a number of packhorse-loads of Gloucester cheese on sale. These were cheeses not already spoken for by factors buying direct from farms. Whole loads of 'best Making' fetched 34*s* a hundredweight (3¾*d* a pound), smaller quantities, down to a hundredweight, nearly 4*d* a pound. Even single cream 'two-meal' cheeses sold at 3*d* a pound. These cheeses, weighing 11–12 lb, went mainly to the manufacturing districts and adjoining counties, but some went to London (sold as Warwickshire, according to Marshall) and some went abroad. Some Double Gloucesters were exported to the United States, but they were probably shipped from Bristol direct.

In the next five years something went amiss. Perhaps the high demand attracted some less competent farms into the cheese market. At Barton Fair in 1788 there were forty waggon-loads of cheese, and prices were from 17 to 25 per

Method of making Single or Double Gloucester
Abridged from an account by William Marshall, 1783

The evening milk was skimmed the following morning, and the cream or the skimmed milk, according to the type, was added (at a temperature suited to the weather) to the fresh morning milk to make it 85°F normally (up to 88° in frost or lower in warm weather).

Annatto-stained milk and rennet were then added. Curd might come in 40 minutes, but it would be tough; or take up to 1½ hours and be very tender. At this point the whey temperature should be 80°F. The curd was then cut with a triple cheese-knife or broken by hand until 'not a lump larger than a bean is seen'.

After about half an hour most of the whey was removed through a sieve into a container. The curd was drawn to the side of the tub, pressed with the bottom of the skimming dish, trimmed with a knife. Then, with the trimmings on top, the curd was passed round the tub to collect fragments of curd from the remaining whey, which was then drawn off. The curd, now in one mass, was cut into squares, then reduced into pieces as small as peas with the triple knife. The heated whey was thrown on the curd and stirred briskly to give an even scalding temperature. The liquid was then ladled off (some dairies waited half an hour for this).

The mould was placed on the cheese ladder over the tub, and the curd crumbled into it by hand, whey being squeezed out, and the mould inclined occasionally to drain whey that had got through. The curd was pressed down into the mould, with more towards the centre. When it was well filled a cheesecloth was spread over it and the curd turned out into the cloth. When the mould had been dipped in the whey, the inverted curd in the cheesecloth was returned to the mould with the cloth under it. Angles formed by the mould were trimmed and the surface partially broken so that the trimmings could be incorporated, and the top was rounded up as before. The cloth was folded over and tucked in and the mould placed in the press. Only the top cheese would need a cheeseboard (or follower), the bottoms of the moulds fitting over each other and acting as followers on the well-packed curd of the moulds below.

After 2-3 hours the mould was removed, the cloth pulled off and washed and the cheese turned and replaced, in the same cloth and mould, in the press. Another 7 or 8 hours later the cheese was removed from the press and (the angles being pared off, if necessary) placed unclothed on the inverted mould for salting with a handful rubbed hard round the edge 'as much hanging to it as will stick'. The same was done on each face of the cheese and the cheese was pressed again, bare.

The next morning and evening it was turned bare in the mould and returned to press, and the third day removed finally after 48 hours of pressing and placed on the dairy shelves. There the cheeses were turned from once a day to once every two or three days, according to weather or other influences. In harsh or dry weather windows were shut; in close, moist atmosphere all possible air was let in.

After 10 days they were immersed in a large tub of whey for up to an hour until the rind was supple. On removal they were scraped with a blunt cake knife to remove cloth marks and all roughness, and give a polished neatness on the edges. After being rinsed in whey and wiped dry they were piled in open brickwork fashion in the window or a similarly airy place to dry, and then placed in the cheese chamber. At the start they were placed singly, but as they matured they could be piled two or four high, the rind being tough enough at one month to 'throw about like old cheeses'. They were turned twice a week.

cent lower than in 1783. Cheese had become 'a drug on the market', in Marshall's words. The widening of the price range suggests more variable standards of making. This sadly unprofitable surfeit started a decline in Gloucestershire cheesemaking which would never be reversed. This turn of the tide coincided with the virtual eclipse of the old Gloucester breed, of which only a handful of pure-bred herds remained by 1790 to keep it from extinction. Longhorns had largely taken their place. They in turn were to yield to the Shorthorn by the end of the nineteenth century, although these were still looked on as primarily a beef animal by some authorities.

The nineteenth and early twentieth centuries

Good cheese was still made. In the early 1800s Charles Lamb said that Gloucester was his favourite; and Professor Low, a Scot, wrote in 1849 that Double Gloucester was still the most generally esteemed cheese in England, and that Single Gloucester was still better than the whole-cream cheeses of other districts. Production, however, had greatly diminished in the Upper Vale and the Cotswolds. That of the Hundred of Berkeley, where most Gloucester was now made, had dropped to between 1000 and 1200 tons by 1849, some of it marketed as Berkeley or Double Berkeley. The two Vales had made over five times as much as this between them only seventy years before.

There was still confusion in the use of the terms Double and Single Gloucester, but in 1854 Double Gloucesters of the proper stamp were being made on Ralph Bigland's old farm at Frocester Court by Mrs Hayward, who contributed part of an article published in her husband's name by the _Farmers' Magazine_ in June that year. Their Double Gloucesters weighed just over 22 lb (five to the hundredweight) and measured $15\frac{1}{2}$ inches in diameter and $4\frac{1}{4}$ inches deep. Singles of the same diameter weighed 14 lb (eight to the hundredweight) and were $2\frac{1}{2}$ inches in depth. These linear measurements still hold good, but weights vary with the way the curd is packed in the mould.

Factory making started in Gloucestershire in 1875 and, to speed up the change from the ancient ways, creameries employed agents to go round farm sales and buy and destroy farm cheese-dairy equipment, to reduce the capacity of farmhouse cheesemaking. Nevertheless, many farms continued to make cheese and in 1893 the Gloucester County Council Agricultural Education Department appointed the first 'Instructress in Dairying', Miss Flora Priday. She taught many farmers' wives and daughters and other students on into the 1920s. This was the period that saw the almost complete change from wooden to metal moulds and from hard, polished to clothbound Double Gloucester.

In 1887 Dr Francis Bond invented his Little Gloucester, a small brick-shaped cheese. He followed this up twenty years later with the Gloucester Roundel, a 2 lb spherical cheese which could be eaten 'unctuous', young and mild, or mature, blue and rich.

At the turn of the century G. S. Kingscote, Sir Aston Lister and G. Herridge (a farmer) set up the Gloucester Dairy Supply Company to make milk products to sell through their own shops and to despatch all over the country retail and wholesale. As well as the two traditional Gloucester cheeses, and Cheddar and Caerphilly, they acquired Dr Bond's recipe and made a 2 lb brick-shaped, thin-rinded Little Gloucester cheese which closely resembled his Roundels in character. It was supplied to Queen Victoria and to the Dukes of Connaught and Cambridge.

In 1908 Dr Bond addressed himself to Gloucestershire cheesemakers, many of whom were now making Cheddar, Caerphilly or even Stilton. Some were calling their Cheddar 'Double Gloucester'. Dr Bond deplored the county's general loss of identity in the cheese world. He thought the demand for smaller, softer cheeses should be met, as he had met it, but recommended that the large cheeses made in the county should be real Double Gloucester, limited though the demand might be. Single Gloucester he obviously thought little of, and wrote off the demand as negligible. If the old cheeses were not quite as dead as he judged, and the old Gloucester breed was still kept going by the Duke of Beaufort at Badminton, the First World War was approaching to give both cheese and breed of cattle another push towards the grave. In quantity and in general quality the cheeses were a mere shadow of their mid-Victorian predecessors, let alone of their ancestors of the 1770s and 1780s. Meanwhile, Dr Bond was selling several thousand of his Roundels each year, alongside an assortment of other soft cheeses made, until 1914, at his Stonehouse dairy. Another county cheese of that era was Cottslowe, a factory product of Cheddar flavour.

In 1927 Avis Colnett, successor to Miss Priday, introduced starter to the farms and began to make a careful and valuable record of farm cheesemaking methods of the time. Looking for profitable ways of using small milk surpluses she evolved, under the sponsorship of Gloucestershire Education Committee, Cotswold cheese (not related to today's Vale of Belvoir product). It was made uncoloured, plain, mild and creamy, in 1 or 2 lb sizes, and ripened at from one to three months. At this stage the bandage was removed and the cheese was scrubbed in cold water, dried, and then rubbed with olive oil. There was a large demand for Cotswold by 1935.

In 1939 there were a dozen entries in the Cotswold Cheese Class at the Three Counties Show, first prize going to Miss Pain of Cam. Her father's Double Gloucester and Cotswold had been bought by the House of Commons, which wanted a regular supply. This was unluckily beyond Mr Pain's resources. Another prize Double Gloucester maker of this period was Mrs Haines, who had started cheesemaking in her home county of Somerset (see p. 8). In the early 1920s she had married and moved, continuing to make Cheddar from the milk of her Shorthorns at Rectory Farm, Slimbridge. She was then taught to make her adopted county's cheese (probably by Avis Colnett). Mrs Haines won first prize and the championship cup nine years running for her Double Gloucesters at the Gloucester Root, Fruit and Grain Show and also won prizes at the last pre-war London Dairy Show.

The last class for Single Gloucester was at the National Dairy Show in 1938. By this time the cheese was normally unbandaged, thinner than the Double, but made of one full-cream milk warm from the cow by a short, less acid method, to ripen at two months. It was often known as 'Haymaking Cheese', most of it being made in May to be ready to enjoy in the hayfield with crusty bread and locally brewed cider.

By the 1930s, however, the larger dairies were taking the market for the bigger cheeses. Several of these factories were run by farmers, and the cheesemaking was supervised by people who had learned their craft on farms - some from Miss Priday and Mrs Haines. The figures of English farmhouse cheese-makers registered in 1939 sent to me by the Milk Marketing Board make no mention of Gloucestershire, but Miss Lilla Smith, who assisted Avis Colnett, has culled from her records and her memory the names of ten farms on which cheese was being made at the time. The Second World War finished off farmhouse cheesemaking on a regular basis, but it was kept alive by a few devotees of the cheese and the old Gloucester breed. Lady Susan and Lady Victoria Hicks-Beach were making it from Gloucester milk at Williamstrip Park, Coln St Aldwyn. Colonel Elwes started cheesemaking at Colesbourne Park in 1942 to stimulate interest in the old breed. As a consequence Vincent Yorke bought a bull and some cows from him and started making on the Home Farm at Forthampton Court, an old-time source of Gloucester cheese. A few farmers made cheese and butter from time to time when small surpluses of milk were left over from the churn collection.

Post-war revival

In 1968 two farmers' wives were making cheese for their families, but there was no commercial cheese production in Gloucestershire at all. However, Avis Colnett's work made it possible for the making of Double Gloucester to be revived in the 1950s at Sturminster Newton Creamery in Dorset and on a few Somerset farms. Mr Look made beautiful farmhouse cheeses at Ditcheat until he retired in the early 1970s, and Martin Biggs, another pupil of Avis Colnett, still makes tasty cheeses, coloured and white, at North Leaze Farm, North Cadbury, in Somerset.

The post-war farmhouse revival striven for by Avis Colnett never got going; but she lived long enough to see the making of native Gloucester cheeses once more by traditional handmade methods, from milk of the old Gloucestershire permanent pastures at Laurel Farm, Dymock. In the early 1970s Charles and Monica Martell felt the call to save the almost extinct Gloucester breed: in 1974 only forty-five head survived. At Laurel Farm they re-formed the Gloucester Cattle Society by approaching all the buyers at the last dispersal sale, and patiently built up their own herd, co-operating with the Ministry over breeding policy. The national total passed the hundred mark in 1979, but the cattle outside Dymock are scattered, mostly in ones and twos, all over England. It would be good to see herds back in Gloucestershire and cheese dairies to go with them, on such historic home grounds as Badminton. William Marshall wrote in 1796: 'For dairy cows, I have not, in my own judgement, seen a better form . . . it was the Gloucestershire breed which raised the Gloucestershire dairy to its greatest height.' My customers and I can vouch for their virtue living on in the Gloucester cheeses produced at Dymock today.

Sources of farmhouse Double and Single Gloucester

GLOUCESTERSHIRE

LAUREL FARM, Dymock
No visitors, please (*The Martells are fully occupied in re-establishing the Gloucester breed, see p. 3, making cheese and selling at market*)
1   Double Gloucester
Usually uncoloured, UNpasteurised; natural unpainted crust; traditional wheels of various weights
2   Single Gloucester
Uncoloured, made with or without starter; also with herbs or nettle; natural, unpainted crust; traditional wheels, some smaller, cylindrical
Single Gloucester made without started is a semi-soft succulent cheese of pronounced flavour; that made with starter is gentler, more open-textured, but firmer
3   Forest Cheese
Double Gloucester creamed with cider vinegar; nut-enriched; 1 lb, 2 lb circular, flat

Cave-ripened in the Forest of Dean to blue naturally; only made occasionally
4   Dymock
Dales type, white, open-textured
To be eaten young
All UNpasteurised
Farmers: Charles Martell and Son; *cheesemaker:* Monica Martell
Gloucester herd; permanent pastures, Old Red Sandstone
Season: May to October
Where to buy: Cirencester: Charles Martell, the Market, 8 a.m.–4 p.m. Monday, Friday; Gloucester: Cattle Market, 9 a.m.–2 p.m. Saturday; Ledbury: Market House, Saturday; Streatley: Wells Stores

See also Home Farm, Newton St Cyres (p. 14), Milk Marketing Board Creamery, Sturminster Newton (p. 16), and North Leaze Farm, North Cadbury (p. 16)

Hereford and Worcester

These counties have no great cheese history. Duncomb's report of 1805 to the Board of Agriculture suggests that Herefordshire was well provided with cheese from Shropshire and Gloucestershire, and that its own cheese had only been made for household or farm use. However, just before he was writing 'improved modes' had been adopted from other counties, and Hereford market had seen local cheese from the Bromyard area 'equalling the best of Shropshire in quality and price'.

Early in the twentieth century Herefordshire produced 'Little Derby', a cheese said to have been a Cheddar-Derby cross, and in 1918 Ellen Yeld invented a 'Little Hereford' for small dairies.

In 1975 Gerard and Titania Molyneux moved from Bishops Castle in Shropshire to Bodcott Farm, Bredwardine, where they make various cheeses between May and October.

Worcestershire was noted by Pomeroy in 1794 as a producer of butter for Birmingham, and consequently also of a skimmed-milk cheese called 'two meals' or 'seconds', selling at 8s a hundredweight, nearly 1d a pound, less than the one-meal whole-milk cheese made by other dairymen. Worcestershire has a number of farmhouses with third-storey cheese rooms in the Gloucestershire style but no evidence of their recent use.

Other cheeses of Gloucestershire, Hereford and Worcester

GLOUCESTERSHIRE

STOWAWAY, Daisybank Road, Charlton Kings Common, near Cheltenham (*B4070 S. out of Cheltenham; turn left off Leck-hampton Hill towards Birdlip*)
Notice required for visitors, tel. Cheltenham (0242) 22767
Soft Goat Cheese
No crust; plastic cartons
Smallholder, cheesemaker: Mrs Anne North
British Saanen goats; permanent rough pastures on limestone
Where to buy: On farm; Cheltenham: Russet's Delicatessen, Bath Road

FREEDOM FARM, Bromsberrow Heath, near Ledbury (*M50 motorway, 1 mile W. of Junction 2; farm just by flyover bridge on Gloucester side*)
Visitors welcome, tel. Bromesberrow (*sic*) (053 181) 519
Soft Goat Cheese
UNpasteurised; no crust; any weight to order, 5 oz–5 lb

Farmer, cheesemaker: Miss B. P. G. Robinson
Season: All year
Where to buy: On farm

HEREFORD AND WORCESTER

BODCOTT FARM, Bredwardine, near Hereford
Visitors by appointment, tel. Moccas (098 17) 257
Herefordshire Cheese
Soft, semi-soft and hard, UNpasteurised; occasional natural blueing; clothbound; 7–8 lb; Parmesan-like when aged
Farmers, cheesemakers: Gerard and Titania Molyneux
Jersey, Welsh Black herds; mixed permanent pastures and leys on red sandstone
Season: May to October
Where to buy: On farm
The Molyneux have made cheese here and at Bishop's Castle for over 25 years by old-fashioned hand methods

Dorset Blue Vinney

Origins of Blue Vinney

In the eighteenth and nineteenth centuries most of Dorset's cattle were to be found in the vales, where dairymen rented the pastures. Particularly in the Vale of Sherborne, cows were often of the deep mahogany, white-behinded Gloucester breed, summering in Dorset. The dairymen sold fresh milk, butter and a little cream. From the residual buttermilk they made their hard, almost fat-free cheese in a dairy often rich enough in natural mould spores to produce a blue cheese without more ado. Vinney, or Vinny, derived from the old English word for mould, *vinew*, which was still in general use in the 1600s. Thereafter its use dwindled, was eventually confined to Wessex, and finally became especially and uniquely associated with Dorset's idiosyncratic cheese – Blue Vinney.

The nineteenth century saw some reduction in cheesemaking in Dorset, as elsewhere, when the railways made it easy to transport milk to the towns. Dorset, however, is not a county of fast change. The old pattern of dairying in the vales with Blue Vinney as a by-product endured into the 1930s; but 1933 brought security of milk sales, and by 1939 Blue Vinney was described as a 'precarious survival'.

The greatest blow to this system was the invention of machine skimming of milk, which leaves too little fat and other solid substance in the milk to make Blue Vinney even at its hardest. The next almost lethal stroke came from the Ministry of Food, when it condemned all the English cheeses except hard versions of Cheddar, Cheshire and Wensleydale at the start of the Second World War. Blue Vinney was hard enough to have survived by logic and sentiment, but neither consideration moved the Ministry. Farmhouse cheesemaking virtually ceased, and milk was taken from the farms to the factories. After the war this comparatively easy way of profiting from milk seemed more secure and less demanding to farming families than butter and cheesemaking; so the Dorset pattern of dairying died. I will leave an account of the few post-war signs of life to the end of this chapter.

Methods of making

One of the early traditions of making was that single Blue Vinney should be made from the milk of one cow. The cream would have been setting for twenty-four hours before it was skimmed off, and several days' buttermilk would be needed for one cheese, so they tended to be very hardy indeed.

Apart from blueing by mould present in the dairy, there are accounts of natural blueing from mouldy old boots kept purposely alongside ripening cheeses: cracking crusts, common in underfat cheese, offered easy access for mould spores. Some cheeses matured in harness rooms, where unpolished, moist, mould-nurturing leather would be the rule. Cheeses kept in the hay-racks of stables and cattle byres were never short of visiting mould either. If bad design or bad floor-laying sloped drainage towards the trough and rack side of the building, the cheeses would have the added sharp gift of ammoniac vapour from below. In the early 1920s Blue Vinney was made 'with a dram of rennet, an ounce or two of salt, and a pinch of flour to help it turn blue'. The blueing method which appeals most to me for its thoroughness was the drawing of mouldy harness through the milk in the vat before cheesemaking began, thus ensuring a spread of vinew throughout the cheese. The austere uncertainty of some of the more chancy methods is illustrated by the account of those cheese-making days given to Ted Gliddon in the 1970s by the son of a notable Dorset character called 'Blue Vinney Ward': 'Only ten out of fifty cheeses came off, and the rest were hard as bloody bullets.' Among other lore told to me by Dorset veterans, not themselves cheesemakers, were these two gems: 'tiert' soil, free of any trace of molybdenum, was necessary for Blue Vinney milk; and when horses drawing milk to the factory were frightened by thunder and the milk landed up in the ditch, a farmer rescued it and made 'marvellous Blue Vinney'.

Dorset cheesemaking had not been confined to small dairymen in the vales. An accidental school of Blue Vinney production sprang from the old tradition of Cheddar making. These gone-wrong Cheddars were full-fat cheeses, but in Dorset eyes and on Dorset tongues they were none the less Blue Vinney for all that. Mr G. A. Patch, now a Hampshire farmer, told me in May 1980 of his own family's experience in this branch of Blue Vinney making. His mother trained as a Cheddar cheesemaker on Longhill Farm, Cucklington, and made cheese on Hill Street Farm in the Dorset Holwell, and then on Home Farm, Downside, until the outbreak of the Second World War. The family tradition is that from time to time during milking the fortunate accident of contamination, *Escherichia coli*, would occur in the pail, making milk, curd and cheese more attractive to local vinew as well as stronger in flavour. This resulted in unsolicited Blue Vinney cheese, which earned quite a premium over the standard Cheddar. Mrs

Patch told her son that his birthpangs had been particularly fruitful. When she took to childbed with him in the thirties, his father had to cope with milking and cheesemaking. This did not come easily to him, and expectant mother had to shout instructions downstairs to expectant father for two days. Father thought he had made a proper mess of it and wasted two whole days' milkings. However, his embarrassment and shame were subsequently erased by the bloom of two splendid celebratory batches of Blue Vinney.

Joyce Ward, now of Leamington and not I think related to her 'Blue Vinney' namesake, collected twenty-eight accounts of the making of Blue Vinney in 1974. A number came from previous makers of the cheese, but no two recipes were alike. This reminds me of the rich goat-farming areas of France with their infinite variety of cheeses, but wilful obscurantism in nomenclature. When I find some new treasure, quite different from anything else I have tasted, and ask the maker or shopkeeper its name, I am told with surprise: '_O, c'est chèvre._'

Purists who say that Blue Vinney must be made of skimmed milk are up against the accidental school and the varying effectiveness of hand skimming. They are also up against William Fream, the _Encyclopaedia Britannica_ authority on dairying, who died in 1907. Well before then he had found the best of Blue Vinney to be 'comparable with Stilton'. The answer in Dorset on historical evidence is 'If it blues, it's Vinney'. Etymologically speaking we cannot cavil.

Post-war Blue Vinney

Little making survived the last war, and of the few makers who tried to resume, some could not recapture the art. Guy Churchhouse, a noted Cheddar cheese farmer, set up a couple who had made Blue Vinney before the war on their Dorset farm, providing all the equipment needed and the services of a graduate-chemist cheesemaker; but it never came off. Nor did the efforts of South Western Dairies. Unigate experimented at Egginton in Derbyshire, mixing one part of whole milk with three parts of machine skimmed milk, and sold some in London. Egginton is no longer a creamery town. My conclusion from these short-lived experiments is that Blue Vinney making requires experience, instinct and a selective but minimal degree of science and hygiene.

Nevertheless, in the late 1950s and early 1960s I had no difficulty in getting cheese through friends living in Dorset: one used to bring me back a couple of cheeses regularly, and others would pick up a cheese or half-cheese from a publican. But the places of making were already being cloaked in a fog of secrecy as dense as that surrounding a Russian military establishment. When my Dorset connections moved away or retired I turned to Guy Churchhouse, who had been getting Blue Vinney from one intermediary (not a maker) for many years, and he spared me some of his supply; but we never knew where it came from.

There are a few established post-war makers. I believe Valerie Pinney made at Horn Park, Beaminster, but stopped when she married and moved away. One of Guy Churchhouse's employees, Mr Surland, saw Blue Vinney being made near Bridport in about 1972, perhaps at Boomerhayes where Mrs Rendell still made for her family at the age of eighty-eight. Finally a Mr Wood came to my shop as a customer a few years ago (unluckily, in my absence), and remarked that he had cleaned out the vats of some Blue Vinney makers in comparatively recent times. My attempts to trace him have failed.

The cheese has eluded many a search, including a foray made in 1971 by the late Kenneth Allsop, who lived in Dorset. He and a BBC 2 researcher eventually landed up independently at the same farm in Cerne Abbas. I know of this farm, which does not claim to make cheese, but only to receive it from yet another 'supplier' who is not claimed as the maker either. Indeed, the cheese obtained by BBC 2 from there was taken to the Milk Marketing Board's Cheddar depot at Crump Way in Wells, where it was ironed by a cheese grader of Vale of Belvoir origins. He declared it unequivocally to be 'substandard Stilton'.

Among journalists only Brian Jackman succeeded in finding and tasting a Blue Vinney of impeccable Dorset provenance. With its 'iron-bound crust' and 'worth its weight in gold', it was made for him late in 1974 only a mile away from his home, 'when there was some spare milk', by May Pitcher of Power-stock, who had learned to make Blue Vinney there over fifty years before. This is plainly not the source of the cheeses now on the market as Blue Vinney.

The death of Blue Vinney

If there were still a farm making Blue Vinney in Dorset on a commercial scale, I could understand the desire of those who marketed it to keep the source secret. The only farm in Gloucestershire making that county's original cheese in the traditional way has found it impossible to get on with cheesemaking without putting a stop to visitors. The burden of letters and telephone calls can become insupportable too. Commercial canniness in guarding the source is another obvious reason for secrecy. Ultimately they could have been guarding the makers against unwanted attentions from the Milk Marketing Board, the Health Inspectors and possibly the tax man. I have personal knowledge of farmers making cheese elsewhere who stay 'confidential' for such reasons, hard though I have tried to persuade them to come out of their shells for the public good. These experiences have naturally made me less sceptical than other cheese lovers, including experts such as Dermot Adamson, about the genuineness of all Blue Vinney over the last ten years.

However, three years ago a Long Clawson Stilton Dairy employee delivering to a Somerset cheese factor identified his own writing on the greaseproof wrappings of some cheeses already in the store. These had been invoiced to his customer from elsewhere as Dorset Farmhouse Blue. They were, of course, Stilton seconds. The Vale of Belvoir has been unwisely ready to loose its down-graded cheeses on the market to any willing buyer, provided he does not sell them as Stilton. This amounts to encouragement of mis-description, and has been an irresistible invitation to the unscrupulous. The customer in this case cut out the supplier who was passing off Stilton seconds as Blue Vinney, but did not prosecute. In August 1978 he found another source of supply in Francombe Farm, Cerne Abbas, the farm at which Kenneth Allsop and the BBC 2 investigator had landed up in 1971. Early in 1980 I wrote to Mrs Stenhouse there, explaining that if Blue Vinney were to feature as an existing cheese in this book, I should need to see it actually being made on a Dorset farm, in the company of an independent witness. Dr Reiter, a noted cheesemaker and bacteriologist, agreed to accompany me. I mentioned widespread scepti-cism, sharpened by the established occasions on which Stilton had been passed off as Dorset cheese, conceded a possible need for confidentiality and suggested that we should register the name of the farm in confidence with the English Country Cheese Council and the National Institute for Research in Dairying. Mrs Stenhouse wrote to me on 26 April that she had passed on my letter to her suppliers, 'leaving it to them to contact you if they wish to'. That is the last I have heard, or now expect to hear, from that quarter.

In March 1980 I had received my last cheeses invoiced as 'Dorset Blue', which I now know to have come from this source. When I came to iron them I identified them as Stilton. On my next visit to the Vale of Belvoir I took them with me and had my opinion confirmed by a fifth-generation Stilton maker and ex-Chairman of the Stilton Cheese Makers' Association, R. H. Watson. He kept one of them and had it analysed to put the diagnosis beyond reasonable doubt. The lapse of time and disintegration of the original wrappings through mould and travel made legal proof of the time of supply of these cheeses a doubtful proposition, but the experience led me in June 1980 to approach the chairman of the Stilton Makers' Association. With the backing of the secretary of the English Country Cheese Council I suggested that Stilton makers should investigate the passing off of their cheeses as Dorset Blue. I also suggested in another letter that they did a disservice to the name of Stilton and to the integrity of the English cheese trade in general by releasing their seconds on to the market. The Association's chairman replied that they could do little to help in the matter and that when someone buys their cheeses and 'does something with it to change its nature, the Stilton Trade Mark is not infringed if they then call the product by another name.'

Meanwhile I followed up a growing suspicion that cheeses which seemed to me and others the most powerful and earthy Blue Vinney over the years had after all been Stiltons: brown-crusted seconds from Colston Bassett, where the only unpasteurised Stilton is made. One of my puzzles, and encouragements, had been that these cheeses were of wider circumference than cheeses made by at least three of the Stilton dairies. Furthermore, these cheeses and a number of less obviously 'genuine' Dorset cheeses appeared to have been irregularly hand-skewered (an old Dorset habit) rather than evenly pricked on the standard mechanical turntable of today's blue cheese dairies.

The extra width is partly explained by wider hoops used at Colston Bassett and Long Clawson, and partly by the fact that an imperfect soft Stilton will settle when removed from the hoop, acquiring an irregular and extended girth. The erratic skewering could be explained by the wish of the original buyer of 'seconds' to spur on to further development some of the reluctant bluers.

Over the years my resistance to the sceptics had been based on these differences in the appearance of most cheeses sold as Blue Vinney from that of Stiltons, and on the greater earthiness and sharpness of character of the 'Dorset' cheeses. Many of them also seemed too good to be Stilton seconds. The final explanation is probably the one I had come to suspect, that the best 'Blue Vinney' had been unpasteurised cheeses from Colston Bassett. Some of them and some seconds from other Stilton dairies may have spent long enough in Dorset to be penetrated, after extra skewering, by a Dorset mould, and to have had their crust enriched by local conditions. The Stilton makers in these circumstances say to the seller 'call the Stilton anything you like except Stilton, and good luck to you'.

37

What is indisputable is that these diverted Stilton seconds satisfied me and many of my customers of Dorset ancestry and upbringing. They even interested Dermot Adamson, the greatest sceptic about Blue Vinney's existence, when he tasted them in my shop. Sadly, I now have little doubt that he was right. I had my last interesting cheeses about three years ago, and it was about then that Colston Bassett ceased to supply anyone in the Dorset region. The cheeses I have seen since then have conformed to the shape and weight and character of Long Clawson Dairy Stilton, with two smaller exceptions in December 1979 which could have been from Webster's Dairy. On 31 July 1980 I had confirmation that the Long Clawson employee who had exposed the passing off of his cheeses two years before was still taking seconds to Dorset, and knew that they were being sold through the farm at Cerne Abbas as 'Dorset Blue'.

In view of this, and as there had been no response from Mrs Stenhouse's 'suppliers', I wrote again, saying that I was forced to the conclusion that all her cheeses were Stilton seconds. This provoked no further word from her. I addressed a copy of my correspondence to Dorset County Council Consumer Protection Department, but perhaps Dorset does not rise to such a service; I am still waiting for an acknowledgement.

Meanwhile in the autumn of 1980 Ross Davies of *The Times*' Business Diary, whom I told of my conclusion about Blue Vinney, did a probe at Cerne Abbas and elicited a statement from Robert Stenhouse of Francombe Farm, who sells 'a score of 17 to 18 lb truckles of Blue Vinny (*sic*) a fortnight'. According to the Diary he said: 'We do not make it. I do not know that I can say where our supplies come from. They might dry up. It could be Somerset or it could be further afield. Anyway it is already blue when we get it and we do not describe it as Dorset cheese because we do not want to tangle with the Trade Descriptions Act.' Robert Stenhouse pointed out that his present cheeses are better than the Blue Vinney he remembered as a child: 'These are made with full-cream milk. They have not got the same sting.'

Sting is not a word I connect with good Stilton, but there is some logic in Mr Stenhouse's disingenuous statement: the cheeses sent to Francombe Farm by Long Clawson Stilton Dairy are second grade, with a ban attached against

Method of making Blue Vinney
As used by Mrs May Pitcher of Powerstock

Use morning and evening milk, fairly acid. If skim milk heat to 80°F, if separated, 76° is high enough. Add rennet (1 dram to 3 gallons) diluted in water. Stir in deep for 1 minute.

Leave 1 hour to coagulate. Cut into ½ inch cubes. Leave 10 minutes. Stir 10 minutes. Leave to 'pitch' in the whey 1–2 hours, until curd is firm and acid.

Draw off whey. Tie up curd in cloth. Leave for 20 minutes. Cut up in 4 pieces.

Turn every 15 minutes until firm and acid enough to break. Break up fairly small. Add salt (1 oz to 3 lb), and place in mould lined with cloth. Put in press.

Next day, turn into dry cloth and back under press.

Third day, should be ready to take out of press and remove from mould. Keep 4 months at least in a cool damp place to blue.

reselling them as Stilton. Mr Stenhouse would not be able to buy them cheap and sell them dear if they were of good, typical Stilton flavour and texture. Mr Stenhouse's own admissions, including the fact that the cheeses arrive from outside Dorset already blue, together with my previous evidence of examination and tasting, and the word of the driver who delivers them to Cerne Åbbas, combine to show that all cheeses emerging from there are, as I surmised, second-grade Long Clawson Stiltons. They cost more than the good ones and they are not Blue Vinney, so shopkeepers and the public should ignore them.

Regrettably, despite Mr Stenhouse's disavowal to _The Times_, they were still being invoiced to trade buyers as Dorset Blue, and described to Adrian Bailey in autumn 1981 as 'Blue Vinney, not Dorset Blue', even after he said he was a journalist. Of the last two cheeses invoiced to me as Dorset Blue I sacrificed one for laboratory examination in Stilton country, and sold the other over the counter as the Stilton it was. There seemed then not a glimmer of evidence from Dorset to dissuade me from describing this account of the county's unpredictable old cheese as Blue Vinney's obituary. Robert Stenhouse was prosecuted by Berkshire Trading Standards Dept in March 1982.

I am delighted to be proved wrong. In April 1981 I learned that there is one farm between Dorchester and Puddletown which has never stopped making. They only supply family and friends, to one of whom I owe this revelation. In the same month I was put in touch with Denis Pitts, who visited and had cheese from a farm which has been making for the last ten years in a small way. This is in the Powerstock area, a traditional stronghold where the veteran Blue Vinney maker May Pitcher lived. Mr Pitts' graduate cheesemaker, who had started at a friend's suggestion on taking over the farm, told him that three other local farms were making the cheese, though she bound him to confidence on names and places. He took home some cheese for which he paid £1.50 a pound, a bargain price proving that it was made there, and not bought in from suspect sources. In the same area Adrian Bailey found a cheesemaker who was given her recipe by May Pitcher. She has been too busy to make cheese in the last three years, but plans to start making Blue Vinney again when time allows. True Blue Vinney may come on the market in 1983 from a young Dorset farmer now busy improving his land and setting up a dairy.

Extinct cheeses of the South and South West

BANBURY, KENTISH; See p. 53
BATH: Soft unripened cheese (like Cambridge or York); pre-1914.
BERKELEY: Golden-marbled version of Gloucester cheese, briefly revived in Somerset about 1972 in two versions, one of them slightly orange-flavoured.
(_Note:_ These are not the usual Gloucester cheeses of this name.)
COTTSLOWE: Factory made Cotswold cheese of Cheddar flavour.
GUILDFORD: Fresh, buttery-flavoured cheese made by Cow and Gate before 1939.

HARMER'S: Made at Redditch in Worcestershire (no description).
NEW FOREST, VICTORIA: Fresh, buttery cheeses made at Guildford, the New Forest half the size of the Victoria.
NORTH WILTS: 5–12 lb loaf cheese of the nineteenth century, probably very close-textured.
PINEAPPLE CHEESE: Made in the late eighteenth and early nineteenth centuries by a farmer called Piko, of Buscot in Berkshire. The cheeses, weighing 5 lb, were hand pressed and made in the shape of a pineapple in wooden moulds like flower-pots.

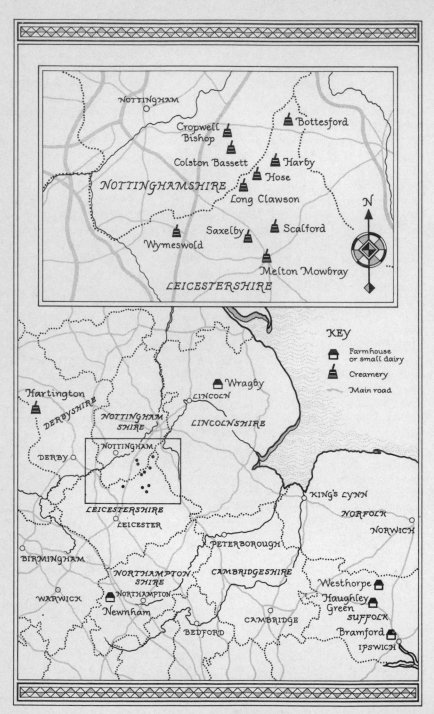

NOTTINGHAM

Cropwell
Bishop

Bottesford

Colston Bassett

Harby

Hose

Long Clawson

NOTTINGHAMSHIRE

Saxelby

Scalford

Wymeswold

Melton Mowbray

LEICESTERSHIRE

N

KEY

Farmhouse
or small dairy

Creamery

Main road

Wragby

Hartington

LINCOLN

DERBYSHIRE

NOTTINGHAM
SHIRE

LINCOLNSHIRE

NOTTINGHAM

DERBY

KING'S LYNN

NORFOLK

LEICESTERSHIRE

NORWICH

LEICESTER

PETERBOROUGH

BIRMINGHAM

CAMBRIDGESHIRE

Westhorpe

NORTHAMPTON
SHIRE

Haughley
Green

WARWICK

NORTHAMPTON

SUFFOLK

Newnham

CAMBRIDGE

Bramford

BEDFORD

IPSWICH

2
Cheeses of the Midlands

Leicester

The closest source of joy for the London-based cheese hunter is Leicestershire, in the heart of the foxhunting shires. Common interest has preserved fine rolling pastures surrounded by bullfinch hedges, double oxers and other beautiful and less frightening challenges to horse and rider, to serve dairymen and foxhunting people impartially. They have combined to keep most of the countryside and its dairying unchanged, to the delight of the human eye and the nesting bird, while other less privileged regions have been laid waste by hedge-hating corngrowers. Even the art of cutting and laying hedges, which seemed dead a few years ago, shows evidence of local revival in 1980.

Melton Mowbray is a hunting and a cheesemaking centre of fame, where Tuxford and Tebbutt's long-respected dairy turns out excellent traditional 20 lb and 45 lb deep-red Leicesters, a steady 25 per cent of its Leicester production, the rest of which is rindless cheeses or block for the supermarket trade. Finely cut curd and the unusual double use of the shredder-type mill before moulding, followed by two days' pressing, gives these cheeses a uniquely close texture, and a flavour at six months which some addicts find even richer when the cut cheese is exposed and hardens. Polythene wrapped versions develop none of this bite, mellowness or beauty of texture.

Early history

Leicester became independent of the vast original Cheshire cheese region well before the eighteenth century. In the 1700s and 1800s the big, hard, red cheeses were being made on many farms, particularly in south Leicestershire, where certain villages achieved local fame for excellent cheeses. Monk, when reporting to the Board of Agriculture in the 1790s, found some among them which he preferred to the newer, but more nationally renowned Stilton. The Leicester town crier used to recite a list of penalties against sellers of short-weight cheese, or cheese below a required standard of quality. To this day the town crier's salary, paid at Christmas, is a bottle of port and a Stilton.

The first factory to make Leicester was established in 1875. Farmhouse cheesemaking had diminished considerably from the middle of the century; it declined still further during the First World War, and died out before the Second. Dairy production had been increasing. Leicester was made alongside Stilton, using up the surplus milk, so from being a purely local cheese it shared the marketing channels of Stilton makers and was introduced to the capital, though it was still described in *The Epicure's Companion* by Edward Bunyard in 1937 as 'not often seen in London'.

In 1933 the Milk Marketing Board was formed to guarantee dairy farmers a market for their milk and for cheeses of adequate quality; but no Leicestershire farms remained to be included in the 1938-9 register of farms making cheese. The former Leicester and Stilton Makers' Association became purely a Stilton makers' preserve.

Leicester was still made during the Second World War, but colouring was not permitted. This was most upsetting to Midland devotees, who had always loved it deep-dyed, and had eaten almost all the cheese locally; and white Leicester was unlikely to attract London customers only recently introduced to the red. The traditional dark colour from annatto is stronger by far than that of any other English cheese, and equalled only by the rare good Mimolette made for long keeping in the Lille region of France. Far from hiding faults, as used to be suggested by outsiders, the colour reveals them by becoming mottled instead of smooth and even; and, despite the verdict of the chemist, I believe it to contribute to the flavour, which is unique. I have tasted some tolerable farm cheeses called Leicester made outside the county, but others have tasted like Double Gloucester with an overdose of annatto, which is not at all the same thing. I have also tasted block and prepacked versions of Leicester with only the annatto to remind one of the name, and with a bland, soggy consistency, quite irreconcilable with the genuine article.

However, it does seem probable that Leicester evolved under South Western influences, seeping from Gloucestershire through Warwickshire. Leicester is nearer in shape and external appearance to Double Gloucester, even to the tradition of blueing the crust, than to any other cheese.

Despite pasteurisation, something survives in the milk of this lush region and this, with the traditional method of making, marks the flavour of the Melton Mowbray cheeses. The curd is packed in the widest hoops of any English cheese, 20 inches across and 6 inches deep. The cheesecloth used is much lighter than that of other cheeses, and Dr Davis recommends that it should be removed for the last two weeks of the ripening period to let blue mould coat the surface. The resultant juxtaposition of blue and deep red is enchanting, as is the occasional happy accident of natural blueing.

Leicester can be eaten at three months, but my recommendation is to give it at least six and preferably nine months. Some of its devotees like it really hard, when it acquires an extra nuttiness. This can be achieved by leaving the cheese unwrapped in a dry atmosphere. The crust is always palatable.

Sources of Leicester

CHESHIRE

CHORLTON LODGE FARM, Chester (*for details of farm see p. 62*)

LANCASHIRE

SINGLETON'S DAIRY, Longridge, near Preston (*see p. 70*)

LEICESTERSHIRE

TUXFORD AND TEBBUTT, Melton Mowbray (*see p. 49*)

The only producer of the cheese in its native area and in the original 45 lb flat wheels

SOMERSET

NORTH LEAZE FARM, North Cadbury (*see p. 16*)
Hard, deep red, pasteurised; hard natural, clothbound; 17–20 lb, 45 lb wheels
Where to buy: North Cadbury: Longman's Farmhouse Fare, North Leaze Farm; Longridge: Singleton's Dairy, Preston Road (all wholesale); other reputable cheese factors

Stilton

North east of Leicester lie vales rich in brooks, pastures, fences and trees. They encircle Melton Mowbray and culminate beyond in the Vale of Belvoir, presided over from an isolated rise by its fairy-tale ducal castle. In this much-loved corner of the Shires, threatened now by coalmining proposals, within the fifteen miles between Quenby and Cropwell Bishop, are the pastures and the house that first gave birth to Stilton. There too are all but one of the dairies making today. They embrace the north east of old Leicestershire, Rutland, and green tracts of Nottinghamshire, with iron as well as coal beneath the soil, iron that is said to encourage the blueing of its native cheese. Outside this area only the beautiful Dale of the Dove is legally permitted to make Stilton, England's most internationally respected and only protected cheese.

The origins of Stilton

The first evidence of the cheese's existence dates back to the years before 1720 when Elizabeth Scarbrow was housekeeper to the Ashbys at Quenby Hall, Hungarton, two miles north east of the outskirts of Leicester. She saw cheese being made there from a recipe headed 'Lady Beaumont's Cheese' and learned to make it herself. Known locally as Quenby cheese, it was sold within the first quarter of the eighteenth century to the Bell Inn at Stilton in Huntingdonshire, a Great North Road coaching-house thirty miles away. The Bell served and sold enough of it for Stilton to have become 'famous for its cheese' before

Daniel Defoe passed through in 1722 on his *Tour through the Whole Island of Great Britain*. The cheese was never made in, or even near, Stilton; but eighteenth-century travellers, gratefully remembering the place where they found it, called it Stilton Cheese; and Stilton Cheese it has remained ever since.

These few facts are historically beyond dispute. It is not so simple to unravel whether the recipe originated at Quenby or elsewhere, or which Lady Beaumont conceived or sponsored it. Geographically the nearest candidate for inventor's honours would have been the wife of one of the Beaumont Baronets of Stoughton Grange, five miles south west of Quenby, but there is no evidence connecting this family with the Ashbys. Their cousins the Beaumonts of Cole Orton, twenty miles north west of Quenby, on the other hand, were connected through the sixteenth-century marriage of Anne Beaumont to Thomas Ashby of Loseby and Quenby. Squire de Lisle, the present owner of Quenby, thinks that Thomas and Anne lived at Loseby and could have invited Anne's stepmother, Elizabeth Beaumont, to spend her widowhood at Quenby Hall, where she might have used the recipe. As she was married before 1553, her tenure would have been from the latter part of the 1500s until, at the latest, 1618, when George Ashby inherited the house and immediately started rebuilding it in its present form. This theory presents two difficulties: first, Elizabeth might have been called Mistress or Dame but she was never Lady Beaumont; second, more than a century elapsed between her time and the earliest report of cheesemaking at Quenby, a period disturbed by two decades of rebuilding, and by the Civil War. Nevertheless a family relationship had been established between Ashbys and Beaumonts which was a degree closer than that of county neighbours. If this did not bring the recipe to Quenby then, it may well have led to the Ashbys' inheritance of it later.

The most likely introducer of the recipe was Mary, daughter of Sir Erasmus de la Fontaine of Kirby Bellars, seven miles north of Quenby. From being a young neighbour of the Ashbys she became a family connection, marrying the only descendant in the male line of Anne Ashby's father.

Mary's husband, the last Baronet of Cole Orton and last Viscount Beaumont of Swords, died in 1702. The childless widow could have returned to Kirky Bellars, but might well have been invited by the Ashbys to live at Quenby. Professor W. G. Hoskins thinks that the cheese recipe originated in her family at Kirby Bellars in the seventeenth century. If this is so, Lady Beaumont would seem to have brought her recipe to Quenby after leaving home, because the Quenby copy bore her married name. Whether she found it at Kirby Bellars or devised it there or at Quenby, there can be little doubt that it is to Mary, Lady Beaumont that we owe its preservation; and it is to Elizabeth Scarbrow that we owe its propagation.

For the fame of Stilton to have been recognised by 1722, the first cheeses bought by The Bell must surely have been not only Quenby by name, but Quenby made. This presupposes a link between hostelry and household in Elizabeth Scarbrow's time as housekeeper, leading to her later business and family association with Cowper Thornhill, the landlord. She may have made some of these early cheeses herself, although she was only reported as having seen the making.

In 1720 Elizabeth married Mr Orton, farming a few miles away at Little

Dalby. John Nichols, in his history of Leicestershire, reported her as starting to make cheese there in about 1730. If he was right, Quenby must have been supplying large quantities of cheese to the Bell after Elizabeth left until at least 1730; but Quenby Hall fell into such neglect about this time or just after that it was described as a shell when Shuckburgh Ashby, a relative, bought it in the middle of the century. So Elizabeth became the only Stilton maker, which may have fostered the legend that one of her husband's pastures, Orton's Close, was the only source of milk from which the cheese could be made. (I am sorry to say that on a brief visit to Little Dalby I was unable to find anyone who could show it to me.)

As well as cheese Elizabeth produced daughters. One of them learned to make the cheese and married a farmer called Paulet at Wymondham near Melton. She joined her mother in supplying The Bell. The whole business was gathered into the family when her sister married Cowper Thornhill. Perhaps that wise and persistent man would have said that he had gathered family and cheese unto himself. At the time, he was selling Stilton of the family make, still unique, at 2s 6d a pound, a price not equalled again, probably, until after 1945.

In 1756 there were still only three Stilton makers: Mrs Orton and her daughter Mrs Paulet, and one other who could by then have been a Paulet daughter. Mrs Paulet was still living in Wymondham in 1790. By that time the family monopoly had long been broken. Nichols wrote that the cheese was now made from 'not one but from almost every close in this parish [Little Dalby], and in many of the neighbouring ones'. Marshall, writing of the same period, reported that Dalby, which 'first took the lead', was said to pay its rent through cheese alone, but that cheese was now made in almost every village in the Melton quarter of Leicestershire and in many neighbouring villages in Rutland. Makers sold it at between 10d and 1s a pound to all the innkeepers within a radius of between fifteen and twenty miles, who served it and sold it to take away at 12d to 14d a pound 'makers' weight'. This meant that the customer accepted weight loss, but was compensated for it by maturity. The cheese was often described as 'cream cheese', not in the modern sense, but as a cheese generally made from full-cream milk with the addition of cream taken off a further equal quantity of milk. For his 1794 report to the Board of Agriculture Monk investigated Stilton making in most of the villages around Melton Mowbray, but he could not wheedle the secret out of any of the farm dairies. He was eventually helped by Major Cheselden of Somerby (a parish adjoining Little Dalby), who extracted a recipe from one of his tenants. Making varied in the number of separate curds used, three curds gradually giving way to two, but the recipes handed down from mothers to daughters changed little before the First World War. One noted Edwardian Stilton maker, Mrs Musson of Wartnaby, told Rider Haggard that 'Stiltons, with the exception they make no noise, are more trouble than babies'.

The decline of farmhouse Stilton making

In 1910 the producers organised themselves to improve methods of production and the making 'passed from the stage of a secret recipe guarded by a few farmhouse makers to become an ascertainable process'. The nature of the cheese, and the region of pastures and Stilton-making dairies, was defined.

Basically the cheese remained the same, but the era of farmhouse Stilton was near its end.

Few farms were making Stilton in 1918. One of the last which survived into the 1930s was that of the Watson family, then fourth-generation Stilton makers. The son, R. H. Watson, learned the art too: he practised in the dairy, not on the farm, became president of the Stilton Makers' Association in the 1970s, and now sells the cheese in Market Street, Bingham, alongside many others.

The 1870s brought the first factory-scale making of Stilton, but their methods did not suppress the cheese's character. J. Marshall Dugdale, visiting most of them in 1899, found such individuality that no two dairies were carrying out all the stages of Stilton making in the same way.

The first removal of Stilton from its close-knit traditional pastures came when a farmer whose herd had been stricken by foot and mouth disease took over the dairy opened by the Duke of Devonshire at Hartington in Dovedale. This Derbyshire venture became famous as Nuttall's, and was finally bought by the Milk Marketing Board in 1962. Dovedale milk has for many years reinforced local supplies for Melton Mowbray cheeses, but expansion of Nuttall's enabled much more of it to be used there by the end of the 1970s.

Legal protection for Stilton

Cheese called Stilton has been made elsewhere. I was once misled by the sight of a napkin-surrounded drum into asking for Stilton at a restaurant in Henley, only to be repelled by a close view of its ashen-white flesh and cindery black mould. Later investigation of Henley grocers' shops revealed in one window the image of my restaurant nightmare proudly displayed as 'Winnie Wilts Prize Stilton'.

Such disservice to the name of Stilton is, fortunately, no longer legal. In 1969 the Stilton Makers' definitions of 1910 were given the backing of a High Court judgment: Stilton is a blue or white cheese made from full-cream milk with no applied pressure, forming its own crust or coat and made in cylindrical form, the milk coming from English dairy herds in the district of Melton Mowbray and surrounding areas falling within the counties of Leicestershire (now including Rutland), Derbyshire and Nottinghamshire.

The judgment came too late to exclude pasteurisation, which all except the Colston Bassett Dairy have adopted since the Second World War. Nuttall's explained to me in 1974 that their bulked milk (from forty-nine farms then) might contain antibiotics, and that yeasts associated with mould could cause the milk to froth over in the vat; they had to pasteurise to kill it. It is regrettable that sloppy dairy farming should be allowed to change cheese. One Hartington resident told the wife of a senior MMB official, herself an old devotee of Nuttall's cheese, that the cheese had never been the same since.

The 1969 judgment, in specifying the shape of the cheese, rules out block Stilton and any imitation from outside the prescribed region, but it does not lay down enough detail in the method to eliminate a certain amount of shortcutting. Some Stiltons have a suspiciously smooth interior and scarcely any coat, suggesting quite severe departures from tradition. Another problem not properly dealt with is sub-standard cheese (see p. 37–8). However, the general standard of present-day Stilton which has been sufficiently matured, and not refrigerated or smothered in sweat-inducing plastic, is high.

The character of Stilton

When Defoe first met the cheese for which Stilton was famous, he wrote that it is 'called our English Parmesan and brought to the table with the mites and maggots round it so thick, that they bring a spoon for you to eat the mites with, as you do the cheese'. The mite tradition was taken very seriously. Even in this century some of the dairies would not let cheeses out until the mite had got such a hold that their floors were carpeted in the living brown dust they shed from their coats. J. G. W. Stafford, who was introduced to Stilton making about 1907, said that any cheese not having a mite-infested rough coat was looked upon with suspicion by old hands among the factors and merchants.

The nickname English Parmesan made me at first think of another use for the spoon Defoe mentions, which no doubt developed into the cheese scoop. One of those old cheeses (one 1812 devotee liked Stilton at two years) must have broken the knife and caused a claret-filled host to turn the port decanter upside down over it to make the cheese malleable before he worked away with a spoon. Mrs Beeton was still using the term English Parmesan in 1861, when she gave a recipe for Stilton to her readers.

On the other hand early reports also remark on the creaminess of the cheese, which was indeed made by taking the cream off the overnight milk and adding it to the full-cream morning milk, milk from pastures renowned for their lushness. There are also early traditions of wine being dripped on the curds during the making, and of whole cheeses being put under a beer tap, or having port or sherry poured over them, the cheese sometimes being pricked. These practices, not accidental dripping from a pipe of port over a whole cheese in the cellar, are the origins of the custom of putting port in Stilton. The wine on the curd could have been for the encouragement of mould rather than to enrich the flavour; but with the general use for many years of three different curds and the absence of pressing, mould development can have presented few problems. I wonder whether wine could have contributed to the virtues of a Stilton sent by Thomas Allsop to Charles Lamb in 1823. Lamb's letter of thanks included this passage: 'Your cheese is the best I ever tasted ... yours is the delicatest, rainbow-hued, melted piece I ever flavoured.'

Some cheese may have been eaten young, but Stilton does not have to be young to be soft and creamy – rather does it start firm and then soften as it blues. Maturing a new cheese is always a mixture of accident and experiment, seasonal over-production often necessitating the first trials of longer keeping, as for instance the eighteen months mentioned early on. A year was considered the ideal time in the late eighteenth century; but with an unpressed cheese there is always great variation in texture and therefore in speed of development, even between factory cheeses of the same batch made from pasteurised milk. Before starters were cultured, the milk for cheese ripened naturally, and cheeses were often slower to make and mature, and softer in maturity. A pressed cheese made in the old way can develop into a semi-soft cheese (compare Single Gloucester) which will keep better than its firmer, starter-made counterpart. Even with a modern starter, a good unpasteurised cheese can develop and retain a remarkably soft, creamy consistency in full maturity: I have recently sampled an eighteenth-month-old Green Fade (see p. 61) which was softer than the average three-month-old Cheshire. Finally mould itself breaks down protein in the cheese and works alongside the enzymes in ripening it after bacterial activity has ended.

Good Blue Stilton ready to eat has the protection of an uncracked, tough, hard crust; the interior is cream-coloured to yellow, not white, and its veins reveal a well-spread greeny blue rather than a blue-black or cindery aspect. The texture varies largely with the tightness of packing of the curd in the hoop, and offers a range from crumbly to smooth, from soft to firm, wide enough to suit many different palates. I am thankful for this as I iron my Christmas cheeses, and match their potential characters with the specified requirements of my splendidly demanding customers. These variations come within the products of a single dairy, but the dairies still retain their own individuality too, and long may it remain so.

A total of 6000 tons of Stilton was made in 1980, equal to the annual cheese consumption of a million Britons. Yet Stilton curd and crust are still largely hand-made, and each finished cheese must be gently hand-turned daily. In August 1981 Mr Wiles, Chairman of the Stilton Makers' Association, was looking forward to changes which could bring 'the consistency of product quality which the public requires'. My advice to Stilton makers, before they invest in machinery which might remove the variety and individuality which is the very essence of Stilton, is to attend to two easily rectifiable shortcomings. They should keep their second-grade cheeses off the market, and they should watch with more care the stage of maturity at which their good cheeses are released. Ironing Stiltons as they came to me in autumn 1981, I had to reject at least half for complete or almost complete absence of blueing.

Immaturity puts off more potential Stilton customers than any other factor. 'Consistent quality from every Stilton dairy' is Mr Wiles's admirable aim; but if consistency of quality is confused with uniformity of character, Stilton will lose old customers faster than it gains new ones. The range of taste among the faithful is richly wide; long may the products of the Stilton dairies vary enough to cater for them.

I am delighted to be able to end this story of Stilton cheese with happy news. In April 1981 work began on restoring the long-derelict Bell Inn at Stilton. It will be reopened by Turnpike Inns for its original purpose. I am assured that we shall once more be served good Stilton on the premises where that excellent landlord, Cowper Thornhill, first made the cheese famous in the early eighteenth century.

White Stilton

White Stilton has been eaten for many years as a different cheese. Kirwan wrote in *Host and Guest* in 1864 that 'Epicures prefer cheese with a green mould, but the best are ... without any appearance of mouldiness'. It is a refreshing and very individual cheese, far removed in consistency and flavour from the Blue.

Sources of Stilton

LEICESTERSHIRE (MELTON MOWBRAY AND THE VALE OF BELVOIR)

TUXFORD AND TEBBUTT (Express Dairies), Thorpe End, Melton Mowbray

This is the southernmost dairy and the nearest to the possible birth places of Stilton. Quenby is eight miles to the south west; Kirby Bellars is on Melton's doorstep, just over a mile to the west south west, and Little Dalby is within three miles to the south east. Although the dairy belongs to a giant concern, it keeps up tradition in its Stilton and Leicester cheeses. Its Stiltons have a notably creamy colour and are about 14 lb in weight.

WEBSTER'S DAIRY, Saxelby (*3 miles W.N.W. of Melton Mowbray*)

Webster's cheeses, with the smallest circumference of all makes, have an old-fashioned creamy texture and colour and uneven blue in larger streaks, suggesting methods closer to tradition than some other dairies. In 1981 they started making a coloured version of their cheese, marketed as Royal Blue, stopping in October.

WYMESWOLD (*8–9 miles W. of Melton on Ashby Road*)
SCALFORD (*3 miles N. of Melton*)

These two dairies are subsidiaries of J. M. Nuttall and Co., Hartington (*see below*). I have seen good-looking cheeses from Wymeswold with a well-spread but noticeably pale blue mould.

LONG CLAWSON DAIRY, Long Clawson (*6 miles N. of Melton*)

This dairy started as a farmers' co-operative. Its cheeses average about 17 lb, though they are not quite as broad as those from Colston Bassett.

Long Clawson came first in the class for two open half Stiltons at Nantwich in 1980, showing cheeses of extremely creamy aspect. Over the years I have found them firmer than Nuttall's and greyer in crust, but late 1981 cheeses were softer.

The company is still farmer-owned. It also owns the HOSE STILTON DAIRY (*2 miles N.E. of Long Clawson*), which it took over and modernised in the early 1970s,

and has turned TYTHBY FARM, Harby (*2 miles N. of Hose*), over to Stilton making too. All three dairies make Blue and White Stilton according to demand, which has grown considerably. These dairies regret that they have not the facilities to receive visitors.

ST IVEL (Unigate Dairy), Harby (*7 miles N. of Melton*)

St Ivel Stiltons tend to have a smoother exterior, a skin rather than a crust. Their interiors are usually smooth too, but the well-blued half Stiltons they showed at Nantwich in 1980 were rather uneven in texture.

NOTTINGHAMSHIRE

COLSTON BASSETT AND DISTRICT DAIRY COMPANY, Colston Bassett (*6 miles S.E. of Nottingham*)

This dairy makes the broadest Stiltons, in 10½ in. hoops. Unpasteurised milk gives them a deeper, richer flavour, distinctive from those of any other dairy. Their rich brown powdery coats are also notable.

SOMERSET CREAMERIES LTD, Cropwell Bishop, near Nottingham

This is the only Stilton dairy of whose cheeses I have no personal experience.

DERBYSHIRE

J. M. NUTTALL AND COMPANY (Dairy Crest), Dove Dairy, Hartington, near Buxton

This dairy's large cheeses are like Tuxford and Tebbutt's in size, smaller in circumference than Long Clawson, but larger than Webster's. They have a distinctive rough golden crust, and are generally fat, full-flavoured typical Stiltons, if properly looked after. They vary considerably in texture: light moist crumbly, creamy soft, creamy fat, firm, and gradations between. The firmer cheeses are slow to blue, and need patience which ought really to be exercised at Hartington before they are sold; but I like the variety and seldom find a poor cheese. Nuttall's won a first prize for two whole Blue Stiltons at Nantwich in 1980.

Cheeses with added flavouring

Vale of Belvoir, Leicestershire and Nottinghamshire

These cheeses are made by breaking up Cheddar or Double Gloucester at the required stage of maturity (unblued Stilton, too, in the case of Walton, see list below) and either mixing in the chosen ingredients with the curd before re-milling or, as in the case of Windsor Red, pouring wine over the re-milled curd. It has been an immemorial custom in many respected cheesemaking regions to use wine, herbs, spices, charcoal and leaves in or on cheeses, so there is no call for contempt of the practices evolved by these enterprising Midland dairies. The cheeses are usually presented in 10 lb drum-shaped form, crustless except in the case of Walton, which is coated with nibbed walnuts, and Charnwood with its paprika skin.

VALE OF BELVOIR

All the following cheeses are made at TYTHBY FARM DAIRY, Bottesford, Nottinghamshire (now also 5 lb halves)

Charnwood
Medium, moist Cheddar, smoke-flavoured and coated with paprika; 10 lb drums

Cheviot
White Cheddar with chives; 1 lb, 10 lb drums

Cotswold
Double Gloucester with chives and onions; 1 lb, 10 lb drums

Huntsman
Two layers of Stilton curd sandwiched between three of Double Gloucester curd; 10 lb drums

Nutwood
Medium Cheddar with cider, raisins and hazelnuts; 1 lb, 10 lb drums

Rutland
Medium Cheddar with beer, garlic and parsley; 1 lb, 10 lb drums

Sherwood
Double Gloucester with pickle; 1 lb, 10 lb drums

Walton
Cheddar and Stilton curd with finely chopped walnuts and a nibbed walnut coat; 1 lb drums, 3 lb flat rounds, 6 lb flat drums

Windsor Red
Medium, moist Cheddar, marbled with bright red elderberry wine from Merrydown, East Sussex; 1 lb, 10 lb drums

Derby

Derby is one of the oldest of British cheeses to become distinct from the ancient widespread type once common to all the Midlands, which led to the Cheshire we know today. Derby was also the first cheese to take to factory processes. It was an early subject of co-operative enterprise among farmers in the county, which culminated in the conversion of an old Derby cheese warehouse in 1870. Soon afterwards the first purpose-built cheese factory was opened at Longford, and within six years there were six in Derbyshire (the rest of England could only boast seven). One factory, at Brailsford, specialised in the five-layer Derby Sage.

Of all this there is now nothing left. The only traditional cheesemaking in Derbyshire is that of Stilton by Nuttall's Dairy at Hartington in Dovedale. This dairy also blues Wensleydale cheeses made at Kirkby Malzeard in North Yorkshire, where the mould spores were causing trouble in a dairy mainly devoted to white cheeses. By a curious irony, it is there among those white Yorkshire cheeses that the only Derby following the full traditional recipe is made today. It may be a sort of revenge, but I find such geographical contradictions a sad element in modern cheesemaking. However, the Wensleydale-made 'Derby' is good cheese.

When it was made on farms, Dr Davis tells us, each farm had its own method, and 'those farmers who were able to make better cheese than their neighbours kept the method a family secret'. This helps to explain the cheese's demise. Cheesemaking recipes are as precious as the results of scientific research, and, like them, should be published to the general good, to keep the best practices alive for posterity.

Towards the end most of the cheesemakers had passed through the Midland College at Sutton Bonington, which introduced starter and standardised the recipe. A little farmhouse cheesemaking in the south of the county survived the First World War. Etchells Farm at Church Broughton made until 1925, and other farms nearby made cheese when their milk was returned (usually from London) until the Milk Marketing Board took over milk distribution in 1933.

The traditional maker set out with 30 gallons of whole milk to make a cheese softer, whiter and less acid than Cheddar. The outward result was a cheese 14–16 inches across and 4–6 inches deep, weighing 28–30 lb. Today's cheeses are waxed over the cloth, but Mrs Gibson of Coxbench in Derbyshire, who trained at the Midland College (now the University of Nottingham's Faculty of Agriculture) in the interwar years, tells me that the cheese 'gray', the coarse stuff cheesecloth, was pasted on with a flour and water paste, and that wax was not then used, as it has been for some time in coating cheeses of creamery manufacture. Mrs Arthur of Church Broughton, who has made a study of old Derbyshire cheesemaking, tells me that in earlier days the paste method, though used, had been frowned upon by the best makers. They used calico for top and bottom and a cheesecloth bandage round the outside of the cheese.

Despite its slightly softer nature Derby lived on through the Second World War as a creamery cheese, though only 700 tons were made in 1950–1, less than a quarter of 1939 production. By the late 1970s this had increased to nearly 1300 tons, but most of this was in block form or as small rindless cheeses. For some years now we have had to thank Kirkby Malzeard for the only traditional Derby.

Derby Sage

The smaller, Derby Sage cheeses of about 14 lb (waxed, tubby clothbound cheeses also from North Yorkshire) are made of Derby curd. After the milling and salting process the curd is coated with sage steeped in chlorophyll, which results in a striking green-marbled effect when the cheese is cut. Because of its pervasive flavour it should not be eaten just before any other cheese.

The original sage cheeses were produced in spring for harvest eating, though I have seen mention of autumn making for Christmas too. They were made quite differently from their marbled successors of the last ten years. Two vats were used, one holding two-fifths of the milk which was flavoured and coloured with the strained juice of pulped fresh sage leaves, the brownish colour being corrected with spinach leaves or some other natural green agent. The factory at Brailsford stained its sage with juice squeezed from potato tops. When the curd had been milled and salted it was shovelled into the clothlined hoop, usually in five alternating layers of uncoloured and coloured curd. When cut the cheese had an attractive, somewhat 'Neapolitan' look. Unfortunately the black mould, to which moist Derby is particularly vulnerable, did tend to penetrate between the layers, a disadvantage avoided by the modern marbling method. A friend of mine remembers eating Derby with a single one inch layer of sage in the centre on a farm at Glutton Bridge, near the Staffordshire border, during trout fishing seasons in the 1930s.

Sources of Derby

NORTH YORKSHIRE

KIRKBY MALZEARD DAIRY, near Ripon (Wensleydale Creameries)
1 Derby
Hard, full-cream, pasteurised; natural, clothbound, waxed; 28–30 lb wheels
Softer and whiter than Cheddar, reaching a distinctive rich, tangy flavour in 8 months
2 Derby Sage
Hard, full-cream, pasteurised; natural, clothbound, waxed; 14 lb tubby, barrel-shaped form
Of green marbled appearance, strong in colour and in sage-chlorophyl flavouring
Where to buy: Neither widely available, though Derby Sage more commonly sold than real plain Derby; Crewe: Embertons; North Cadbury: Longman's Farmhouse Fare; Stockton-on-Tees: Whitelock's (all wholesale); Streatley: Wells Stores

Other cheeses of the Midlands and East Anglia

Cambridge

This cheese was originally an unsalted cheese with a fresh cream slice in the middle which gave it the orange layer, now regrettably replaced by coloured curd. It was made in the Isle of Ely and surrounding areas. York recipes were like Cambridge and included the sage layers. A similar cheese called Lancashire Cream Slice used to be made to use up odd surplus milk. Mollington Grange Farm near Chester (see p. 71) makes a larger, round, entirely apricot-coloured version, and an uncoloured cheese.

Colwick

Originally of skimmed milk, as made now at Fox Covert Dairy (and in recent years in the Vale of Belvoir by Tythby Farm Dairy and Long Clawson Stilton Dairy), this cheese traditionally went with cucumber sandwiches for tea in Nottingham on summer Sundays before 1914.

The Ministry of Agriculture classes it, despite local lore, as a full-fat cheese, which is how the School of Agriculture at Sutton Bonington made it when Dr Hinch was there thirty years ago. This version is made by Neal's Yard, Covent Garden, and sometimes recalls the Slipcote described below. Dr Hinch plans to make full-cream Colwick in addition to her present skimmed-milk cheese.

Slipcote (also Slippcott, Slippcoat or Slipcoat)

This cheese describes itself, outwardly speaking, and was probably a full-fat cheese similar to Colwick, casting its coat with creamy exuberance as it liquefied under it on ripening. I have seen some Neal's Yard cheeses behaving this way and looking most succulent.

Slipcote was written of in 1699 as made of 'good morning milk putting cream to it'. In 1858 *Simmonds' Trade Dictionary* called it 'new made cheese; a small and very rich variety of Yorkshire cheese, not unlike butter, but white'. It was familiar in Rutland until 1914, remembered later as something like a Camembert, sold on straw, with a volatile coat. Although the 'new made' Yorkshire suggests York curd cheese (unsalted), this does not normally crust.

Extinct cheeses of the Midlands and East Anglia

BANBURY: This was probably a flat, round, rindy cheese, made with what was left of Banbury milk after cream- or butter-making. It was proverbially thin: Shakespeare wrote of 'a thin affair . . . like a Banbury cheese, nothing but paring'.

COTTENHAM: This Cambridgeshire cheese was variously reported in the past as 'like Stilton, only thicker' and as resembling Lancashire. It was made of new milk. (I have never seen a Cottenham, and it is not even listed in Dr Davis's massive work *Cheese.*)

ESSEX: This cheese was mentioned by William Bulleyn in 1550, and rated low in order of merit by Barnaby Googe (1557): followed only by Kentish, 'the very worst'. We may suppose Essex to have been halfway between Banbury and Suffolk (see below) in shape, size and severity.

ESSEX EWES' MILK CHEESE: Ewes' milk cheese from the Essex marshes is recorded as being exported to the Continent as early as the eighth or ninth century. Huge, hard, sharp-flavoured cheeses produced in Essex from skimmed ewes' milk were sold to London in Elizabethan times.

NEWMARKET: This cheese is mentioned as 'Queen's Cheese' in the 1744 edition of E. Smith's *Compleat Housewife*, which gives a recipe. It was made 'to eat at two years old'. One report describes it as a 40 lb marigold-coloured cheese naturally ripening, with scalded cream and rennet added after the curd had formed. After removal of the whey and hand pressing of the curd under cloth, the curd was packed into the vat (mould). It was later removed, sliced, redrained, wiped, treated with 'a handful of salt' and 1 quart of cold cream. It was then hand worked and repacked in the vat and left overnight under a 1 lb weight. The next day it was put under 'normal pressure'.

NORFOLK: The dairymaids of Norfolk were much looked down upon, and one report describes their cheeses as being often mere bags of maggots.

READING YELLOW: This 10 lb, close-textured, waxy cheese was a dairy school invention. It was made of washed curd, salted in a brine bath, coated with wax or resin, and eaten at 14 days, or 2–3 months in colder weather.

SUFFOLK: Henry VIII was given some Suffolk cheeses, and the donor is not known to have lost her head; so the cheese must have come down in the world afterwards. This 'hard, horny, flet-milk' cheese became even more notorious than Banbury for its meanness, but was much exported to Scotland before Dunlop gave the Scots a taste for a full-milk cheese. The adjectives quoted above were used in a 1655 description, which adds that it was a cartwheel in shape, and called 'bang' by farmworkers. It was made from what was probably the most thoroughly skimmed or 'flet' milk in England.

WARWICKSHIRE: This cheese had a reasonable enough reputation in the eighteenth century for some Gloucester cheeses to be sold under its name in London. The cheese market was at Atherstone. My belief is that this cheese was similar to Gloucester, and that a further development of it produced Leicester.

Other cheeses of the Midlands and East Anglia

NORTHAMPTONSHIRE

GREEN COTTAGE, Newnham (*about 3 miles S. of Daventry, 1 mile E. of A382*)
Visitors tel. Daventry (032 72) 4221
1   Hard Goat Cheese
Natural rind; 4 in. cube
Kept for periods between 3 weeks and a year, when it is strong and as hard as Parmesan
2   Soft Goat Cheese
Full-cream; 4 oz tubs
Both UNpasteurised, ripened naturally without added starter
Farmer, cheesemaker: Joy Williams
Saanen goats
Where to buy: On farm
Joy Williams is planning to milk her Dorset Horn sheep for cheesemaking

LEICESTERSHIRE

WEBSTER'S DAIRY, Saxelby
Royal Blue
Stilton-textured, coloured blue
For details see p. 49

LINCOLNSHIRE

FOX COVERT DAIRY, Holton-cum-Beckering, Wragby
No visitors
1   Cambridge
Soft, unripened, medium-fat, white with horizontal orange layer in middle (sometimes with sage-stained layer) on straw mat; no crust; $4\frac{1}{2}$–$5\frac{1}{2}$ oz flat, rectangular
2   Colwick
Soft, skimmed-milk cheese (under 2 per cent fat), lightly salted; natural crust, white; 4–5 oz flat, round
Cheesemaker: Dr Helen Hinch
Where to buy: At dairy (wholesale only); Arnold, Beeston, Newark and Lincoln markets; Bingham: R. H. and J. Watson, Market Street; Navenby: J. W. Welbourne and Son; Wragby: Market Place Stores
Dr Hinch's great-grandmother made Stilton at Moorcot

Note: Neal's Yard Dairy, Covent Garden

(*see p. 19*) also make Colwick. Although they do not call it Slipcote, I have seen one slipping its coat in the most appetising fashion in summer

SUFFOLK

BULLEN CAPRINE DAIRIES, Keepers Cottage, Bullen Lane, Bramford, near Ipswich
Goat Cheese
1   Semi-hard matured Mendel, Liptauer type
2   Soft: plain or with herbs or nuts
No crusts; 12 oz–4 lb
Farmers, cheesemakers: Mrs M. Lamb, Mrs Cooke, Mrs L. Hetherington
British Toggenberg, ⋅ Saanen, Anglo-Nubian goats
Where to buy: On farm (will post also)

SHRUB FARM, Haughley Green, near Stowmarket (*3 miles N.N.E. of Stowmarket; turn right off A45 2 miles out of town*)
Visitors by appointment, tel. Haughley (044 970) 311
Haughley Green Cheese
Unripened, soft
Farmer, cheesemaker: Mrs Morris
Jersey herd; permanent pastures on heavy loam
Where to buy: On farm; Stowmarket: Betta Foods

LADYWELL, Westhorpe (*on B1113, 6 miles N. of Stowmarket*)
Visitors tel. Bacton (0449) 781544
Ladywell Goat Cheese
1   Soft, lactic; no crust; 4 oz packets
2   Smallholder
Natural crust
Both UNpasteurised
Farmer, cheesemaker: Mrs Frances Case
British Toggenberg goats; permanent pastures on chalk-based clay
Where to buy: On farm, end April to autumn (notice required for Smallholder)
Mrs Case gives occasional demonstrations but does not teach theory

3

Cheeses of the North West

Cheshire

Cheshire, Britain's oldest named cheese, was the child of a mild climate and a region of vales and gently undulating hills. This countryside is drained by the Dee and its numerous tributaries, and the soil ranges from light sand to lower-lying clay. Marls and sandstones predominate, the soft marl decomposing to form the underlying rock salt to which the characteristic flavour of Cheshire's cheese has long been attributed.

Origins of Cheshire cheese

Cheese was probably made in quantity in the North West before Roman times; but the Romans had such an extensive experience of dairying and such a well-supplied international cheese market that they must have contributed consider-

ably towards its improvement and increased production. Unlike the cheeses of the North and of Scotland, most of which were first made of ewes' milk, Cheshire was a cows' milk cheese from early days. It became the standard dairy product not only of Shropshire, Cheshire and north-east Wales, but of the whole of the Midlands and the lower-lying parts of the North West.

Gradually Leicestershire and Derbyshire were to develop their own characteristic differences in cheesemaking, as did the County Palatine of Lancaster, only formed from parts of Cheshire and Northumbria after Domesday.

The cheese was mentioned in the _Domesday Book_, and its making was a matter of pride among well-born families in the succeeding centuries. Geraldus Cambriensis wrote of the herd of kine kept by Constance, wife of Hugh Lupus (cousin to Henry I, and Earl of Chester), and praised the good cheese she made of their milk.

From the sixteenth century the original cheese continued to flourish in south Cheshire, the Vale of Clwyd (until recently shared by Flint and Denbigh), Shropshire and north Staffordshire. Thomas Fuller, writing in 1601, marvelled that cattle kept out all the year round, so presumably hardy, should not only prove 'best for quantity and quality' but should 'yield the tenderest cheese'. He found the farmers of the Vale prospering in its production and spoke highly of their soil. Attempts were made to copy the cheese elsewhere, some imitators even taking Cheshire soil with them, but to no avail. They would have had to take the saltbeds too.

Fuller found the butter less praiseworthy, which indicates that the cheeses were generally made of full-cream milk and the butter of whey, a Cheshire farm practice still holding good. The whey was described by a later eighteenth-century explorer of Cheshire as 'the constant beverage of servants and labourers'. In fact this drink was really 'fleetings' (the liquor left after butter making), into which some proper whey was poured. What remained after all this from the milk of eight to ten cows was only enough to feed one pig. Today more of the whey goes to the pigs. They are the usual complement to the cheese-dairy herd and sometimes have a farm to themselves alongside the dairy farm.

Celia Fiennes, travelling in about the year 1700, noticed that milk from two or more farms was being combined for cheesemaking (as Fuller had observed in Somerset a century earlier), resulting in bigger cheeses. This practice was little seen in subsequent years until the 1950s when most of the few remaining cheese farms started buying the milk of neighbouring farmers (co-operators) to expand their cheese production.

In the late eighteenth century one-third of Cheshire farmland was pasture, allowing from two to three acres per cow, with further acreage of arable producing winter feed. The county's annual cheese production was between 8500 and 9200 tons, so the total for the five counties in the cheese region may well have equalled the 23,000 odd tons of Cheshire cheese made by farm and creamery in England in 1980. In the Vale of Cheshire the average cow gave enough milk for 2½ cwt (280 lb) of cheese every season. In the Wirral almost every farm had a dairy, but the overstocked land was poorer, there was little 'old grass', autumn feed was scanty and winter feed usually straw only, according to Henry Holland. As a result the Wirral cow produced under 2 cwt of cheese.

Across the Dee estuary, in contrast, the rich Vale of Clwyd averaged 3 cwt per cow. The problem of the limited season was being faced. Cheshire farms were starting to stall-feed green crops in autumn, extending lactations up to a further month.

Dairying in Staffordshire and Shropshire at this time was commented on by visitors in less detail; but cheesemaking went on right through southern Shropshire where farmers were reported to be crossing Lancashire Longhorns with Leicestershire cattle for dairy purposes. It was only over the Hereford border, where the old white-faced breed prevailed, that cheese seemed of little account and the bias was towards beef.

This was the peak of Cheshire cheesemaking. On the larger farms all the servants, women, men and boys, helped with the milking or the making in summer. There were cheese fairs at Shrewsbury, Market Drayton, Ellesmere, Chester, Nantwich and Whitchurch. These last three towns still held fairs every three weeks up to 1939. The trade was organised to cover much of England. Cheshires went down the Staffordshire canal for the Midlands, and to Stockport and Manchester for Lancashire and West Yorkshire. Cheese was the only Cheshire product noted on the London food market. It was either shipped there from Chester, or collected at Frodsham for the Liverpool factors, who employed a special fleet of vessels for their London cheese trade. In the 1790s the price of good-quality cheeses was from 5*d* to 7*d* a pound according to maturity, not very different from that of the 1930s. Keeping cheeses were matured for between one and two years.

In this connection it is of interest that the labour which went into finishing the cheeses was very much greater, more complicated and more prolonged than it is today. This is partly because modern presses are more efficient, but partly because the cheeses were made to stand up to a long maturing period in considerably higher temperatures over much of the year than most cheeses undergo today. One of the processes called for repeated skewering of the cheese through holes in the cylindrical mould, penetrating it through the lining cloth to the centre of the cheese. This went on through a succession of pressings and turnings of the cheese, with renewal of the cheesecloth, over at least two days. Subsequently the cheesecloth was renewed five times, usually without further skewering, each successive cheesecloth being finer, to smooth the surface. After the final cheesecloth had been pasted on, the cheese was subjected to days of brine bath and external salting before going to a cheese room carpeted with 'sniddle' (sedge), dried aftermath hay, or straw. The latter was least desirable because it marked the cheeses.

To ensure the necessary warmth the cheese room was commonly over the cowshed and under a thatched roof. Larger farmhouses often had the dairy at one end, and the cheese room at second-storey level under the eaves. Most of these have now had windows installed and been converted into bedrooms, but the height of the windows betrays the original purpose of the upper storey. I slept in such a room at Chorlton Lodge Farm recently. My host and I felt that the cheeses must have been overheated in the summer, unless more of these farmhouses were thatched than one would have expected.

The first setback in the Cheshire region came when prices dropped after 1815 and depressed cheese production. Later the railways made it easy to satisfy urban demand for fresh milk from the farms, and to transport farm milk to factories. The first two of these in the region started in 1875, one in Cheshire and one in Staffordshire. Nevertheless, there were still over 2000 farms making Cheshire cheese in 1914.

The twentieth century

Within thirty years, two wars with an intervening agricultural depression transformed the farming and cheesemaking pattern. In 1939 there were 405 farms producing 5000 tons of cheese, perhaps less than a quarter of what their 1790s predecessors made; even 13,000 tons of creamery cheese could not fill this gap. By 1949 the number of farms and the amount of farm cheese were one-tenth of the 1939 figures. The Ministry of Food had allowed Cheshire to survive through the war, but in a harder and drier form than the traditional cheese of the area. The grading standards still operate compulsorily for the eighteen farms operating today under the Milk Marketing Board scheme. It is as though we had retained not merely 'utility' clothing, but wartime rationing too; for the Board reduced the milk available for farmhouse cheesemaking in the 1977–8 and 1978–9 seasons, and would not allow newcomers into the scheme. Officially this restriction only operated if no farm gave up, but I am told that would-be farmhouse cheesemakers have been excluded despite six retirements since the early 1970s, and twenty-six since 1949. Productivity has greatly increased, with present farms using the milk of forty-four co-operator dairy farms; but of the 4500 tons of farm Cheshire made in 1979–80 (against 5000 tons of 1939 farm production), 2100 tons were made in block form by two farms. The latter should be classed with the creamery production, which was about 21,500 tons (compared with 13,000 tons in 1939).

All farmhouse Cheshire is now made from unpasteurised milk; and, except for the Blue and the block, methods are still broadly similar to those of the eighteenth century. The eye, the hand and the instinctive judgement of the cheesemaker are still vital, even where physical labour and guesswork have been eased by piping the milk from milking parlour to vat, by water-jacket heat-control, and by mechanical working of stirrers, cutters and the curd-mill. The weather, the season, the pastures and the cattle all influence the detail and timing of the operation. The cheesemaker is like a navigator without radar: he can never set a constant course to be followed blind without inviting disaster.

The biggest general change, apart from reducing moisture, is in the finishing of the cheeses. Early spring cheeses remain the most difficult to make because of the higher acidity and greater unpredictability of milk from cows newly turned out to flush pastures. They are, as they always were, cheeses to sell young. Summer cheeses used to be kept for medium maturity, except for some outstanding June cheeses. These, with the autumn cheeses, came harder and were left unwaxed to mature for up to eighteen months, then considered the ideal age. At Nantwich Show in 1980 I tasted a cheese of this age made at Mollington, and even with its natural green fade (the Cheshire term for blueing) it had a surprisingly gentle mellow flavour, and was agreeably moist through the working of its mould. In fact this cheese had been matured in the wax which coats the cloth of all but a small minority of Cheshire cheeses these days. This is a change deplored by Lance Appleby, the producer of the Supreme Champion and other prize Cheshires at Nantwich Show in 1980. None of his cheeses is waxed, so other farms who have changed to wax in recent years may pause to reflect on his success. He says that waxed cheeses tend to sweat, a long-standing worry of Cheshire cheesemakers, some of whom once talked of special sweating rooms at different temperatures for different makings, not a very practicable answer. Most cheeses are now waxed and graded for eating young, a deprivation for lovers of mature rich Cheshire. The waxed cheeses present maturing problems, exacerbated by the Board's plastic publicity bands stuck round their waist. These should be removed as quickly as possible to reduce the damage they do to the cheese.

The extreme differences in making and finish occur in block cheese, which is really not Cheshire but a distinct sub-species. Being made of unpasteurised milk (unlike its Cheddar counterpart), Cheshire farmhouse block is at least superior to the creamery product; but the farm curd still has to vary from the traditional Cheshire. In Dr Davis's words: 'a drier curd must be produced, the film must have a very low oxygen transmission value and sealing must be effective as Cheshire cheese is particularly susceptible to mould growth.' It also has to undergo greater pressure than the cylindrical cheeses. Creamery cheeses are pressed immediately after making instead of being left to drain at 70°F in the cheese 'oven' overnight without pressure, as used to be done at Four Crosses in Powys. In the opinion of a cheesemaker who worked there and is now making traditional and block cheeses on a Somerset farm, this change did much to destroy the old crumbly texture proper to Cheshire. Furthermore, in the cause of speed and tidiness, the pressure in making block cheese can be up to 100 tons, as against the traditional maximum of 25 cwt gradually reached over two days on the farm. The result is a harder, stodgier product which has to be kept at a very low temperature to avoid its blowing the plastic coat. This factor combines with its denser consistency to slow down ripening severely. As for creamery block made of pasteurised milk, this needs twice as long again, on Dr Davis's calculations, to mature properly.

A few years ago cheesemakers in Cheshire said that creamery starters were not what was wanted on farms, where they should make their own cultures for 'built-in flavour' and hardiness. I was told that in the old days 'freedom' immunised starters against contamination, whereas cosseted factory starters were more susceptible and vulnerable. One maker of clothbound unwaxed keeping cheeses had used the same starter for eighteen months when he was advised to change. He never made another superfine grade cheese, and went out of cheesemaking. Now Hansen's starters seem to be more widely accepted. Single-strain starters make for dullness.

The final distinction to be drawn between farmhouse and creamery cheese arises from the milk supply. Even the Cheshire farmer who needs more milk for cheesemaking than his own herd can supply uses co-operator dairy farms on his doorstep and does not pasteurise their milk. Local characteristics are therefore preserved in the cheese flavour. The only more distant case I know of is the use of milk from the Mayalls' notable organically farmed Ayrshire herd near Shrewsbury, for making the Matsons' special vegetarian farm Cheshire at The Twemlows, near Whitchurch (see p. 63). This milk is kept separate and gives these cheeses the full natural character of its provenance, unweakened by artificial fertilisers or by pasteurisation.

Ministry visitors to Cheshire recently were troubled by bacterial counts in milk and inclined to encourage pasteurisation to save cheesemakers from any trouble. Fortunately Cheshire farmers know that the trouble is worth enduring to produce cheese whose character, Mr Bill Lloyd the head grader says, cannot survive pasteurisation. Creameries have to accept the milk the Board sends them. One manager told me that it may be up to three days in the tanker, when a sudden flush of milk, surplus to local needs, has to be cleared from a distant part of the Kingdom. Furthermore, the tanker of 3000-gallon capacity mixes the milk of numerous farms regardless of character and quality (it could take the yield of fifteen herds averaging over sixty milkers). This factor destroys the local character of creamery cheese and, because it necessitates pasteurisation, leads to the elimination of most of the other natural flavour arising from the milk.

In 1922, when Cheshire was fetching 2d a pound (less than half what good eighteenth-century cheese fetched), a Cheshire Cheese Publicity Committee was formed, and its members met cheese buyers who complained of uneven quality and said they would pay 1d a pound more for graded cheese. Miss Bennion (a name still found in the roll of farmhouse cheesemakers) was appointed grader and established the first standards. The Publicity Committee then became the Cheshire Cheese Federation, and came under the wing of the Milk Marketing Board when it was formed in 1933. My impression was that the Ministry's wartime grading standards were responsible for reducing the moisture in Cheshire and hardening it; but Oulton Wade points out that farmhouse cheesemaking stopped altogether with the war, so its own grading was dormant. Afterwards the grading became more systematised, but it was the retail trade's post-war pressure for 'bright', less crumbly cheese and the cheesemakers' hurry that brought about a change in the character of Cheshire. Between 3 and $3\frac{1}{2}$ hours used to be the time for making Cheshire. One cheesemaker told me in 1974 that if her cheese came between 2 hours 55 minutes and 3 hours she knew it would be of superfine grade. Now many cheesemakers worry if they have not finished in 2 hours and 40 minutes. They use more starter and work for a quicker, more acid cheese which will be drier, harder and silkier in aspect but will not keep well.

As an old hand in the Cheshire trade put it to me in September 1981: 'they work by the clock, not by the curd'. He thought farmhouse Cheshire 'nothing like as good as twenty years ago', with the exceptions of clothbound cheese made by the Appleby and Wade families (among the latter's cheese he had tasted 'delicious, if uneven', Green Fade), and waxed Cheshire from some of the farms which use only their own milk. A further cause of lost flavour is the change in farming practices pointed out by Mr Cope of Adderley Hall and dealt with in detail in Chapter 9.

Sources of traditional farmhouse Cheshire

Note: Genuine farmhouse Cheshires are stamped with the number of the farm, together with the date of making and 'Superfine' or 'Fine' grading. Waxed cheeses not so marked may not be sold as farmhouse Cheshire

CHESHIRE

MOLLINGTON GRANGE FARM, Mollington, near Chester **No 4**
Visitors by appointment, tel. Great Mollington (0244) 851226
Traditional UNpasteurised; clothbound, waxed; 52 lb
Farmers: Oulton and David Wade; *cheesemakers:* David Wade, Mark Beavan
British Friesian; permanent pastures on medium loam
Where to buy: At farm shop; Crewe: Embertons (wholesale)

CHORLTON LODGE FARM, Backford, near Chester
Traditional UNpasteurised; clothbound, unwaxed; 52 lb
Details are as for Mollington Grange, but cheeses are distinct in character, with some Green Fade (see p. 64). Blue Cheshire (p. 65–6) is made here too

OLD BEACHIN, Churton, near Chester, **No 360**
Visitors by appointment, tel. Broxton (082 925) 268, 270
Traditional UNpasteurised
Farmers: Rutter brothers; *cheesemaker:* Mrs Anne Rutter
Friesian herd; heavy clay
Where to buy: On farm; Crewe: Embertons (wholesale)
Cheese has been made here by the Rutters for over 55 years; they were prizewinners at the Nantwich Show in 1980

THE BANK, Malpas **No 282**
Visitors by appointment, tel. Threapwood (094 881) 214
Traditional UNpasteurised; clothbound, waxed; small (up to 7 lb) and full size
Farmers: H. S. Bourne Partnership; *cheesemakers:* Mrs Harold Bourne and her son, H. S. Bourne
Friesian herd; heavy loam under clay
Where to buy: On farm; Crewe: Embertons
Traditional cheesemaking has gone on here for over 50 years

CRABTREE FARM, Cuddington, Malpas
Traditional UNpasteurised; clothbound, waxed
Cheesemaking has recently ceased here, and resumption is still uncertain

OVERTON HALL, Malpas **No 44**
Visitors by appointment, tel. Malpas (094 883) 257
Traditional UNpasteurised; clothbound, waxed
Farmers: Mr and Mrs Henry Barnett and their sons; *cheesemakers:* Richard Barnett, Dorothy Williss and Colin Johnson
British Friesian herd; permanent pastures on clay
Where to buy: On farm; Crewe: Embertons (wholesale); Whitchurch: Edward Jones, Alkington Cheese Supplies, 10 Chester Avenue (by post also)
The Barnetts take pride in the 'quality and unique flavour' of their cheeses, made here for nearly 50 years; they were 1st in the open class for two cheeses at Nantwich in 1980

THE DAIRY HOUSE, Edge, near Malpas **No 388**
Visitors by appointment in special circumstances, tel. Hampton Heath (094 885) 530
Traditional UNpasteurised; clothbound, waxed; from 5 lb up
Farmer: A. K. Wolley Dod; *cheesemaker:* David Morrison
Friesian herd; very old permanent pastures, long and short leys, medium loam
Where to buy: On farm for the special visitor; Crewe: Embertons (wholesale)
Cheese had been made on this farm for centuries until the Second World War; making was resumed in 1962

CLWYD

KNOLTON FARM, Knolton, Overton-on-Dee **No 297**
Visitors by appointment, tel. Overton-on-Dee (097 873) 278
Traditional UNpasteurised
Farmer: Robert Latham; *cheesemaker:* Dennis Edison
Friesian herd; medium and heavy clay
Where to buy: On farm; Crewe: Embertons (wholesale)

SHROPSHIRE

ABBEY FARM, Hawkstone, Weston-under-Redcastle **No 125**
Visitors by appointment, tel. Whitchurch (0948) 40221
Traditional UNpasteurised; clothbound, unwaxed
Farmer: Lance Appleby; *cheesemakers:* Mrs Appleby, David Collins
Where to buy: On farm; Crewe: Embertons (wholesale)
The Applebys won the Supreme Championship at Nantwich in 1980

MILLENHEATH FARM, Higher Heath, Whitchurch **No 271**
Visitors by appointment, tel. Whitchurch (0948) 40299
Traditional UNpasteurised; waxed
Farmer: V. J. Hares
Where to buy: On farm; Crewe: Embertons (wholesale)

TWEMLOWS HALL, Whitchurch **No 96**
Visitors by appointment, tel. Whitchurch (0948) 3239
1 Traditional UNpasteurised
2 Special UNpasteurised Vegetarian
Made with organically produced Ayrshire milk from Lea Hall, Harmer Hill, Shrewsbury, the famous Mayall farm (*see p. 60*)
3 Sage 20 lb
All waxed
Farmers: R. L. and R. T. Matson
Where to buy: On farm; Crewe: Embertons (wholesale)

LODGE FARM, Black Park, Whitchurch **No 150**
Visitors by appointment, tel. Whitchurch (0948) 2958
Traditional UNpasteurised; waxed
Farmer: W. J. Windsor; *cheesemaker:* Paul Holland
Friesian herd; permanent pastures

HINTON BANK FARM, Whitchurch (*for details of farm see p. 66*)

ADDERLEY HALL, Market Drayton **No 145**
Visitors by appointment, tel. Market Drayton (0630) 3841
Traditional UNpasteurised; waxed
Farmer: R. A. Cope
Leys
Where to buy: On farm; Crewe: Embertons (wholesale)

CHESHIRE

HAYFIELDS FARM, Audlem, near Nantwich **No 31**
Visitors by appointment, tel. Audlem (0270) 811394
Traditional UNpasteurised; waxed; 4 lb, 20 lb, 56 lb
Interesting mellow flavour; will keep for 4–6 months
Farmer: Philip Huntbach; *cheesemaker:* Peter Pilsbury
Where to buy: On farm; Crewe: Embertons (wholesale)
Cheshire champions at Nantwich in 1981

TOWN HOUSE FARM, Hankelow, near Nantwich **No 37**
Visitors by appointment, tel. Audlem (0270) 811214
Traditional UNpasteurised; clothbound, waxed
Farmers: R. C. and S. R. Bonell
Where to buy: On farm; Crewe: Embertons (wholesale)

MANOR FARM, Hankelow, near Nantwich
Visitors by appointment, tel. Audlem (0270) 811207
Traditional UNpasteurised
Farmers: Elliot Hulme, J. G. Hunt; *cheesemaker:* Harry Hanlin
Ayrshire (75 per cent), British Friesian (25 per cent) herd; permanent pastures
Co-operator: R. T. V. Maughan, Monk's Hall, Hankelow

THE ROYALS, Aston, Nantwich **No 90**
No visitors in the dairy
Traditional UNpasteurised; clothbound, waxed
Farmer: B. Goodwin
Where to buy: On farm; Crewe: Embertons (wholesale)

Sources of creamery Cheshire (traditional)

ASTON CREAMERY (Dairy Crest), Newhall Hill, Aston, near Nantwich
Visitors by appointment, tel. Crewe (0270) 780 491
Creamery Cheshire Cheese
Pasteurised; natural, waxed; 8 k, 20 lb (block also made)

Manager: E. B. Pritchard; *cheesemaker:* Fred Mitchell
Traditional Cheshire is also made at Reece's Diary, Malpas (sold at Lewis's, Manchester) and by T. H. Goodwin in Whitchurch

Green Fade and Blue Cheshire

Given an opening in a good cheese, mould is not slow to take advantage. So the old Cheshire habit of draining the last drops of whey out of cheese by skewering must have pleased many a roving mould spore. Unfortunately the result was not enjoyed by Cheshire cheesemakers, who called it Green Fade and threw much of it away. A little was put in the medicine cupboard to treat sores, ear aches and infected wounds, and some was sold cheap by the more fortunate or more enterprising makers to the itinerant market cheesemongers of the day. This was how Yorkshire miners became the first really appreciative customers for Green Fade; and they, too, used it medicinally.

The first intentional exploitation of Cheshire's blueing tendency I know of was the making of cheese called 'Stilton' Cheshire for private consumption by a few farmers in the last century. The term suggests the use of Stilton methods; but I believe it was employed loosely to describe cheeses made more open in texture, with a fifth to a seventh part added at the salting stage from the previous day's curd which had been partially exposed to attract mould spores. To encourage receptivity to mould the cheeses were pressed lightly if at all, and matured in a moist atmosphere. Val Cheke associates the idea of this cheese with the year 1894.

The natural Green Fades were found among Cheshires given the optimum ripening period of eighteen months. William Fream remarks in his pre-1907 *Encyclopaedia Britannica* 'Dairy' article that these cheeses were often permeated with 'a blue-green mould' and acquired 'a characteristic flavour which is much appreciated'. No one appreciated them more than Geoffrey Hutchinson, who started in the cheese trade at Hampton, near Malpas, in 1904. As he came to know and love them he discovered that they were the moistest, fattest and most acid of the flakier-textured cheeses. With this knowledge he toured the best farms, ironing cheeses to detect the potential Green Fades. As farmhouse cheesemaking achieved more uniform standards the likely faders dropped to one in a thousand, and even some of them could be matured for a further six to twelve months, only to prove a failure. Those which succeeded often went to London clubs and shipping companies as Blue Cheshire, thus spreading their fame abroad. Maurice des Ombieux, the French gastronome, called it 'a cheese fit only for heroes'.

In 1922 Geoffrey Hutchinson began storing his cheeses in old beer cellars belonging to the cheese factor Sam Biggins, at Alkington Road, Whitchurch, in Shropshire, where natural mould was to flourish for the cheeses' enrichment for over fifty years. When they had blued effectively (after from six to twelve months of keeping), he sold them as Old Blue Cheshire.

In 1933 the new Milk Marketing Board started buying and marketing cheese from the farms, with Emberton's of Crewe as their agents in the North West. The collection of cheese there simplified Geoffrey Hutchinson's task, as he could make periodic calls at Emberton's to select his blueing candidates from a wide range of white and coloured cheeses, instead of having to visit the individual farms which made them. So he continued, except for the war years, until the end of the 1950s.

After Geoffrey Hutchinson died in 1961, the Board bought his business and

Tom Hassall carried it on in the Alkington Road premises under Sam Biggin's son Dennis (now head of Westry Roberts of Whitchurch). The only changes were the pricking of all the cheeses at two to three months to make the mould penetration more certain, and the removal from the cellar walls of some of the mould accretion, which had never before been disturbed.

In 1968 at Hinton Bank Farm, Whitchurch, where her mother had started cheesemaking in 1931 because milk prices were so low, Mrs Hutchinson Smith made the first purpose-built Blue Cheshire. She was a graduate agricultural scientist as well as a hereditary cheesemaker, and had been abroad as a Nuffield Scholar in 1952 to study the feeding of dairy cattle for high-quality milk production. She consulted with the Ministry of Agriculture's Crewe laboratory under David Wych, and with their dairy husbandry advisers, particularly John Hughes. She also had help from the Milk Marketing Board's research workers at Thames Ditton, of whom she cannot speak too highly. In her own words, 'everyone helped and put in bits and pieces of information and research results to make Blue Cheshire'.

Mrs Hutchinson Smith's pride lies particularly in the achievement of a new and consistent British cheese, with a stronger flavour than the sometimes quite gentle Green Fade, or the sweet-smoky blues of Alkington Road. It is a faster, more acid cheese than standard Cheshire, and all the cheeses are annatto-coloured. The curd is less finely cut than ordinary Cheshire and is milled by a traditional Cheshire mill. The result is a very leafy curd, recalling Geoffrey Hutchinson's mention of the flaky texture of his chosen cheeses, not a typical Cheshire characteristic. The milled curd falls on a platform with twelve holes which fit over a dozen calico-lined hoops into which the curd is shovelled. This calico is the final cheesecloth. On it is stamped the date of making.

Vertical presses are used, with pneumatic action which adjusts sensitively to the slightly varying size of each cheese. It was found that the usual modern horizontal press did not work satisfactorily, the centres of cheeses often failing to blue, a fault which had puzzled me. Pressure is less than half that used on plain cheeses, beginning at 5 cwt and never exceeding 10 cwt in the normal two days. Seasonal variation allows for slightly more pressure to drain the volatile May cheeses; but, with the reservation that too little pressure means no skin formation, the rule is the lighter the pressure, the better the cheese. 'Skinning', as it is called, is a tricky two-week operation conducted in a special room kept in the high 60s (Fahrenheit) at a high level of humidity. The fat in the calico cloth plays a part in forming the skin. The next stage is three weeks in a cool cheese room. Too low a temperature stunts the cheese's development, but if it is too high the protein in the cheese can be broken down excessively.

At between four and eight weeks of age the cheese is pierced by compressed-air jets, which process replaces the conventional needling on the turntable. This is timed to occur three weeks before the date for which a batch of cheeses has been ordered. A really blue cheese is achieved in under two months, through the quick spread of the mould in the acid cheese and its ability to break down the protein. Mrs Hutchinson Smith thinks that eight to nine weeks from the date of making is the ideal time for eating her Blue Cheshire.

In mid August 1980 David Wade started making Blue Cheshire by the Hinton Bank methods at Chorlton Lodge Farm, Backford, near Chester, from the milk of the farm's British Friesian herd. This is part of the Wild farming enterprise run by the brothers Oulton and David Wade under the name of their mother's family, which farmed there for generations before them. Chorlton Lodge is Oulton Wade's home. The cheeses are now marketed under the Board's Hutchinson label alongside those from Hinton Bank.

Independent of the Board, Elliot Hulme started producing Blue Cheshire at Hankelow Manor Farm from the milk of his own herd (75 per cent Ayrshires, 25 per cent British Friesians) and that of his neighbour R. T. V. Maughan, of Monks' Hall, Hankelow. Elliot Hulme had made cheese on this farm before, and his father was a very good cheesemaker before him. The cheesemaker, Harry Hanlin, had worked at Hinton Bank Farm, so the methods used were similar. (They also make Shropshire Blue, see below.)

These three Blue Cheshire farms were on different soils, their pastures were differently treated, and their herds were of different breeds. It is interesting to learn that differences were soon detectable in the cheeses' flavours, despite the penetrating and pervasive element of the mould. Unfortunately the Hankelow enterprise has not survived; I believe that use of horizontal gang-presses was one of the reasons.

Sources of Blue Cheshire

Lightly pressed, coloured, UNpasteurised, blued; natural skin, clothbound, pierced; 18–20 lb tall cylinders and 7 lb size
For names of farms and where to buy, see below

SHROPSHIRE

HINTON BANK FARM, Whitchurch
Visitors by appointment, tel. Whitchurch (0948) 2631
Farmers: Group-Captain D. W. and Mrs Hutchinson Smith; *cheesemaker:* Miss Ruth Harrison; *co-operator:* Leslie Walley, Fernyleas Farm, Prees
Dairy Shorthorn herd; mostly permanent pastures (naturally manured) on clay
Where to buy: On farm (minimum of 5 lb

or ¼ cheese); Crewe: Embertons (wholesale); Whitchurch: Alkington Cheese Supplies, 10 Chester Avenue (also by post); most good cheese shops
This purpose-made Blue Cheshire was invented by Mrs Hutchinson Smith, whose mother made cheese on the farm here 50 years ago; at the Chester Show in 1981 it won a class open to any European blue cheese

CHESHIRE

CHORLTON LODGE FARM, Backford, near Chester (*for details of farm see p. 62*)
Where to buy: Crewe: Embertons (wholesale); Mollington: Mollington Grange Farm Shop

Shropshire Blue

One of the blue cheeses made for some years at Castle Stuart Dairy, Inverness, was sponsored by Adamsons of Short Street, London, who sold it as Shropshire Blue. Andy Williamson, much respected in the Stilton world, went back to Scotland to make the new cheese, a lightly pressed blue with a deep red curd, which found a ready sale throughout the country in good cheese shops. Then orders were refused in spring 1980, with a promise of 'more later'. For unexplained and unfathomable reasons the North of Scotland Milk Marketing Board had closed the dairy and the 'more later' came from Hankelow. Elliot Hulme and his Blue Cheshire cheesemaker Harry Hanlin showed their first public Shropshire Blue at Nantwich Show in July 1980. They had been helped with advice from Charlie Chisholm, who managed the Castle Stuart Dairy when the cheese was made there.

All the milk for the cheese was unpasteurised, and came from Hankelow pastures. Mr Hulme had to quote EEC regulations against monopolistic restraint of trade to persuade the Milk Marketing Board to let him buy extra milk for his new enterprise from his co-operator.

Mr Hulme told me in September 1980 that first Shropshire Blues from Hankelow had proved a little firmer and deeper red than the cheeses made in Inverness. He has since ceased production, but in 1981 John Adamson and Company got Long Clawson Stilton Dairy interested in this cheese, coming back to the nineteenth-century conception of Stilton Cheshire.

Lancashire

Until after Domesday the part of north-west England which became the County Palatine was divided between Cheshire and Northumbria. It was probably well after that time that Lancashire cheese became distinct from Cheshire; which it certainly was by the eighteenth century, when today's territorial differences between England's cheeses had become firmly established.

The northern parts of the old county had their distinctive dairy pattern of making butter and using the buttermilk for an inevitably tough cheese called 'Wang' or 'Whey', like the harder Dales and Lakeland cheeses (see p. 84). Further south, towards the centre of the county, Lancashire cheese developed as we have known it, until recent abuse of the name for a completely different product began to adulterate the market.

The real Lancashire was and remains a semi-soft, loose-textured, crumbly, buttery cheese, unlike any other in flavour and resembling only the softer Dales cheeses in consistency. Until this century making was done by rule of thumb, the overnight milk ripening to start the cheese when the morning milk was mixed with it. Additional starter was first used in 1910, and even then only 0.1 per cent was used in relation to the quantity of coming milk. Within Lancashire the flavour varied between youth and maturity, and from farm to farm, according to the lie of the land and the pastures. The cheese was often made in the farm kitchen.

The first dairy making Lancashire started at Chipping in 1913, and others followed; but making was still on a small scale. The laborious methods needed to achieve this fragile cheese do not lend themselves to factory practices. For instance, after the whey has been drained from the vat the curd is scooped into clothlined tubs, covered and pressed with periodic adjustment before cutting. After this it is broken up by hand, re-wrapped, pressed and re-cut three to five times in an hour and a half. Only then is it ready to be mixed with the previous day's curd or stored back in the vat, to be mixed with the next day's curd. The two curds are salted and milled, then re-milled into the clothlined moulds to become the finished cheeses. Some farms made cheese of three days' curd.

In 1939 there were still 202 farms turning out 1260 tons of Lancashire cheese a year, dairies bringing the year's total to nearly 4800 tons. It was all made from unpasteurised milk in the traditional way from two days' curd. But in 1940 Lancashire became a casualty of the hard-cheese, factory-making edict by the Ministry of Food, acting on the advice of Professor Capstick. Lancashire loyalists can hold their fire; this Yorkshire dalesman (if his name means anything) killed the traditional softer white rose cheeses of his own Dales too.

In 1948, in the limited post-war revival, twenty-two farms were making cheese; but by the early 1970s numbers were fluctuating between five and seven. S. D. O. Brown, a milk tester in the Advisory Service, had tested the milk on every farm in Lancashire and tasted the cheese of every farm that made it. He told me in 1973 that the best cheeses came from five farms near the Trough of Bowland. They were all on permanent pastures with up to five generations of cheesemaking experience to support them. Of the remaining lower-lying farms one was too near sea-level, with a high water-table, and had trouble with its milk; the last was a mixed farm with rotations and 'essential herbs were missing from its pastures', depriving its cheese of flavour. Now the only farms making are north of Preston in the villages of Inglewhite, Goosnargh and Catforth, and there are dairies at Longridge and Chipping, Garstang and Bay Horse.

In comparatively recent years Mr and Mrs Kirkham, senior, of West Lea Farm, Goosnargh, have retired because of ill health and cheesemaking has ceased at Winn House Farm, Inglewhite, on two farms at Chipping, and at Ribchester, Clitheroe and Thornton, where Miss Wood had followed an old custom of greasing her cheeses. The four remaining farms make about 240 tons of cheese a year. This includes some sage cheese from two farms, traditionally a Christmas treat but available now from New House Farm, Goosnargh, all through the year. The total is less than a fifth of the pre-war farmhouse cheese; but our loss is far greater than that. Pre-war creamery production was the real thing, whereas all of it now is pasteurised, and most of it bears no relation to Lancashire cheese at all. New House Farm and Beesley Farm at Goosnargh and Lower Barker Farm at Inglewhite alone make nothing but the delicious, inimitable traditional Lancashire.

I have explained why the traditional cheese cannot be convincingly copied, made in block form, or prepacked by factory processes. This used to make me feel secure about its survival, despite mechanisation. Alas, with connivance of the Board, which should have been the cheese's protector, the large-scale, prepacking cheese handlers solved the problem by inventing New Lancashire. This product, convenient for commercial interests, has none of the characteristics which interest a lover of real cheese. It is aroma-less, tasteless and has the consistency of small lumps of stodgy dough stuck together with flour paste.

I took some to Mr Lloyd and Mr Ted Hassall, the graders of farmhouse Cheshire and Lancashire at Crewe in 1974, and they could not even guess what it was supposed to be. In 1978 a disgruntled Lancastrian submitted a more 'mature' sample to his county analyst, who described it in his annual report for 1978-9 as 'harsh and acid-like' and obviously 'intended for quick consumption'. My last taste of this block version in October 1979 indicated that one maker had read that comment: the object looked and tasted like nothing more than block-salt; yet my innocent host had bought it as Lancashire.

At Nantwich Show in July 1980 I was horrified to find that the 'New' qualification had been quietly dropped in favour of 'Single-acid', not a term likely to help the ordinary cheese customer. The cheese is made more acid to speed it up, and uses only a single day's curd (a wartime method for a drier, hardy cheese), which changes everything. Even worse, the cheese is being made by reputable creameries and by Barron's Farms, Catforth, in waxed cylinders, externally indistinguishable from the real cheese. To say I was given a taste would be an exaggeration, but I put some in my mouth; the consistency was that of gritty pin-head oatmeal. A senior Board official of long experience said to me: 'It hasn't any flavour at all.' Mr Vale of Singleton's Dairy admitted: 'It's a bastard cheese; they call it sawdust in the South. I don't like to see any on my shelves after two weeks.'

Grading on farms is done at two to four weeks by the graders from Crewe. Creamery grading is no longer compulsory, but Mr Vale likes to keep it up at Singleton's to provide a yardstick. He does criticise it, however, as being 'grading for early eating', and not taking account of the special virtues required in keeping a cheese. It is difficult to see how 'single-acid' cheeses can be graded on anything more substantial than appearance, since they lack the qualities of aroma, flavour and consistency which really matter in cheese.

It is not surprising that sales of Lancashire cheese went down by one-third between 1974 and 1978. The tragedy is that the baby goes down with the bathwater. The single-acid cheese which the Board should never have allowed has debased the market and put off innumerable customers, like the famous lifelong Yorkshire cheesemaker and Lancashire cheese lover Kit Calvert, who told me last summer at Hawes: 'I shall never eat Lancashire again.' I hope that, rather than accept defeat, lovers of the cheese and those who wish to sample it will press their local cheese shops to stock the real thing. They can start with 20 lb cheeses. Their customers will soon notice the difference.

In an attempt to assess the general trend of sales I asked the Lancashire Cheese Association, which represents the small dairies and creameries, what kinds of cheese its members were producing and the proportions of traditional to new. The secretary sent me a list of seven dairies but was 'unable to supply the rest of the information requested'. This inability to provide such information suggests a lack of commercial acumen, as I can only risk mentioning here those which I know to be making genuine Lancashire. The member who forwarded my letter to the secretary made good cheeses in 1974, but would not tell me what he was making now himself.

Fortunately Mr Vale of Singleton's Dairy at Longridge has no such inhibitions, and this dairy's recent experience shows a significant revival of demand for traditional cheese of all kinds. During the year up to August 1980, in which their production doubled, the proportion of block cheese they made went down from 60 per cent to 25 per cent, a reduction in quantity terms; but the proportion of clothbound cheeses rose from 40 per cent to 75 per cent, increasing almost five fold their output of traditional cheese. The market is there for those who seek it.

Sources of farmhouse Lancashire and Sage Lancashire

LANCASHIRE

Semi-soft, UNpasteurised; natural smooth, clothbound, waxed; about 46 lb (some 3 lb and 20 lb), cylindrical with rounded edges This cheese has an unmistakable tang, even when young; medium maturity is 3 months and over, full maturity over 6 months and up to a year. The sage version has finely chopped sage leaves mixed in the curd, giving a broader, more natural flavour than Sage Derby
Where to buy: On farms; Crewe: Embertons (wholesale); most good cheese shops
For names of farms, see below

NEWHOUSE FARM, Goosnargh (*4 miles N. of Preston*) **No 61**
Visitors by appointment, tel. Goosnargh (077 476) 250
Farmers: W. and M. E. Shorrock; *cheesemaker:* R. Wilkinson
Friesian herd; clay–loam mixture

BEESLEY FARM, Mill Lane, Goosnargh **No 39**
Visitors by appointment, tel. Goosnargh (077 476) 325

Farmer: J. J. Kirkham; *cheesemaker:* Mrs R. Kirkham
Friesian herd; heavy clay

LOWER BARKER FARM, Inglewhite (*5 miles N.W. of Preston*) **No 7**
Visitors by appointment, tel. Brock (0995) 40334
Farmers: T. and R. Butler; *cheesemaker:* Mrs J. M. Butler
Friesian herd; clay
Where to buy: As above (left) and Inglewhite: Post Office and Village Store; Streatley: Wells Stores
These cheeses won 1st and 2nd prizes at the Nantwich Show in 1980

AMBROSE HALL FARM, Catforth Hall, Woodplumpton (*6 miles N. of Preston*) **No 11**
Visitors by appointment, tel. Catforth (0772) 690111
Farmer: K. Leeming; *cheesemaker:* Sean Finn
Friesian herd; medium loam

Sources of creamery Lancashire (traditional)

LANCASHIRE

SINGLETON'S DAIRY, Mill Farm, Preston Road, Longridge (*8 miles N.E. of Preston*)
Semi-soft, pasteurised and vegetarian; natural, smooth, clothbound, waxed; 22 lb, 44 lb slightly conical (truncated) for all full-sized cheeses, cylindrical for half sizes
A vegetable renneting agent is used for the vegetarian cheese; Sage Lancashire is also made here, in 22 lb cylinders
Where to buy: At dairy (wholesale); Clitheroe: Mrs Alpe, 14 Shawbridge Street; many good cheese shops

MILK MARKETING BOARD CREAMERY, Inglewhite Road, Longridge
Semi-soft, pasteurised; natural, clothbound, waxed; 13 lb, 20 lb, 30 lb, 45 lb cylindrical

Manager: D. J. Slater; *cheesemaker:* F. Cruse
Where to buy: At creamery (*note:* 'fatty' traditionals are made alongside 'single acid' New Lancashire, so care must be taken when ordering)

Note: Traditional creamery Lancashire is also made at the following creameries:

DEW LAY PRODUCTS, Green Lane West, Cabus, Garstang (*half way between Preston and Lancaster on A6*)

GREENFIELD DAIRIES, Syke House Lane, Goosnargh (*4 miles N. of Preston*)

WOLFEN MILL DAIRY, Chipping (*N.E. of Preston*)
Wolfen Mill Dairy makes 1 lb, 4 lb and medium-sized cheeses

Other cheeses of the North West

LANCASHIRE

SINGLETON'S DAIRY, Longridge, near Preston (*for details of dairy see p. 70*)
1 Dairy Vegetarian Cheshire Cheese
Pasteurised; natural, waxed; cylindrical
Made with vegetable renneting agent
2 Cheddar
White and black waxed
3 Leicester
Where to buy: At dairy

SYKES HOLT, Myerscough Road, Balderstone (*7 miles E. of Preston, 4 miles W. of Blackburn on A59*)
Visitors welcome, tel. Mellor (025 481) 2336
Soft Goat Cheese
White; no crust; 5 oz tubs
Smallholder, cheesemaker: Norman Young
British Toggenberg, English goats; permanent pastures on heavy clay and woodland grazing
Season: March to December
Where to buy: On farm

CHESHIRE

MOLLINGTON GRANGE and CHORLTON LODGE FARMS, near Chester (*for details of farms see p. 62*)
1 Farmhouse Mollington
Soft, unripened, coloured (pale apricot), UNpasteurised; no crust; 2 lb (smaller individual cheeses may now be available), flat, round
A mild crumbly cheese related to Cambridge
2 Farmhouse Cheshire
Two-week-old cheeses broken up and mixed with spring onion, pickle, farm-roast ham, walnut, pineapple, and remoulded
UNpasteurised; rindless; 3 lb drums
3 Green Fade (Chorlton Lodge)
Hard, white or coloured, UNpasteurised, naturally blued; natural, clothbound; not pierced; sizes as Farmhouse Cheshire, cylindrical
Where to buy: At farm shop (Wild's); Crewe: Embertons; Stockton-on-Tees: Whitelocks (both wholesale); Streatley: Wells Stores

STAFFORDSHIRE

ADAMS FOODS PROVISIONS DIVISION, Leek
Double Gloucester
With chives, chives and onion, onion, or parsley and garlic; natural, clothbound; 5 lb drums

SHROPSHIRE

TWEMLOWS HALL, Whitchurch (*for details of farm see p. 63*)
Farmhouse Vegetarian–Organic Cheshire
UNpasteurised; natural, waxed; cylindrical
Made with vegetable renneting agent
Where to buy: On farm; Crewe: Embertons (wholesale)

FORDHALL ORGANIC FARM, near Market Drayton
Visitors welcome, tel. Tern Hill (063 083) 255
Cream Cheese
Farmer: A. Hollins
Mixed herd; permanent pastures
Mr Hollins has been working for many years to re establish multi-species permanent pastures with all year round grazing in the old tradition of this region.
Where to buy: This cheese is made only for the farm restaurant, not for general sale

RIVERSLEA, Clunton, Craven Arms
Hard Goat Cheese
Farmer: C. M. Mason

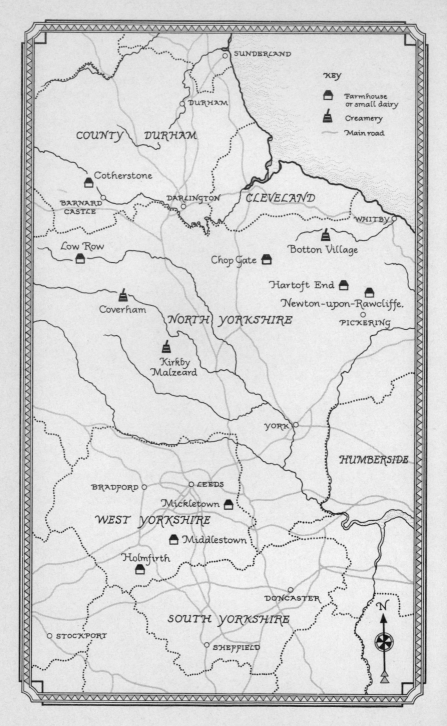

KEY

🏠 Farmhouse
or small dairy

🏭 Creamery

〜 Main road

SUNDERLAND

DURHAM

COUNTY DURHAM

Cotherstone

BARNARD
CASTLE

DARLINGTON

CLEVELAND

WHITBY

Low Row

Botton Village

Chop Gate

Hartoft End

Coverham

NORTH YORKSHIRE

Newton-upon-Rawcliffe.

PICKERING

Kirkby
Malzeard

YORK

HUMBERSIDE

BRADFORD

LEEDS

Mickletown

WEST YORKSHIRE

Middlestown

Holmfirth

DONCASTER

SOUTH YORKSHIRE

STOCKPORT

SHEFFIELD

N

4

Cheeses of the North

The Dales

The historic cheesemaking Dales are those of the Tees and the Swale, and Wensleydale, the valley of the Ure. These rivers, rising high up on the eastern slopes of the Pennines, cut their way down towards the Vale of York. The Tees, the most substantial of them, winds on its own irregular way to the sea north of the Vale and the Cleveland Hills (the northern range of the Yorkshire Moors). Swale and Ure turn south easterly and join forces in the Vale before swelling the Ouse at York itself.

The earliest trace of cheesemaking in the area is a curd strainer found in a Roman fort at Bainbridge, overlooking Wensleydale. Local history then suffers the usual missing pages of the post-Roman era; but, although much of Wensleydale was forest when the Normans arrived, the Dales were already well settled when *Domesday Book* was compiled.

From the thirteenth to the early twentieth century, stone was quarried and lead and coal were mined, lead extensively. In the last two centuries the plentiful water supply invited the addition of textile mills. Some of the buildings and many of the scars remain, but few car-bound travellers would suppose today that this had so recently been an industrial region, with a population to match.

Ewes' milk cheeses

'The shepherd milks his ewes twice a day and makes butter and cheese.' This is one of the answers to questions for students about various professions and trades in *Aelfric's Colloquy* , a late tenth-century educational publication. However, if the Saxons were making cheeses in the Dales, they obviously did not come up to Norman requirements. After the Conquest the invaders stationed in Wensleydale seem to have expressed enough discontent with Yorkshire diet for their complaints to have come to the ears of King William. An uncle of his, the Abbot of Savigny, was called upon for help. Monks had long been established as pioneers of cheesemaking in the French dairy world. Their ewes' milk cheese, ripened in the *caves* of Cambalou near Roquefort, had been famous for three centuries. Wensleydale lore has it that the Dales cheeses familiar until 1939 were first made by monks acquainted with Roquefort methods, who were gathered at William the Conqueror's request by the Abbot of Savigny, after rumblings of discontent about English food from Norman troops. The first monks came over from Savigny as Benedictines, but early in the twelfth century they submitted to the reformed order of Cistercians, whose fount was in Burgundy at Cîteaux, a house still famous for cheese. Monks from still further south must have responded to our Abbot's call, but his *Abbaye* was at Savigny-sur-Braye in the soft cows' milk cheese region round Paris, not at Savigny-les-Beaune as might have been expected.

Whatever their mother house, French monks came over to exploit the summer milk of Wensleydale ewes and the mould which flourishes amid the local stone. Demanding enough land to make them independent, they were granted parts of the only freehold available, the Forest of Wensleydale, westward from Askrigg for fifteen miles on the sunny side of the Dale to the watershed of the Pennines. These slopes are still known as Abbotside.

The first great monastic institution was eventually built at Fors, near the place later called Dalegrange, and an Abbey inventory for 1150 includes cheeses. However, Fors proved excessively exposed and did not survive long. Fifteen years after the first grant the community was given Jervaulx. The Abbey, more kindly and intelligently sited there, with its better land, became a fount of agricultural expertise. As the size of this and other monastic estates swelled through grants and bequests, they were put to organised farming, with a series of granges, such as Dalegrange, in which produce was stored. The cheeses came from the evening milking of the ewes, when they were separated for the night from their lambs, which they rejoined in the morning on Abbotside.

This system spread northward into Swaledale and Teesdale and eastward to the Cleveland Hills. As their land increased beyond the limit of their capacity to farm it, the surplus was let to lay farmers. The monks instructed their tenants in the making of cheese, which could then form at least part of the rent they paid to the abbeys. In 1310 Bolton Abbey in Lower Wharfedale consumed nearly a ton of ewes' milk cheese. By the late thirteenth and early fourteenth centuries one tenant was paying four stones of cheese (half a hundredweight) and two stones of butter per cow, a sign of changing husbandry. These rents in kind were delivered to the granges and brought thence by the agents to the Abbey cellars to mature. The internal character of the cheese was probably that of a soft, open-textured Roquefort, susceptible to the abundant natural mould of the rock-hewn cellars. The exterior probably developed the same natural grey-moulded crust that Swaledale cheeses have today, which the modern surface treatment of Roquefort inhibits.

At the Dissolution of the Monasteries tenant farmers, reinforced by some of the dispersed monks, carried on the cheesemaking. Jervaulx gave its recipe to the landlord of the Cover Bridge Inn. Harrison, in his _Description of England in Shakespeare's Youth_, says that by that time housewives were using predominantly cows' milk, but adding 'a lesser proportion of ewes' milke unto so manie kine' to keep their cheese moist and mellow. By the mid seventeenth century Shorthorn cows had largely displaced ewes as the source of milk in the Dales.

To the north the making of ewes' milk cheese continued into the nineteenth century. Large quantities were reported as selling cheaply in the Cheviots in 1816. Some of these cheeses could be kept for three or four years, becoming extremely pungent and 'in considerable esteem for the table'. In Cleveland ewes' milk cheese survived on at least two Farndale farms into the early twentieth century. Its making has now been resumed in England, not in the Dales, but in Oxfordshire, Hampshire, Devon and Sussex.

Dales cheeses of the nineteenth century

Wensleydale is first known to have been used as a general name for local cheeses in 1840, when cheese fairs were first held at Leyburn. Making usually started in mid May: 'buttercups out - cows out', I was told in 1980 by one Swaledale couple who still make cheese. 'Grass cheese' was the term used for the first products of the season, 'pasture cheese' for mid-season's sure bluers, and 'fog cheese' for the products of the hay aftermath.

Cheeses weighed from 5 to 20 lb, most of them in the 10–15 lb range. Early spring and late autumn cheeses were made in the flatter, millstone form. June to September cheeses were more often of Stilton shape and could be kept for Christmas. Full-cream overnight milk ripened naturally to be mixed with and start the morning whole milk. The rennet used was made locally from the vells of the cows, and called prezzur, directly descended from the French _présure_, a good Norman inheritance. When natural rennet was short, a black snail was sometimes substituted, which allegedly had the same effect as rennet. Just after making, most cheeses were salted in a brine bath for a period of from one to three days. Some were salted externally, and a few were salted in the heart of the curd before brine washing. Later some makers adopted the more general English custom of salting the curd for their winter cheeses after the milling, and some did this for all their cheese. As long as farmhouse cheesemaking survived in Wensleydale the traditional brine washing was considered to produce the best results: cheeses softer, moister and more pungent in character. They even acted as a weather guide to the farmer: 'Cheeses is runnin', we'll get on wi't' hay.'

Most of the farms had from three to seven cows in milk, normally Shorthorns. A farm with seventeen or eighteen cows was considered really large-scale. Cheesemaking traditionally finished with the first frost. Any winter cheese made in the old days was called, for obvious reasons, 'hay cheese'; it was usually tougher and harder than proper seasonal cheese, and at its worst was termed 'Old Peg'.

Cheeses were brought to market by their makers, or collected from the farms in payment for goods by the provision merchants who supplied their needs, or by cheese factors, who matured and marketed the cheese themselves. One such factor called Whitelock started in a small way in 1882, collecting from farms and selling mainly in October at the year's final large-scale outlet for late and matured cheeses at Yarm Cheese Fair. Over the years he built up a business still famous in the North East. Now under the Milk Marketing Board, Whitelock's continues to sell cheese wholesale from Stockton-on-Tees to retailers all over the region, and to buyers abroad.

Until late in the last century Wensleydale and its other Dales cousins remained the traditional natural blue cheese, only the source of its milk having changed since monastic times. Wensleydale was softer than Stilton, and appreciated for being spreadable with a knife (but my advice is not to spread such cheese, rather to enjoy the full glory of its texture in slices). Cotherstone, the Teesdale cheese, and Swaledale were even softer and more prized. They could be kept for up to a year, and it was common for provision merchants to book extra cheeses made during the rich flush of the late spring and the second growth of early autumn. These were more likely to be of the fat, moist, open character most hospitable to the beneficent green mould present in the cheese room and most encouraging of its speedy internal development. Pricking was used by some makers for further acceleration of blueing.

The new White Wensleydale

Farmhouse cheesemaking in the Dales first started diminishing when the new railways made it easy to transport fresh milk to the industrial regions of the North. Then, just before 1900, a provision merchant called Chapman grew dissatisfied with the uneven quality of the cheeses he was offered on his contracts with farmers. There was an element of straight barter between farmer and merchant, and no merchant wanted to lose an outlet for his wares by refusing the poorer cheeses; so Chapman decided to buy milk from the farms and control the quality of his cheeses by making them himself at Hawes. This, the first factory, or creamery, in the Dales is still making cheese, but none of it now in traditional form. Soon after the turn of the century a farmer called Rowntree started buying his neighbours' milk and making cheese on a factory scale at Masham, where cheesemaking continued until a few years ago. Before and during this period the recently established Department of Agriculture at Leeds had been encouraging the study of cheesemaking methods and had established an advisory service in the Dales and a dairy school at Gosforth which lasted until 1929. This brought about some standardisation of practices, and probably reduced the amount of naturally blueing cheese coming from the farms. The school was well attended, but the numbers of farms making cheese continued to decrease.

To avoid variations in consistency and keeping quality, the factory cheesemakers salted the curd in preference to brine washing and made a firmer-pressed cheese. This eliminated both the long waiting period needed for the ripening of the traditional cheese and most of its chances of blueing naturally. With the dulling of public taste, the new cheese could be sold at three weeks, as much of it is today, an attractive financial advantage.

In the 1920s Durham miners began to show a distaste for their old Dales blues and took to the infant white. They thus show more affinity with their Caerphilly-loving Welsh mining cousins than with their Yorkshire brothers, who had been the first customers to appreciate Cheshire Green Fade. This was a period of general deterioration in British taste and cuisine, a bleak trend not reversed until the advent of strong cosmopolitan influences on British eating habits in the late 1950s.

The early 1930s were hard years for farmers. Wensleydale sold for as little as 6d a pound (2$\frac{1}{2}$p) against the 8d to 11d of the 1840s. The dairies established at Askrigg, Coverham, Hawes, Masham and Kirkby Malzeard came on thin times. Some only survived under the guidance of Kit Calvert, who, with the help of the new Milk Marketing Board, formed a Wensleydale Cheesemakers' Association. Three factory and three farmhouse makers, representing Wensleydale, Swaledale and Teesdale, conferred together.

Most farmers were now selling their milk to dairy or creamery, where all the cheeses produced were white. Yet in 1939 there were still registered cheesemakers, on 176 farms in Wensleydale and 257 in Swaledale and Teesdale combined, making cheese in the traditional way. With few exceptions they were farmers' wives and daughters. Cows were still being milked in the upland pastures, their milk coming down to the farmhouse dairy in backcans or budgets, some strapped to the shoulders of women or children, others placed in crates or hebbles astride Wensleydale donkeys and Swaledale ponies. Headcans were the only item of traditional equipment which had gone out of use. Eighteenth-century stone and wooden cheese presses, usually sited out of doors in porches, or in alcoves in the farmyard, were still employed on the many farms which had not invested in the newer cast-iron presses.

When the Ministry of Food centralised cheesemaking and eliminated the softer varieties, the Dales farmhouse cheeses in their traditional form were doomed, condemned by utilitarian standards for their very virtues: softness, moisture and moderate acidity. Kit Calvert did manage to save the firmer, all-white dairy cheeses, first from the Ministry's bureaucrats and then, with the backing of Whitelock's, from takeover threats by Express Dairies.

Wensleydale post-war

In 1946 only nine farms still had a cheesemaker: Ministry control of cheese production and sales persisted and cheese rationing did not cease until 1954. Milk Marketing Board representatives then descended on Wensleydale with a list of the 176 cheesemakers of 1939 and the commendable intention of reviving their tradition. Kit Calvert, who had been collecting milk off the farms for his creameries all these years, warned the Board's men that it would be a waste of time; but they insisted that he take them round in an attempt to encourage resumption of farm cheesemaking. The effort was wasted, because wartime rules were not softened to match their goodwill, despite Kit Calvert's objection to compulsory grading by outsiders and to the standards laid down. Pre-war Dales cheeses, graded at Barnard Castle and Hawes, had a moisture content of over 50 per cent, or in the case of a good fog cheese, up to 55 per cent. The wartime standard set a limit of 46 per cent which condemned even the cheeses of the show prize-winners, and this was not relaxed. The handful of farmers

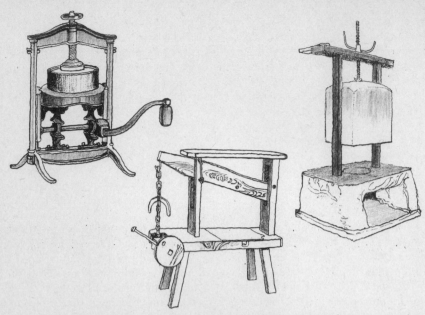

Cheese presses were made in a variety of materials: (left) a nineteenth-century cast iron press; (centre) a wooden press from Thwaite, in Swaledale; and (right) a stone press from Ghyll Head Farm, Oxnop.

who persisted found their cheeses up against a standard attuned to the foreign character of the harder, more acid wartime product, not to the sweet, soft, rich native beauty of their time-honoured artistry. It was like suddenly facing Royal Academicians with a hanging committee formed exclusively of industrial technologists, who had never attended an art class in their lives and never looked at an original painting. Some farms would have gone on cheesemaking off the register, but they were forced to hand over their milk, although this often made economic nonsense. Kit Calvert's lorries had to travel many extra rough miles daily for the odd five gallons, which could much better have been left for the cheesemaker, whose produce could accumulate until it was worth marketing or having collected.

Bewildered and disgusted at this perverse injustice, the few Wensleydale cheesemakers gave up. The last farmhouse cheese was made in 1957. The last of the few backcan donkeys still working after the war died in honourable retirement at Castle Bolton in 1967.

To the south east of Wensleydale, between the lower stretches of the Ure and the Swale near Boroughbridge, Wensleydale cheese was still being made good enough to win the Supreme Championship at the first post-war and the 1958 Dairy Shows at Olympia. Miss Betsy Mudd had been famous for her cheese throughout much of this century. She went on making proper Wensleydale and maturing it in her mould-rich cellar at Aldborough Dairy until a few days before she died in September 1960 at the age of eighty-three. This establishment which had produced cheese eaten with joy by two generations of customers was not

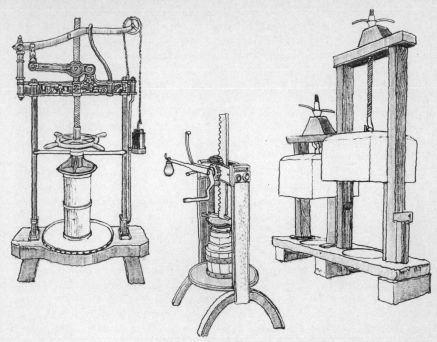

An early nineteenth-century vertical iron press with pulleys (left); a simpler screw press from Swaledale (centre); and (right) a screw press with stone weights from Leigh in the Vale of Gloucester.

good enough for the Board. They would not allow cheesemaking to continue there, and bought the dairy only to close it.

Kit Calvert had fought to preserve some traces of tradition in his dairies, but his hope died with the advent of bulk tanker collection of milk. Good milk, indifferent milk and milk from every sort of soil was mixed together. Contact between farmer and cheesemaker was broken, and pasteurisation was forced upon the dairies as a result. This killed the local flavours. The Board bought Hawes and Kirkby Malzeard, and took over Whitelock's as their North Eastern depot. Coverham went on making under Unigate until 1979, when it too, with most of Unigate's other cheesemaking interests, was sold to the Board.

Revival of Blue Wensleydale

Some farmhouse Blue Wensleydales were available up to 1941 and the odd one until 1957. The source of other blue cheeses long remained a secret between supplier and customers. Mr Tennant, the provision merchant at Middleham, used to buy large numbers of autumn-flush dairy cheeses in pre-pasteurisation days from Kit Calvert, who was much puzzled. He and Mr Tennant's heir only found out after Mr Tennant's death that, with the late Colonel Christie's benign consent, these cheeses had been stored in the cellars of Jervaulx Abbey, to appear well 'greened' at Christmas and Easter.

In the 1960s William Taylor, a lifelong research worker and practitioner in the blue cheese world, re-established a Wensleydale Blue culture at Kirkby Malzeard. He matured cheeses made to a more traditional standard of softness and open texture. Those that blued successfully were of very high quality, the best of them close to farmhouse forebears in their impact on tongue and palate. Unfortunately the Board decided that it was untidy to have these lovely spores flying around in this dairy in their home county, now mainly given over to the production of white cheeses; so the job of blueing Wensleydale cheeses was handed over to Stilton makers in the Derbyshire Dale of the Dove at Hartington. In the same county, at Egginton, Unigate had made a Blue Wensleydale type in the 1960s, but although they took it round the Dales and claim to have had approving comments, it does not survive.

Nuttall's Blue Wensleydale cheeses are pleasant, and quite distinct from their Stiltons; but they mature firmer than when Mr Taylor saw to it all, and are more reluctant bluers. They should be called Dovedale Blue and sold as the new type of cheese they really are.

Cheeses of the Dales today

Wensleydale

The clothbound Wensleydales found in shops today are the tubby barrels of Kirkby Malzeard or the Stilton-shaped cylinders of Coverham. Because any cheesecloth seems romantic amid a sea of polythene some shops call them 'Farmhouse Wensleydales'; but I have bought and tasted such cheeses, and even when I have not been able to see the dairy numbers on their cheesecloths, I have had no doubt that they were of dairy, not farm origin.

Aldborough Dairy, now bought back from the Board by Miss Mudd's niece, Mrs Foster, and her husband, sells Kirkby Malzeard cheeses, including a special order of smaller autumn cheeses to mature in the old cellar for Christmas sale.

After probing very wide and very deep personally and with the help of such far-flung, all-embracing networks as the National Farmers' Union, the veterinary profession and the Women's Institutes, I must regretfully conclude that farmhouse Wensleydale is no longer made, even for fun. The spirit of traditional cheesemaking died along the Ure and its tributaries after the verdict of that hung jury. Although the same verdict ruled out any official reprieve by the Board for the other farm cheeses of the Dales, they refused to die. Swaledale and Cotherstone persisted in their unchanged courses outside the hard grading rules of the Board in more or less private '*salons des indépendants*'.

Swaledale

In Swaledale, behind shrouds of misty reserve, farms have gone on making for themselves and their friends. Most of the makers were convinced after their post-war clash with the graders and the Board that their lovely cheeses were illegal, yet it was of such cheese that Kit Calvert said: 'When you do manage to get some real Wensleydale you realise just what a loss it is to cheese lovers everywhere.' He heard that a farm cheese had been seen at a harvest festival in Swaledale in the early 1970s and with enormous difficulty tracked it down and had one made for a special Dales' event. The maker of that cheese has since taken a job in Reeth, so Arkengarthdale, where it came from, is now cheeseless. Further west, across the Swale from Gunnerside, cheese was made until 1950 at Hill Top Farm, Oxnop, where the porch sheltered two old stone presses, one

Method of making Swaledale cheese
Still in use on a Swaledale farm

1 Take 3 gallons of milk straight from the cow and strain into a clean bucket.
2 Add 1 teaspoon of rennet (milk should be approx 90°F). Leave for one hour.
3 Break curd into fine pieces. Leave for one hour.
4 Pour off whey and put curd into a muslin cloth.
5 Hang up for 12 hours to drip.
6 Crumble curd by hand very fine, sprinkle in salt and mix.
7 Put salted curd into fine muslin cloth.
8 Place in cheese vat and press for at least 12 hours.
9 Remove, peel off cloth and cheese is ready for drying.
10 Place on wooden shelf in a well-ventilated position and turn daily.
If cheese is very soft a cloth is wrapped round sides and sewn tight to keep the cheese to its proper shape, i.e. small 3 lb Stilton shape.

Cheese can be eaten after 3 weeks if preferred soft, or it can be kept for several months if preferred dry and crumbly. The crust becomes rough and grey. Some cheeses blue naturally.

of which was probably the last to be used. Ghyll Head Farm, Oxnop, also had a stone press in its porch not long ago. Very good cheese was produced by Mrs Thwaite at Walden until she died in the late 1970s.

Three farms still keep up the succulent tradition of the Dales for their own private satisfaction. The higher farms have gone out of milk production and into suckling calves, which means that they only have surplus milk when the cows first go out to grass in spring and in the 'fog' time. (A remarkable change occurs in the cheeses when the cows go out to grass in the spring: the delicate white of the winter-fed cheese turns suddenly to deep yellow.) Recently a retired accountant and his wife, Mr and Mrs Vernon Bottomley, have settled at Daleside in Low Row and re-established the right of public access to Swaledale cheese. Under a Ministry of Agriculture licence they produce as much cheese as they have time and milk for, but not nearly as much as their customers would gladly buy and eat. Their Melbeck herd of Jerseys, pastured on the north side of the Swale, is named after the moor above Low Row and Gunnerside. The cheeses are curd-salted and clothbound, acquiring a fine grey mould as they mature. The recipe is a local traditional one.

Reluctance to sell to strangers seems to stem from fear of disobeying Milk Marketing Board regulations, an inhibition not shared by Cotherstone sellers in the next dale to the north. In any case, as the English Country Cheese Council says, the Board does not lose by their cheesemaking and will not interfere with it. The Farmhouse English Cheese Public Relations Office and the English Tourist Board both take an encouraging, sympathetic view towards small farm producers, including those not under the umbrella (and form-filling burden) of the MMB scheme, so perhaps the fears of the secret Swaledale makers can be swept away. Their praiseworthy contribution to England's shrunken list of regional foods should be expanded and sold openly with pride and joy. The demand is plainly there for much more than the Bottomleys can produce.

Cotherstone
The most famous maker of Cotherstone cheese was Mrs Birkett, who made at West Park until 1940. Her family believe that the village name first became

attached to Teesdale cheeses early in this century, certainly during her lifetime. However, Cotherstone is mentioned by this name as a Yorkshire cheese in the pre-1907 'Dairy' entry of the 1911 edition of *Encyclopaedia Britannica*, the writer preferring it to most Stilton because it was softer. The makers' attitude by the 1930s can be judged by a comment from the Teesdale farmers' representative when the Wensleydale Cheesemakers' Association was formed: 'I've never made a Wensleydale cheese in my life. We make a Cotherstone cheese.'

Mrs Birkett made her cheeses from the milk of a Shorthorn herd and dry-salted them, although a lot of Teesdale farms then making salted by washing their cheeses in brine. The cheeses were bound before pressing, but the binding was removed afterwards for the crust to form naturally. If the cheeses turned out on the wet side they would be re-bound and left until the crust had formed. Cheeses of 1 lb in weight were moulded in treacle-tin vats for tourists, but most of the cheeses were 4 or 5 lb, of which some were sold young. From June onward cheeses of 7-14 lb were also made for special orders, most of them being kept for Christmas. They were not pricked, but a minority blued naturally. In 1938 West Park cheeses were going all over the country at 1s 3d a pound until late in the year, when they went up to 1s 6d in their mature state.

A young granddaughter of Mrs Birkett told me in 1980 that her aunt had recently made a cheese for a family occasion at the farm, but that there were regrettably no signs of its becoming a habit again.

Seven miles beyond Middleton (north west of Cotherstone) a farm near Langdon Beck was making until a few years ago, an activity appreciated by guests at the local youth hostel. Unfortunately the feedstuff prices rose so much that the labour was no longer worth while. Like so many Dales farms, they have gone in for suckling the calves on the cows. Another former Cotherstone cheesemaker lives at Staindrop, where the curator of Raby Castle, Mrs Elizabeth Steele, has been hoping to find a willing student to learn from her and then make cheese in the castle dairy.

Fortunately Cotherstone cheeses made quietly on two farms with a family tradition are on sale in and around Barnard Castle. Their sides are convex and their unbound crusts sometimes develop the pinky-gold appearance of a French soft cheese, especially if they are removed from the cheese room in warm weather before the crust has firmed up. Most of them are eaten at three weeks or younger. This is probably best for the smaller cheeses, and for larger cheeses too if their crust is tender; but a well-crusted larger cheese kept in a cool, moist atmosphere may go on developing flavour without drying out for another two months or more.

Sources of Cotherstone

DURHAM

Made on two farms near Cotherstone
Semi-soft, full-cream, UNpasteurised; natural crust, becoming granular (sometimes pinkish gold like that of Camembert); 2 lb, 5 lb millstones
Season: Traditionally spring to first frost, but now almost all year round

Where to buy: Barnard Castle: Kidd (Butcher) and V.G. Stores, near Buttercross; R. Morrell and Sons, 82 Galgate; Partners, Star Yard, Horsemarket; Cotherstone: Post Office Stores; Darlington: Market (David Wilson); Romaldkirk: Eggleston Hall; Staindrop: V.G. Stores; Streatley: Wells Stores

Other North Country cheeses

Cleveland

The persistence into this century of ewes' milk cheesemaking in Cleveland has already been mentioned. They were made in Farndale on Stilton House Farm, Helmsley, and Low Hagg Farm, Fadmoor, from surplus milk remaining with ewes after their lambs were weaned, and were kept to eat at harvest time. The commoner cows' milk cheese of Cleveland was once as famous as Wensleydale. It was of the salted-curd type, was pressed for three days, and did not blue. The last I know of was made at Ajalon House Farm, Fryup, in 1940.

Cheesemaking of the soft kind, and of a vegetable rennet Wensleydale type, has started again in Cleveland at Botton, between Castleton and Danby, where it is hoped to establish a local recipe. (I have suggested that they use the old Ajalon House recipe.)

Method of making Cleveland cheese
As used at Ajalon House Farm, Fryup, from 1930 to 1940

Strain night's milk into cheese kettle; stir occasionally during evening to prevent cream setting on top.

Strain morning's milk into this and heat to 84°F. Add 1 dram rennet to every 4 gallons milk, stirring gently for 3 or 4 minutes to mix thoroughly. Cover and leave 50 minutes, by which time it will be junket.

Cut in criss-cross fashion and leave to settle for 10 minutes. Then gradually raise temperature to 94°F, stirring gently and thoroughly all the time (this should take at least 20 minutes).

Leave for an hour, then drain off whey and remove curd to draining tub, shovelling it into a large linen strainer. Tie the corners crosswise, place a wooden board on top and leave for an hour.

Cut into large squares every hour, mix up, re-tie cloth and place small weight on top of board, increasing weight each time it is cut. In 3 or 4 hours, when it seems acid enough, heat a heavy poker in the fire, apply a piece of curd to it, then draw away, and when you can draw fine threads about an inch long, it is ready to vat.

Now weigh, chop fairly small or put through a curd mill, and add salt at rate of 1 oz to 3½ lb curd, mixing well. Line vats with strainer cloth wrung out in cold water and fill with curd, press down well and fold surplus cloth neatly over on top. Put in the lid, place necessary sinkers on top and put in cheese press (metal), applying light pressure.

Next morning, take out of vat and put upside down on same strainer, put back in vat and fold surplus over, put on lid and more sinkers if necessary as cheese gets smaller through pressure.

The following morning, take out of vat, put upside down on fine butter-muslin strainer, put back in press with more pressure still.

Next morning, take out of vat, discard strainer, cut off any thin bits round edges to make a good shape, and run a rather hot poker round cut edges to seal. Rub sparingly with butter or lard, put a calico bandage round and stitch securely in place.

Store on shelves in cool darkened room and turn every day for 6 weeks, then every other day until mature, when it will have developed a blue mould on a fine skin and will need turning only occasionally.

Craven

In this vale near Skipton village partnerships for smaller farms and cottages were common in the eighteenth century. In 1740 every householder of Linton-in-Craven kept a cow.

Dent

In this west Pennine dale of the Upper Dee tons of cheese was made in the eighteenth century. In 1926 a provision merchant started the Dinsdale Dairy, but this was moved to Sedburgh in Cumbria in 1950. It is no longer in operation.

Pickering

In the Vale of Pickering skimmed-milk cheese was made of a quality compared by an eighteenth-century visitor with Gloucester. They were at their best after a year's maturing. Use of the comparatively new-fangled cheese mill was noted here in 1792.

Ribblesdale

The only evidence of past cheesemaking in this Dale is one of the few surviving stone cheese presses at Studfold.

Other Dales

In the area north west from the Ribble almost as far as the Tyne, in the Pennines and the North Yorkshire Moors, cheesemaking was carried on extensively, notably in Garsdale, Ravenstonedale, Nidderdale, Baldersdale, Colsterdale and Hintondale.

At the turn of the seventeenth century Celia Fiennes remarked on cheeses in the Newcastle area as being 'very indifferent; black-looking, soft sower things'.

Yorkshire skimmed-milk cheese

South of Wensleydale in Wharfedale and the Craven district, towards Skipton, and westwards towards the Lakes, were great butter-making areas, when this was the only form of fat easily available. Consequently almost all the cheese of the area was made from skimmed milk and hardened quickly. The cheese of Yorkshire origin was called Whangby, derived from *whang*, a thong, describing its tough, leathery nature. (Whillymoor Wang, the Lakeland equivalent, is mentioned below.)

The Lakes

Wordsworth reported that every cottage seemed to have two or three cows and a cheese press near the door, each family making its own butter and cheese. The butter-making meant that most of these were skimmed-milk cheeses of the kind described above. One such, called Whillymoor Wang, was made on the very poor land called Whillymoor between Arlecdon and Moresby. A native of Arlecdon, Mrs Dora Marley, told me recently that *wang* meant leather shoelace, and 'the cheese was just as tough'. Mrs Marley remembers some Cumbrian farms making cheese for their own consumption in the twenties, but knows of no farm making now. In 1926 the Bells at Aigle Gill, Aspatria, engaged a cheesemaker because they could no longer sell their milk. He came from Cheshire, and Cheshire he made, but not for very long. When the Aspatria

Creamery was able to take their milk the Bells gave up, and the family farms have sent it there ever since. Aspatria makes block Cheddar for the Board, and Cumbria can boast no local cheese today.

Sources of traditional and other Yorkshire cheeses

WEST YORKSHIRE

MANOR HOUSE FARM, Mickletown, Leeds
Capra
Pure goat lactic (like French Banon), UNpasteurised; no crust, coated in various herbs or spices; 2 oz rounded discs
Farmers, cheesemakers: Peter and Margaret Edginton
Anglo-Nubian, British Saanen, Toggenberg goats

LONGLEY FARM, Holmfirth (*4 miles S. of Huddersfield via A61 and B6106, 1½ miles from centre of Holmfirth*)
Visitors tel. Holmfirth (048 489) 4151
Longley Farm Cheese
Low-fat cottage cheese, plain or with chives, pasteurised; no crust; 25 or 125 g. tubs, heat-sealed
Farmers: J. and E. Dickinson
Jersey herd: permanent pastures on Millstone Grit and sandstone
Where to buy: On farm (retail and wholesale); London: Harrods, Knightsbridge, S.W.1; Partridges, 132 Sloane Street, S.W.1

ADAM'S RIB FARM, 51 Sandy Lane, Middlestown (*S. of Wakefield, off A642 to Huddersfield*)
Visitors tel. Wakefield (0924) 272322
1 Goat Cream Cheese
4 oz cartons
2 Smallholder
1½ lb cylindrical
Both made from UNpasteurised goats' milk
Farmer, cheesemaker: Lynn Eve
Mainly Saanen goats (not pedigree); loam sown with a view to permanent pasture
Where to buy: On farm

NORTH YORKSHIRE

York (sometimes called curd cheese)
Unripened, medium or full-fat soft, unsalted, white with central layer of fresh cream, or cream mixed with a small proportion of the curd (or the desired proportion of curd sage-stained or coloured with annatto); no crust; flat, rectangular; on straw mat

Where to buy: Isle of Wight (*see p. 18*); Hampshire (*see p. 18*); London (*see p. 19–20*)

Note: Cheese termed 'York' or 'Curd' sold for cheesecake-making is unlikely to be in the traditional form described, but see also Cambridge (p. 54)

KIRKBY MALZEARD DAIRY (Wensleydale Creameries) (*6 miles W.N.W. of Ripon*)
1 Blue Wensleydale
Firm, blue, pasteurised; natural, clothbound, pricked; 9–10 lb cylindrical
The cheeses are sent to Nuttall's Dairy at Hartington in Dovedale to be blued; blueing is often irregular
2 White Wensleydale
Hard, white, pasteurised; natural, clothbound, hardening with maturity; 14 lb tubby barrels (2 lb and 4 lb cheeses for Christmas)
Note: 'KM' identifies cheeses, in place of old number
Season: All year, but spring and autumn cheeses may develop more richly and occasionally blue irregularly
Where to buy: Boroughbridge: Aldborough Dairy; most cheese shops; Whitelock's, Embertons, most factors (wholesale)
Many of these cheeses are sold at 3 weeks; their fine-grained light texture can be refreshing, but the flavour is also light. The best cheeses will mature to a sweet richness of flavour and texture at 4–9 months.

COVERHAM DAIRY (Dairy Crest), Coverdale (*1½ miles W.S.W. of Middleham*)
Hard, white, pasteurised; natural, clothbound; 14 lb cylindrical
Where to buy: As above (wholesale only)

Note: Rindless White Wensleydale is made at the Milk Marketing Board Creamery at Hawes (see p. 77, 79)

DALESIDE, Low Row, Swaledale
Swaledale
Soft or semi-soft, full-cream, UNpasteurised; natural (usually clothbound), grey

surface mould; 1½–2 lb, 3–3½ lb (and occasionally larger) millstones or truncated cylinders
Jerseys on permanent pastures
The demand is much greater than Daleside's present pastures can supply
Farmer, cheesemaker: Vernon Bottomley

Note: This cheese is also made on two farms near Gunnerside and one near Grinton, but not for sale

BOTTON VILLAGE CREAMERY, Danby
1 Botton Cheese
Hard, full-cream, UNpasteurised, made with vegetable rennet and sea salt; natural, larded and flour-pasted, clothbound 25 lb, 50 lb (probably changing to 8 lb, 25 lb) cylindrical, made to Dales recipe
2 Danbydale
Semi-soft, crusted Dales cheese; with chives, or celery seed, or marjoram and basil; 12–15 oz
Farmers: Camphill Village Trust on four farms; *cheesemaker:* Miss Inez Vermaas
Dairy Shorthorns (75 per cent), Ayrshires (25 per cent) on organically farmed pastures
Where to buy: Botton: Village Store and Creamery (between Castleton and Danby); Guisborough: Market and Electra; Whitby: Shepherd's Purse; York: Wholefood Bakery,Gillygate; Wholefood, Micklegate

LAVEROCK HALL FARM, Chop Gate (*8 miles N. of Helmsley, S. of pub and church, before Fangdale Beck*)
Bilsdale
UNpasteurised semi-hard goat cheese; waxed
Of the firmer Swaledale farmhouse type; close but melting texture and delicious goat flavour
Farmers: Jeremy and Anne Alston (*cheesemaker*)
Where to buy (*when available*)*:* Streatley: Wells Stores

HIGH FARM, Hartoft End, near Pickering (*3 miles W. of Pickering or 5 miles E. of Kirkby Moorside*)

Visitors by appointment, tel. Lastingham (075 15) 268
Semi-hard Goat Cheese
Made to adapted Wensleydale recipe; waxed crust; about 1 lb cylindrical
Farmer, cheesemaker: Philip Rheinberg
British Toggenberg, British Saanen and most other breeds of goat; long-term ley, brown earth on glacial clay
Where to buy: At many health food shops in North and West Yorkshire and Humberside (not always in winter)

MELHOUSE, Newton-upon-Rawcliffe (*4½ miles N. of Pickering, in middle of village facing green*)
Melhouse Hard Goat Cheese
Wensleydale type, UNpasteurised; waxed crust
Smallholder, cheesemaker: Mollie Croysdale
Anglo-Nubian, White British Saanen goats; well-drained plateau, light, sandy soil
Where to buy: At house

GREENDALE FARM, Boltby (*4½ miles N.E. of Thirsk, 3 miles N. of A170 and Sutton-under-Whitestonecliffe*)
Visitors welcome, tel. Thirsk (0845) 597306 if distant
1 Cheddar-type
Cloth-bound; 25 lb
2 Yorkshire Curd
Bagged
3 Coulommiers
All cheeses from UNpasteurised milk
Farmer, cheesemaker: Rosanne Pearson
Jerseys on permanent pastures (over 20 plant species, varying from hilltop to dale) on marginal land
Where to buy: on farm; Northallerton: Lewis and Cooper, market Place; Stockton: Covered Market (Sundley's Dairy)
Cheddars, made mainly for family use, are given a little extra rennet because of Jersey milk

5

Cheeses of Scotland

Scotland's mountains are not confined to the Highlands. It has to be remembered that while they are less rugged than those of the north, the Lowlands contain much of Scotland's highest-lying countryside. The odd part out is the south west. Ayrshire, the damp green heart of Scotland's real lowlands, was nurturing the domestic cow when most of the rest of Scotland was inhabited by clansmen and sheep. There were scatterings of spectacularly hairy and horny beasts in the Highlands and some representatives of the black breeds further south, few of them living in conditions conducive to milk production.

Early cheese history

From at least the thirteenth century the Scots were making many and varied cheeses, but little is recorded of their character. The oldest historical record of an existing Scottish cheese is a recipe for the oatmeal-coated, buttery Caboc as made by Mariota de Ile, daughter of a fifteenth-century Macdonald of the Isles. Mariota's recipe was passed down in the female line to her descendant Susannah Stone, who has revived it in Ross-shire. Mrs Stone has also helped to give new life to Scotland's simplest and oldest cheese of all, the traditional skimmed-milk Crowdie (porridge) cheese.

KEY

Farmhouse or small dairy

Creamery

Main road

Swannay

Kirkwall

ORKNEY

N

Tain

HIGHLAND

INVERNESS

GRAMPIAN

ABERDEEN

FORT WILLIAM

TAYSIDE

DUNDEE

PERTH

FIFE

CENTRAL

STERLING

EDINBURGH

LOTHIAN

Howgate

Islay

GLASGOW

Gigha
Island

ARRAN

Kilmory

STRATHCLYDE

BORDERS

HAWICK

Bonchester
Bridge

DUMFRIES &
GALLOWAY

Lockerbie

DUMFRIES

Dalbeattie

Annan

In the 1700s there were records of cream and whole-milk cheeses ripened for three or more weeks, sometimes in ox bladders. The only cheese widely known before Dunlop was Orkney. It must have been a hard cheese to have travelled far in those days, and was sought after for funeral feasts. Cheeses, and poultry, could also be used to pay university fees in Scotland.

The earliest mainland hard cheeses were commonly made from the butter makers' skimmed milk. Their character can be guessed at from the fact that the notoriously rocky Suffolk was popular with the Scots, who imported it in considerable quantities.

The first 'sweet-milk', or full-cream hard cheese originated in the parish of Dunlop in Ayrshire. It is attributed to the cheesemaking skills acquired in her exile by Barbara Gilmour. She is thought to have gone to Ireland, certainly not historically renowned for its schools of cheesemaking, during the reign of James II. Whatever the school she learned in, Barbara Gilmour settled with her farmer husband in Dunlop in 1688 and made the first whole-milk cheeses which stood up to travel. Dunlop therefore not only pioneered the improvement of Scotland's basic cheese, but its marketing in town and cities.

Dr Davis suggests that the credit for the cheese's virtues should be shared between Barbara and her Dunlop cows, which is also to praise their pastures and the favourable rainfall. The local Dunlop cows spread through surrounding Cunningham and then throughout Ayrshire, adopting district and county name in turn as their fame grew.

A system of leasing cattle for cheesemaking, called 'bowering' or 'boyering', arose around 1740. The lessee, or boyer, paid hire to the farmer and made what he could from making the milk into cheese. I had supposed it must have been a short-lived idea, as there is no mention of it in the parish reports of the 1790s. Some of the farmers who tried it may indeed have seen their neighbours profiting more from making their own cheese and decided to join them; but Dr Crawford tells me that the system, later known as 'bowing', survived into the 1950s.

By the 1750s the receptive farmers of south-west Scotland had exploited their local breed of cattle, their lush pastures, and Barbara Gilmour's recipe to such advantage that Dunlop cheeses and Ayrshire beasts had become nationally renowned. These cheeses were driving out the less attractive skimmed-milk veterans, and most of the ewes' milk cheeses, which only persisted in any quantity in the Lothians and the mountainous regions on either side of the border.

In the 1790s the _First Statistical Account of Scotland_, a remarkable assessment of the state of the realm parish by parish, was prepared and published. It recorded that the much deforested Forest of Ettrick in Selkirkshire was one of the areas in which ewes' milk cheese was still of importance. The parish of Ettrick, to which no reliably passable roads then led, exported mutton and cheese to the market fifteen miles off from its flocks of 30,000 sheep, whose fleece was too coarse for wool buyers. There was not a waggon in the parish, so, when carts could not get through, pack-horses must have carried the cheese while the mutton went on the hoof.

Further north on the line of the Moorfoot and Lammermuir Hills, Heriot too was still a ewes' cheese parish, but its big locally bred sheep produced good wool, as well as a cheese 'inferior to none in quality, cleanliness and relish' which sold at $3\frac{1}{2}d$ a pound, the same price as Dunlop elsewhere. For a nine-week season it engrossed 'almost the whole attention of the busy house-wife and her maids'.

The growing popularity of Dunlop

The new full-milk hard cheesemaking derived from Dunlop naturally centred on Ayrshire. A number of parishes and districts were already proud of their cheesemaking 'after the Dunlop manner, or what is known by the general name of sweet-milk cheese'. Fenwick was one, benefiting from rising prices in the 1790s as trade flourished in Glasgow and Paisley. Dalry and Galston too prided themselves on their fine Dunlop-style cheese, sent to Kilmarnock, Paisley and Glasgow, and in Galston's case to Edinburgh as well, a new venture in distant marketing following Dunlop parish's own enterprising example. East Monkland sent its cheese the sixteen miles to Glasgow, but was also noted for its local cheese 'equal to Stilton (perhaps not inferior to Parmesan), made by some families; but this superior kind is mostly made for private consumption'. The tenant farmers of Beith paid their rents chiefly from their dairies, almost all making sweet-milk cheese, after the Dunlop fashion, which fetched $3\frac{1}{2}d$ a pound. The average surplus over family consumption was £3 10s worth of cheese a year.

Hoddon was one of the odd parishes out, not having made cheese until the farm of Relief was let in the 1790s to 'a person from Cheshire'. He brought the English county's method of cheese and whey-butter making with him and got $4\frac{1}{2}d$ a pound for his cheese. In an unfavourable year he made £140 worth of cheese from forty cows, to which ten milkers were added the following season.

Kilmaurs was another parish noted for the quality and quantity of its Dunlop. By this time the cheese was being made throughout the surrounding district of Cunningham, and marketed mainly in Paisley and Glasgow. East Kilbride was producing over a ton of Dunlop cheese annually 'from every farm of a plough of land', which must have been of 'superfine' grade as it fetched almost $4d$ a pound. (A plough of land, or ploughgate, was an old Scottish measure latterly interpreted as 50 English to 100 Scottish acres.)

It is fascinating that in Dunlop, the fount of all this expansion of cheese-making and marketing, 'the people were alarmed when questioned about these things'. 'Alleging that this was valuing their farms', they refused to answer questions. The writer of the Dunlop section of the *First Statistical Account of Scotland* 'supposed' there might be about 158 cows kept and well over 100 tons of cheese produced annually, fetching £3714. To this reward they were well entitled, the writer went on, unsoured by their uncooperative attitude. 'For as this is the produce of the richest pastures and the best cows, so nothing can exceed their integrity and cleanliness in manufacturing it.' He remarked that, like some English county cheeses, Dunlop was nothing much when young 'but improved by age and proper keeping'.

In the first half of the 1800s the making of Dunlop continued to spread; but its quality became more variable than the earlier high standard indicated by those confident reports of the 1790s. The Ayrshire Agricultural Association was worried enough to investigate cheesemaking in Gloucestershire, Somerset and

Wiltshire. As a result Joseph Harding was invited to do for Scotland what he had already done for his home Cheddar county (see p. 7). His improved method, combined with the advent of more practical and hygienic dairy equipment and better temperature control, had some effect. John McMaster furthered this progress in the 1860s with the Somerset double-jacket steam-heated vat, and improved designs of both dairy and cheese store.

The 1870s saw a further worrying relapse. On the Scottish Dairy Association's initiative the Canadian Cheddar system was adopted, with its better methods of control, particularly in the preparation and use of rennet, and the use of the hot iron to test acidity. Until then, rennet had been measured in 'teacupsful' of greatly varying size. The second of the Canadians to help with this reform movement, R. J. Drummond, swept away much ancient untidiness and became head of the Kilmarnock Dairy School. As a result hard cheesemaking generally improved, and, while the Dunlop type continued to rule in Ayrshire and Kirkcudbrightshire, most Wigtownshire cheesemakers adopted the harder Cheddar.

The only further significant changes were the introduction of cultured starters at the end of the nineteenth century and the later raising of cheesemaking temperatures, a practice common to the whole Cheddar world. Old hands considered the latter change to have softened the curd unduly, but Dr Davis thinks this may be more attributable to such new factors as an increase in mastitis milk, modern emphasis on bulk as against quality in milk production, and changes in cattle feeding.

At the height of Dunlop fashion almost all farms in the south and south west of Scotland, including those of Robert Burns, were said to have made cheese. Even as late as 1930 the number was 300. Mrs Margaret Menzies Campbell remembers the days when Dunlop was widely made on farms. Each farm had a fully matured cheese open for cooking and a softer one for eating. At breakfast, porridge was followed on alternate days by bacon and eggs or toasted cheese on a scone made of home-ground flour eaten in front of the fire. Mrs Menzies Campbell says she has never tasted such good toasted cheese since.

Post-war Scottish cheesemaking

As in England, cheesemaking on Scottish farms virtually ceased in 1940, but it revived after the war until there were twenty-two farms making cheese in 1960. A rapid decline then set in. The number was only six in 1967, by which year 95 per cent of all the cheese produced in south-west Scotland was being made in block form. In 1972 the Company of Scottish Cheesemakers' annual farmhouse cheesemaking trophy was presented for the sixth time to J. Brian Finlay, of The Ross, Kirkcudbright, in the presence of his fine cheesemaker, Robert Maxwell. The trophy was handed over in perpetuity to Mr Finlay because no other cheesemaking farmers remained to compete with him. The official speech on the occasion betrayed an element of bureaucratic satisfaction that such an untidy survival was almost disposed of: handing over the old trophy, Mr Lockhart, a director of the Company of Scottish Cheesemakers, said: 'I feel this is the end of an era in Scottish cheese history. Scottish cheese today is made in our creameries, which are among the most modern and best equipped in the world, and the day of the farmhouse cheesemaker is virtually over. I hope, however,

Mr Finlay will be able to carry on with his cheesemaking activities for a while yet.'

In 1974, within two years of the utterance of these pious and complacent words, Mr Finlay felt himself forced to stop. He told me: 'We were the last farm in the Board area, and as such were a nuisance to the Milk Board, who were able to force us out economically.'

In 1980 the old London cheese merchants, Charles Liles and John Adamsons, asked for 200 traditional Dunlop cheeses for an American export order. Only six or seven existed, they were told, and these were made only for shows. Anthony Rowcliffe, another much respected London cheese factor, was given the same answer when he wanted a large quantity of Dunlop for export.

It is the same with Scottish Cheddar: with a traditional cheese made only for the show, the Scottish MMB's Rothesay Creamery won the 1979 Nantwich and South Cheshire Show Supreme Cheddar Championship; but good cheese should be made for eating, not just for show. In the block cheese division, to which the Scottish Milk Boards have devoted all their commercial energies, the Danes, prize-winners in earlier years, won the Company of Scottish Cheese-makers' McLelland Perpetual Challenge Cup for the best Cheddar in 1979.

So much for Scottish traditional cheese. It is not surprising that the plethora of Milk Marketing Boards ruling over Scotland's soulless, tasteless dairy world should accept restrictions on the sale of raw milk which have been resisted in the rest of the United Kingdom. Pasteurisation and cooling plants on the smallest scale cost £12,000 at July 1980 prices. The West of Scotland College is now pushing a 'small batch pasteurisation unit' at £2950. Efficient dairy farmers can do better with such a sum than waste it on removing by pasteurisation just the very individual element of character which sells their cheese. One cheesemaker to whom this was suggested was getting £1.50 a pound (May 1981 prices), against less than 83p a pound quoted on 3 May 1981 for Scottish creamery Cheddar or English farm Cheddar (4 × 5 kilo blocks). So, unless the joint plea of the National Farmers' Union and the Smallfarmers' Associations in Scotland for exemption of small herds is answered, small farmers will be unable after August 1983 to build up profitable dairy herds, and discriminating Scottish milk drinkers and small-scale cheesemakers will be deprived of the natural milk which both require. (That raw-milk drinkers are not an insignificant market was shown in the north of England, where hundreds of thousands signed successful petitions against compulsory pasteurisation.)

Scottish cheese today

It would be good to see a revival of traditional farmhouse Dunlop. England's Single Gloucester and Swaledale had not been made for open sale on their home ground for much longer than the seven years which separate us from the last Dunlop cheesemaking at The Ross, Kirkcudbright. Brian Finlay sees as the only hope of revival the co-operative sharing of milk production and cheese-making on a shift basis, between the staffs of a few like-minded farmers; but his view in May 1980 was that with the creameries under-utilised 'the Board would not allow such a venture to start'.

In 1967 a report in the *Scotsman* based on official Scottish Milk Marketing Board publicity conceded that 5 per cent of its Cheddar and Dunlop production was made 'in the traditional round shape, matured in the rind for the speciality market, i.e. the very high-class retail outlets, who specialise in fancy cheeses'. Now no Scottish traditional hard cheese is acknowledged by the Board's publicity handout as catering for a market which one English supermarket cheese buyer assesses as 30 per cent of his custom. Even a pessimistic cheese merchant in Scotland allowed that 20 per cent of Scots might choose real cheese if given the chance.

The state of Scottish cheese as reported up to this point was assessed after wide enquiries through the press, through shops, and during my own travels. My questions on past and present cheeses had also gone to the West of Scotland Agricultural College at Auchincruive and to the North of Scotland Milk Marketing Board. Answers from the Board were terse and unexplanatory, but they did send me what seemed to be a comprehensive list, 'Cheeses made by the Scottish Milk Marketing Boards', which included a number made by private creameries too. It appeared, as the College had said, that Scotland's hard cheeses were only presented in traditional form at shows. So far as official accounts of traditional Dunlop and Scottish Cheddar went, it seemed that I should have to write their obituary.

Such indeed was my first draft, which I sent to Dr Crawford and Miss Galloway at Auchincruive, who had already helped me with a list of lost and surviving Scottish cheeses. Their two corrections of historical fact I have gratefully used. Their comment on the impact of the chapter was this:

The article in no way reflects the well-recognised excellence and quality of Scottish factory cheese maintained by strong grading standards and the interest to maintain an annual Show of international status for cheese quality. [The grading and the Show had in fact been mentioned.]

Much of the article is factual and interesting but the overall picture portrayed of the Scottish cheese industry is neither true not warranted.

My answer is that I can only speak or write as I find, and as many Scottish cheese customers have found over recent years. It is not just chance that, despite Dr Crawford's claim for 'the well-recognised excellence and quality of Scottish factory cheese', the average Scottish household consumes 20 per cent less natural cheese and 55 per cent more processed than its Southern English counterpart. My contention is that the Scottish Boards and Company of Cheese-makers have been mesmerised by technical excellence and mistaken this for consumer satisfaction.

I had found the official Scottish cheese world's answers to my questions too uncommunicative to take at their face value. The *Scots Magazine*, with the same set of questions, had received different answers, some misleading, some completely wrong. In May 1980 they were told that the 'lost cheeses' they listed were 'all still made in Scotland although not always obtainable'. In fact the dairy where two of them (Morven and Caithness) were made had been closed down years ago. Carrick, as they were told, is made at the College at Auchincruive; but only for demonstration to students. 'Blue Stuart', they were told, 'is made by the North of Scotland Board ... although it hasn't been on the market for eight weeks, it is to be available next month'. But the Board had already told me that the dairy was closed. Finally, having asked about traditional Dunlop (specifically *not* block cheese), they were told that Dunlop was produced on the Isle of Islay. The cheese produced there is only available in block form or (rarely) Cryovac-sealed miniatures, quite unlike the traditional cheese.

Happily the magazine, having through no fault of its own turned up all these wrong answers, turned up for me the right man to put the record straight: John Godsell of the Fife Creamery at Kirkcaldy. From him I obtained a really comprehensive list of Scottish hard cheeses. He told me that he could sell at least ten traditional Dunlops a week, against the occasional five allowed him, and fifty (half as many again as he can get) of the traditional Scottish Cheddars. Perhaps this demand for cheese-shaped cheeses of character is just a nuisance to the Scottish Boards and the Company of Cheesemakers, as was the untidy survival of farmhouse cheesemaking until they suppressed it in 1974. Nothing else can explain the concealment from an interested public of the Boards' best products, their wilfully small output of these old cheeses, and their disregard of a considerable export order offered to the Northern Board, who virtually denied Dunlop's commercial existence. Waxed Cheddar has been sold as Dunlop.

If Scots are to be persuaded to eat more cheese this attitude must change, and knowledgeable cheese-loving Scots must rebel to change it. Meanwhile, they in their homeland and Sassenach lovers of good hard cheese who travel there have no choice but to make do with what little they can find.

Method of making Farmhouse Dunlop

As used by Robert Maxwell, cheesemaker, of The Ross, Kirkcudbright (J. Brian Finlay, farmer)

1 Overnight milk (unpasteurised) ripens to be mixed with morning milk.
2 Cultivated starter added.
3 Rennet.
4 Time from renneting to pitching of curd: 2 hours 40 minutes.
5 Time from drainage of whey to milling: $1\frac{1}{2}$ hours (curd turned frequently).
6 Curd milled to 2 inch cubes and salted.
7 Special cheese press used.
8 Cheese bound in cheesecloth.
9 Recommended maturing time 6 months in cool conditions, turned daily.
Weight of cheeses: 80 lb.

Post-war revivals and new cheeses

One of Scotland's best post-war cheeses was Ayrshire soft cheese. This was of rich creamy consistency and flavour, and sold all over Britain. A few years ago it suddenly disappeared: Express Dairies had bought and closed the dairy. In 1979 it reappeared, thinner in consistency and flavour and, with well-justified modesty, devoid of any label of quality or origin. Enquiries to its distributors, Murchies, elicited not even an acknowledgement, but another Scottish factor tells me that it is made by the Northern Board at Inverness. Murchies do now label their product 'Home Farm Soft Cheese Low Fat'. Whose 'Home Farm', I ask.

In the 1960s Miss Elizabeth Naismith, the milk recording officer for Berwickshire, and her mother started making Lammermoor (cheese of Coulommiers type) at Westruther in the Lammermuir Hills, and later made a peat-smoked version, and Crowdie. Regrettably there is no creamery at Westruther now; Miss Naismith has gone to Canada.

At about the same time M. T. R. Marwick and his partners started the smaller Howgate cheeses at Penicuik, Midlothian.

The 1960s saw the invention of two agreeable semi-soft cheeses called Caithness and Morven, first made on the trainless Lybster railway station. Cheesemaking moved to Wick where the company flourished to the extent of producing 4 tons of cheese a week in 1973 and launched a Drambuie-flavoured version with the American market in view. Regrettably, the dairy closed in the mid 1970s; I am told that the selective cheese subsidies of that time were responsible.

Carrick, a softer cheese of the gold-crusted Saint Paulin type, was also available in those days but is now only 'demonstrated' in cheesemaking instruction for students at the West of Scotland Agricultural College at Auchincruive. The college also demonstrates Caledonian Blue (a modified version of Bleu d'Auvergne), fresh lactic curd cheese of the *fromage frais* or Quarg type, American-type cottage cheese, Gouda, Camembert, smallholder ('mini' Cheddar) and fresh lactic curd cheese made from goats' milk.

Dunlop's name is kept alive on the labels of creamery-made, plastic-wrapped small Orkney and Arran cheeses, but the college at Auchincruive, the arbiter of Scottish cheese grading, carefully describes them now as 'modifications of a Dunlop type of cheese'. The Islay creamery produces cheeses of a more flaky consistency and more subtle flavour, and Swannay Farm Dairy, Orkney, produces a pleasant 9 lb round cheese. Both of these are rindless.

With the exception of Caboc, Crowdie and the cheeses of Aberdeenshire and Banffshire it could be said that Scottish traditional cheese has of late been virtually unobtainable. Elsewhere only the Isle of Gigha regularly produced a hard cheese worthy of the name, an enterprise instituted by the Horlick family during their ownership. Machinery for making block cheese and plastic wrapping did invade the island a few years ago, to the visiting Lady Horlick's dismay, but those who ordered them could still get excellent hard 4-5 lb clothbound truckles, usually coloured, which matured to broad flavour in nine months. Sad to say, having considered reviving its full-size traditional cheeses in response to public demand, the owners found the cost of re-equipping too great and closed the dairy in September 1981. Their milk now sails to Campbeltown Creamery.

At the time of going to press there are some encouraging signs of a revival in the making of traditional Scottish cheeses. The Scottish Milk Marketing Board Creamery at Arran, already making 1-2 ton batches of Dunlop and Scottish Cheddar for several shows a year, is planning to resume production of large traditional cheeses for public sale. The main obstacle is the replacing of equipment (hoops and ripening shelves) destroyed when the creamery went over to block cheesemaking, but by 1982 it is hoped that about 200 of both Dunlop and Scottish Cheddar will be available annually for cheese shops from this creamery alone. Its cheeses have a well-deserved name for flavour

In the 1970s the new Castle Stuart Dairy in Inverness, under a respected Scots cheesemaker from the Stilton world, Andy Williamson, made Scotland's first commercial steps in the blue cheese world. Blue Stuart was a Stilton-type cheese, sold, like Stilton, blue or white. He also made versions of Blue

Wensleydale (praised by Kit Calvert) and Blue Cheshire as well. The latter – usually firmer and redder than the original – was a good cheese in its own right, sold by me at Streatley properly as Inverness-shire Blue. It was marketed throughout the rest of Britain as Shropshire Blue, which caused understandable but misconceived excitement in Shropshire in its early days. In 1980 orders were suddenly refused, with rumours that the cheese would be available later; but the North of Scotland Milk Marketing Board told me, without explanation, that the dairy was closed. Only afterwards did I discover that the Board had bought the dairy some years back, and then deliberately closed it, killing off a few more Scottish cheeses including her only commercially marketed blues. 'The Board had better uses for its milk' were the ironic words of one of its largest frustrated cheese customers.

The most recent Scottish cheese I know of is Bonchester, a pleasant unpasteurised farmhouse version of Coulommiers made at Hawick by John Curtis, from Jersey milk.

The greatest post-war Scottish success, however, has been the revival of Crowdie and Caboc by Reggie and Susannah Stone at Blairliath, their farm on the southern shore of Dornoch Firth in Ross-shire. I am told that Reggie said to his wife in 1962: 'I wish you'd make me some Crowdie like mother made it.' Susannah set to with a whole churn of their milk, straining the results over the bath in a wedding present, a large linen pillowcase. There was so much more than the family could eat that they off-loaded the surplus on a local shopkeeper. As a shopkeeper myself, I can picture his misgivings, but his courage was rewarded by appreciative customers, who were soon asking for more.

The Stones followed this with the revival of Susannah's ancestral Caboc, the fifteenth-century 'Chieftain's Cheese'. Then the family gathered some wild garlic and mixed it into the creamy cheese; they named the result Hramsa, the Gaelic for that all-healing Celtic herb. Further variations on the Stones' cream and low-fat cheeses ensued; these are recorded in the list following. It is unfortunate for English cheese merchants and customers that these cheeses have been sent south in recent years by meat lorry at a temperature quite unsuitable for cheese, unless it is to be eaten as it leaves the lorry, an impossible demand.

In the Grampians and an area astride the borders of Banffshire and Morayshire further north some small farms have preserved their cheesemaking tradition. Twelve farms within reach of Mossat now make 6–7 lb cabics (like English truckles). These are all sweet-milk cheeses, whereas formerly only skimmed milk was used, the cream going to make butter.

Finally, ewes' milk cheese took off again in Dumfriesshire in 1980.

Sources of traditional and other Scottish cheeses

DUMFRIES AND GALLOWAY

WINDERMERE FARM, Annan
Visitors tel. Annan (046 12) 4691
Barac Farmhouse Cheese
Semi-hard, Dales type, made from UNpasteurised ewes' milk; white, lightly waxed crust; 3 lb drums
Farmer: Michael Neilson; *cheesemaker:* Carol Neilson

Friesland sheep on coastal pastures
Where to buy: On farm; London: Paxton and Whitfield, Jermyn Street, S.W.1; Streatley: Wells Stores; see p. 120, 127

EXPRESS DAIRIES CREAMERY, Lockerbie
Dunlop
Hard, coloured, pasteurised; clothbound, waxed; 60 lb flat wheel

Firm, close-textured, ready at 7–8 months
Where to buy: Glasgow: A. McClelland and Sons, Cheese Market, Albion Street; Kirkcaldy: Fife Creamery, Randolph Place (wholesale)
These cheeses are only made for shows, though a few subsequently seep on to the market

SCOTTISH MILK MARKETING BOARD CREAMERY, Dalbeattie
Scottish Cheddar
Hard, coloured, pasteurised; clothbound, waxed; 45 lb cylindrical
Where to buy: Dalbeattie: Hodgson's Home Bakery; and as for Dunlop (*see above, with the same reservations about availability*)

STRATHCLYDE
SCOTTISH MILK MARKETING BOARD CREAMERY, Kilmory, Arran
1 Arran
Softer, modified Dunlop, coloured; $2\frac{1}{4}$ lb small drums, Cryovac-wrapped (also block)
Visitors welcome but 3 days' notice required, tel. Sliddery (077 087) 240
2 Dunlop
Clothbound, waxed
3 Scottish Cheddar
60 lb cylinder
Manager: Neil McLean; *cheesemaker:* George Hotchkiss
Where to buy: Kirkcaldy: Fife Creamery, Randolph Place; Paisley: Scottish Milk Marketing Board, Underwood Road (both wholesale)
These outlets handle some of the traditional cheeses coming on to the market after shows; for recent developments on their availability see p. 95–6

ISLE OF GIGHA CREAMERY
Gigha
Hard, usually coloured; natural, clothbound; 4–5 lb cylindrical truckles (also block)
A close-textured firm cheese attaining very full flavour in 9 months
Unhappily this excellent creamery could not bear the cost of re-equipping to produce large traditional cheeses again, and closed in September 1981

PRIVATE DAIRY ON ISLE OF ISLAY
Islay
Hard; 1 lb, 2 lb (rare), 10 lb, 40 lb millstones, Cryovac-wrapped

Firm cheeses of more open, flaky consistency than Orkney, with a less tangy, more subtle flavour
Where to buy: Glasgow: A. McLelland and Sons, Cheese Market, Albion Street; Kirkcaldy: Fife Creamery (wholesale)

ORKNEY
NORTH OF SCOTLAND MILK MARKETING BOARD, Kirkwall
1 Orkney
Plain, coloured or smoked; hard, modified Dunlop; 1 lb flat, round, Cryovac-wrapped
Close-textured, tangy; the smoked version is of typical smoked cheese flavour, but of pleasanter consistency than imported sausage-shaped smoked cheeses
2 Claymore Crowdie
Soft; $7\frac{1}{2}$ oz tubs
Where to buy: Widely available through normal retail and wholesale sources

SWANNAY FARM
Scottish Cheddar
9 lb wheels, Cryovac-wrapped
Agreeable, light consistency and flavour, comparable to Caerphilly
Where to buy: In Orkney; Kirkcaldy: Fife Creamery, Randolph Place (wholesale)

GRAMPIAN
The following two cheeses are made on various farms throughout Grampian
1 Aberdeenshire Farmhouse
Hard, 'sweet milk'; some natural crust, some clothbound; 6–7 lb cabic (like English truckle)
These wholemilk cheeses, traditional in this area, vary considerably (some are flavoured with caraway)
2 Banffshire Farmhouse
Hard, traditional
Where to buy: Rhynie and Mossat: Anderson of Mossat, (Aberdeenshire Farmhouse); shops in Buckie and Keith (Banffshire)

HIGHLAND
BLAIRLIATH, Tain (Highland Fine Cheeses)
1 Caboc
Buttery curd, double cream; toasted pinhead oatmeal crust; 4 oz dumpy log
A rich, fat cheese agreeably set off by the oatmeal

2 Highland Crowdie
Cottage cheese, low-fat, high-protein;
5½ oz
Moister and more refreshing than the usual
mass-produced cottage cheese; probably
Scotland's oldest cheese
3 Crowdie and Cream
Cottage cheese (⅔) with double cream (⅓);
3½ oz
4 Hramsa
Cottage cheese mixed with chopped wild
garlic leaves in cream; 3½ oz
Wild garlic leaves are more delicate than
normal cultivated garlic
5 Crowdie and Wild Garlic
As Hramsa, without the added cream
(low-fat)
6 Galic
Soft, full-fat, with chopped wild garlic
leaves rolled in flaked oats, crumbled al-
monds and hazelnuts; 4 oz
7 Highland Soft Cheese
Full-fat; sold loose
Mild and refreshing; good for cheesecake
and cooking generally
Farmer: Reggie Stone; *cheesemaker:*
Susannah Stone
Where to buy: Tain: The Cheese Shop, 17
Market Street (trade inquiries, tel. Tain
(0862) 2034); cheese shops throughout
Britain (only Caboc commonly sold in
England)

LOTHIAN

LANGSKAILL Howgate, Penicuik
(Howgate Cheeses)
1 Peat-Smoked Soft Cheese
Smoked, on straw mat
2 Crowdie
Traditional, skimmed-milk cheese
3 Oatmeal Cream Cheese
Lighter than Caboc, double cream
4 Cottage Cheese
a) old type, salt-free
b) with cream and pineapple
c) with cream, garlic and herbs
5 Crusted Soft Cheese
Brie and Camembert type
All the above are UNpasteurised and come
in 3–5 oz sizes
6 Goat Cheese
Farmers, cheesemakers: M.J.R. Marwick
and Partners
Soft, pasteurised (summer only)
Where to buy: On farm

BORDERS

EASTERWEENS, Bonchester Bridge, near
Hawick
Bonchester Cheese
Soft, Coulommiers type, UNpasteurised;
natural, white mould crust; 1 lb round
Farmer, cheesemaker: John Curtis
Jersey herd
Season: March to December
Where to buy: Bonchester Bridge: Easter
Weens Enterprises

Part Two
THE STORY OF CHEESE

6

The Nature of Cheese

Cheesemaking is a craft, not a science ... Whenever in cheesemaking the scientific test results and the judgement of the cheesemaker are at variance he should always rely on his judgement.

Far from expressing a sentimental amateur's wish to put the clock back, these words are the considered conclusion on the nature of cheesemaking of one of the world's foremost authorities on the subject. Dr J. G. Davis, biochemist, bacteriologist and technologist, is sharing with us the lesson of a lifetime's experience of research and practice in laboratory, farm and factory. After years with the National Institute for Research in Dairying he became Scientific Adviser and finally Technical Director of Express Dairies. It is doubtful whether any other man in the world combines such scientific and practical knowledge of cheesemaking from the older surviving traditional methods to the most modern large-scale technology, in which he has been a notable innovator. Nevertheless at the end of all this Dr Davis concludes that the best hope of salvation from monotony in the future is that research will overcome the need to pasteurise milk for cheesemaking in the creameries; and he reminds us that 'the best cheese of all can be made by natural souring of milk on the farm'.

It is not in the nature of real cheese, however well made, to be uniform. Dr Davis says that 'the fact that no two cheese are ever exactly alike' has led to conflict of evidence in research. Cheese is made from milk, the product of soil and pasture (varying from season to season and from place to place); milk varies in content according to the species and breed of the dairy animal. This is what makes it a gourmet's delight and a mass marketeer's nightmare. In the pages which follow I list most of the factors affecting the flavour and consistency of cheese, from its native pastureland to its final handling by trade and customer at maturity.

In this century it has become recognised that biology is more important than chemistry in cheese, but research to identify sources of flavour has been largely unsuccessful. My belief is that plant biology here crosses the frontier between herbage and dairy animal to explain at least some of the individuality which distinguishes such an astounding number of cheeses from one another. Accordingly I have devoted more space to this factor than to any other; and I have connected it with the process which cancels it out: pasteurisation of milk used for cheesemaking. Pasteurisation has eliminated many difficulties for those cheesemakers who call it in aid; but, combined with new methods, it has also brought about a standardisation of textures and flavours which, as Dr Davis has warned us, results in monotony. This monotony is something about which the sensitive public is already complaining.

Some writers have told us that all cheese is made in much the same way. I do not think that anyone following the intricate succession of stages in cheesemaking, and the almost endless permutations with which they can be varied, will ever think that again about real cheese. The sameness is unfortunately true about much factory cheese, where the colouring is often the only clue (and not always an accurate one) to its supposed identity.

Cheesemaking is the exploitation of the rich solids in milk to form a food easier, more compact and more economical to transport and to keep than fresh milk (and only comparatively recently could fresh milk travel any great distance or be kept at all). The process starts naturally with development of acidity (now usually accelerated by a starter), followed by clotting (accelerated by the use of rennet usually from the mammals' own digestive juices). The cheesemaker's job so far has been to know his milk, introduce suitable starter and rennet, and to time their application accordingly, with appropriate temperature control and observation of acidity. From renneting onwards the cheesemaker is actively concerned in encouraging the clotting and expelling the whey until the curd is at the right stage of cohesion and acidity for drawing off the whey (except for cheeses where the curd is removed from the whey and put straight into the hoop or mould). For hard cheeses still more moisture has to be released by cutting and piling up the curd, until at the right point of acidity it is milled and salted, ready to be moulded into its traditional shape. The last care of the cheesemaker is the formation of the skin or crust, and, in most British cheeses, its binding in cloth to protect it through the months or years of ripening, and its regular turning in the correct atmospheric temperature and moisture until it is sold. The final satisfaction of the customer still depends not only on the skill of the cheesemaker but on the subsequent treatment of the cheese by factor and retailer, and by the customer himself.

Factors affecting the consistency and keeping quality of cheese

1 *The character of the milk derives from*:
a Soil and subsoil, including mineral traces which can be natural, or from artificial fertilisers and sprays against weed or pest.
b Climate and season. Even one day's weather can affect milk, e.g. thundery weather is known to cause acid, tough cheese.
c Elevation of pastures.

d Grassland management: artificial or organic manure; old pastures or new leys, etc.

e Herbage varieties, particularly aromatic (e.g. Sweet Vernal) and mineral content (e.g. clover, receptive of iron). This affects hay and silage as well as grazing.

f Hay or other dried grass: stage of growth when cut.

g Silage: how well made and kept.

h Other fodder (non-green fodder in quantity is bad for flavour).

i Cow, ewe or goat, and breed: apart from great differences between these species, breeds vary in yield and in the size and quantity of fat globules and other solids in milk.

j The filter of the rumen.

k The milk-forming process and natural bacterial content of milk.

l Health of animal: e.g. mastitis or antibiotics in milk inhibit development of curd.

All these factors affect the quantities and proportions of fats and non-fat solids in milk, which vary throughout the year. The relationship of fat to casein is particularly important. Too little fat makes a poor, hard, dull cheese. A high proportion of fat causes difficulties for factories seeking a standard product, and may produce a cheese moister and softer than Cheddar graders like today. It has been known to cause rancidity in pasteurised experimental cheese.

2 *The character of the milk is affected before it goes into the vat by its handling:*

a Hygiene: (i) In the milking parlour. Neglect can introduce contaminating bacteria, affecting flavour (taint, if bad) or encouraging blueing; airborne yeast enzymes from bread-making, brewing, or from over-ripe fruit during jam or chutney-making can act like antibiotics in milk (see 1*c* above); strong odours, especially if fat based, e.g. soapy flavours during washing, can affect milk in vat. (ii) In the cheese dairy: Detergents 'swear with cheese'. Hydrogen peroxide, as a killer of fault-producing organisms, damages vitamin C and other easily oxidisable constituents of milk. Excessive use in cleaning utensils can cause metallic flavour. Boiling is best for permeable equipment. Five minutes' immersion in water as near boiling point as possible serves for wood or rush.

b Distance of the milking parlour from the cheese dairy and method of moving milk: chances of contamination, over-ripening; bulk tanker can be up to three days on exceptional journeys.

c Raw or pasteurised milk used for cheese. Pasteurised milk cannot ripen naturally; this results in loss of beneficent as well as harmful bacteria, making cheese twice as slow to mature.

d Skimming of milk (lower fat, usually harder, duller cheese) or part skimming.

e Use of morning or evening (richer) milk; whether used straight from the cow or, more commonly, overnight mixed with morning milk straight from cows.

f Cream added from another milking.

g Standardisation of milk in factories, i.e. adjusting natural fat content to a year-long even relationship with the casein to simplify making and achieve constant type.

h Preservatives: UN Food and Agricultural Organisation deprecates any preservatives in milk (cf. 2*a* ii above).

i Trying to restore flavours or speed of ripening lost by pasteurisation by injecting Lactobacilli and other organisms into the milk can result in inconsistent and sometimes undesirable textures and flavours.

j Use of powdered milk results in uncreamy soft cheese.

k Use of powdered skimmed milk results in a tendency to brittle, crumbly cheese and the possible growth of toxigenic Staphylococci and food poisoning.

l Cream sometimes kept up to a week before making into cheese.

m Hygiene in the cheese dairy (e.g. traces of earlier milk or whey, or of detergents on utensils, can cause taints).

n Acidity of overnight milk and mixed milk, or of single milking. The richer the milk, the higher the acidity, which affects desirable acidity at renneting, which should be slightly higher. The temperature at which overnight milk is kept affects acidity.

o The temperature to which the milk is brought for cheesemaking and the method of doing it.

p There are also various treatments of milk in some factories, which artificially interfere with flavour and texture: e.g. homogenisation to reduce globules to small standard size, reducing fat loss, and making for smoother texture; oxidising agents; introduction of certain bacilli for extra flavour.

3 *Method of starting the cheese:*

a Natural ripening of overnight milk to start the cheese when mixed with morning milk.

b Addition of soured whey from previous day; this can perpetuate tainting of faulty milk.

c Addition of cultured starter: locally produced, representative of local character of milk ripening naturally; or standard commercial starter; or selectively cultured starter to feature certain bacteria.

d Temperature of milk at this stage.

e Colouring (annatto, carotene, etc.) or mould in some blues.

f Length of time cheese is left before renneting, and acidity reached; acidity here should not be invariable but related to the acidity of the original milk.

4 *Renneting:*

a Type of rennet used, and its compatibility with the starter; quantity used (some makers using Jersey milk with its large fat globules increase the amount of rennet). Vegetable rennet appears to result in milder cheese. Excessive rennet can cause a bitter taste; overheating before renneting can cause hard, dry cheese.

b Effective stirring in of rennet.

c Length of time and acidity reached before curd is ready for cutting (the more acid the milk the quicker this must be done, but see 2*n*).

For more information about rennet, see p. 106.

5 *Cutting* (this and later operations may be done by hand, or with power assistance, or by completely mechanised factory processes):

a Type of cutter used and gentleness of action: rough treatment can fracture fat globules and lose fat in whey.

b Length of time and acidity reached before scalding.

The terminology of dairy utensils can be confusing. Here is shown what used to be called a tub (modern term, vat) with cheese ladder over, on which rest three metal vats (now moulds) in a wide wooden Double Gloucester vat (or mould). The cheesemaker is holding a curd breaker, and a curd mill, or grinder, is between her and the vats.

6 *Scalding* (certain cheeses only):
a Temperature at first scald. Whether temperature is maintained by jacket heating or by extracting and heating the whey and returning it to the curd, it must be kept even throughout by constant stirring.
b Second scald, if any (usually at a higher temperature). The temperature must be raised gradually or the curd may harden on the surface, sealing in moisture and thus leading to poor consistency, colour and possible taints in cheese. High temperature produces harder cheese (even rubbery if very high), e.g. Emmentaler; lower temperature or no scald gives softer cheese.

7 *Pitching:*
When the scald is at a higher temperature the vat is stirred until the curd is ready for pitching (settling on the bottom of the vat in the whey) and drawing off of whey. The right acidity to be reached before this stage is 0.01 per cent

below that of the acidity at renneting for Cheddar (acidity rises at about 0.01 per cent every quarter of an hour). When the curd is firm enough and the acidity has reached the point indicated for the particular cheese, the stirring ceases, allowing the curd to settle.

In the old Cheddar world Harding (see p. 7) was for leaving it thirty minutes, Candy and Cannon for fifteen minutes; Cannon and Lloyd qualified the latter as being subject to the curd's being firm – 'if sweet it should be left until almost the pre-renneting acidity of the mixed milk'; if curd is fast working whey must . be drawn off as quickly as possible.

8 *Drawing off the whey:*

In the old days this had to be done by scooping out most of the whey and then draining; now it is usually done by raking the curd to the outside of the vat, freeing a centre channel for drainage; the small-scale maker can line a sieve with cloth over another container and empty the tub over it, collecting the curd in the cloth and the whey beneath. There should be a filter of some kind at the outlet of the vat to collect any curd swept out with the whey.

9 *Piling or Cheddaring:*

This is the orderly piling of the curd into masses – at either side of the vat in the case of large vats – the strained crumbs of curd being placed on top and pressed in. The masses of curd are then cut into appropriately sized squares and piled again, the lower curd being placed on top.

The curd may be – it almost always used to be – covered with cloths of varying thickness (thinness if too acid – if very acid it might be not piled but just turned and removed to a cooler). It was cut into blocks, broken, cloth wrapped (unless too acid); the cheeses were then placed one on top of another and pressed. The looser the state in which the curd is kept, the crumblier the cheese will be.

In some modern factories the 'tower' process of draining the curd by its own weight is self-descriptive. Naturally it results in a very close, smooth texture. This stage continues until the curd is at the right stage of ripeness and consistency for the particular kind of cheese; acidity of whey still draining from curd is the measure of readiness. With Lancashire and Stilton part of one day's curd is reserved to mix with the next day's.

Moisture content is finally controlled at this stage. Maxima under British regulations are: Cheddar 39 per cent; Stilton 42 per cent; Cheshire 44 per cent; Wensleydale 46 per cent; Lancashire 48 per cent.

10 *Milling:*

A peg- or a chip-mill is used according to whether the curd is shredded or cut into knobs. Leicester and Double Gloucester curd is milled twice. Herbs, wine, etc. may be introduced after milling.

11 *Salting:*

Some fresh cream or curd cheeses are not salted at all. Some cheeses are brine bathed after making, some washed repeatedly during ripening. Most English cheese is salted as it comes from the mill before packing into the mould.

Internal salting makes for a less smooth internal texture and rind than brine salting, the latter being preferred by old Gloucester and Wensleydale makers

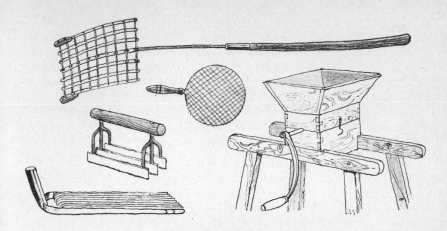

Various kinds of curd breakers (top) and cutters, and a curd mill or grinder.

particularly. External treatment helps to form rind or crust, and washing attracts a russet mould to some cheeses (Pont l'Evèque, for example).

12 *Packing into the mould (vatting):*
The mould is usually lined with cheesecloth of varying thicknesses for different cheeses (or different stages of making). The firmness, evenness, looseness and irregularity of packing the curd affects the texture of the cheese. If smaller pieces of curd are not kept to the outside of the mould the skin may not be close textured and smooth. The size and shape of mould vary according to tradition. Harder cheeses tend to be cylindrical, softer cheeses flat wheels.

13 *Treatment of skin or crust:*
Some cheeses go through repeated changes of cloth, or other treatment. Butter, lard and wax are used with or without cheesecloth. Today plastic coats are often used, regardless of the need of cheese for air. Saran and Pukkafill do allow breathing.

14 *Pressing:*
Variations and times of pressing or its absence (e.g. in Stilton) make for great variation in cheese. Cheeses destined for rectangular moulds and plastic coating have to be pressed far harder than traditional cheese to withstand handling and machine cutting. Horizontal gang-presses facilitate pressing of a number of cheeses together, but have proved unsuitable for blue cheeses, as they inhibit the spread of mould.

15 *Maturing:*
Blue cheeses are usually pricked during ripening to ensure entry of mould spores and to give them space to move.

A temperature of 55–60°F is suitable for most cheeses; higher temperature speeds ripening, very low arrests it. Freezing can make cheese stodgy and ammoniac, and indigestible, unless it is eaten immediately after thawing out. Block cheese is usually kept at a low temperature to avoid its 'blowing' its coat, as it cannot breathe out excess gas. This tends to exacerbate the stodginess already caused by high pressure.

Moisture is important for soft and blue cheeses. Hard cheeses need a drier atmosphere, but not the dehydration of central heating. Airiness is good, but draughts are not. The length of time, varying from weeks to years, affects the flavour and texture. Pasteurisation doubles the time needed for ripening.

Cheeses not turned often enough in their early stages can lose shape. Failure to turn them regularly at a later stage can cause drying out at the top, internal cracking and external doming; the underside may become soggy, which affects texture and flavour.

Methods of making rennet

Preparing rennet in Gloucestershire, from an account by William Marshall, 1789

1 Salt 3 quarts whey till it bears an egg, left overnight.
2 Skim and 'rack off' clear in the morning.
3 Add 3 quarts of water brine.
4 Put in sweet briar, thyme, hyssop or other 'sweet herbs' tied in bunches, a little black pepper, saltpetre etc., and leave a few days before removing herbs.
5 Put in 4 English or a proportionate number of Irish vells (see Glossary).
After three or four days the rennet is ready for use.

Author's note: No heating, let alone boiling, was practised. Some dairies used only cold salt water, and one so doing was noted by Marshall as being scarcely equalled for good cheese; but Marshall favoured neutralisation of the natural vell flavour by some aromatic infusion, preferably spices.

Preparing rennet in Cheshire in the eighteenth century
It was the Cheshire custom to choose a calf's stomach with residual 'curd' or 'chyly matter' in it rather than an empty one. It was cleaned and cured before use, but lack of thoroughness at this stage may have accounted for the 'rank disagreeable flavour which some Cheshire cheeses emit' (Wedge).

'Maw skins', as the cured rennet skins were called in Cheshire, were taken out of brine and drained, then powdered on both sides with salt and rolled smooth. A splint of wood was stuck across each to extend it for drying, a general practice in the North of England. For extracting the rennet from the skin this was an 'improved method, similar to, not identical with Gloster' as reported by William Marshall.
1 Take the season's skins pickled and dried.
2 Fill open vessel(s) with 3 pints pure spring water per skin and soak for 24 hours. Keep this first infusion.
3 Remove skins into other vessels and soak them in 1 pint spring water per skin for 24 hours.
4 Take skins out and stroke by hand into second infusion; discard skins.
5 Mix the two infusions, sieving liquor through fine linen.
6 Salt *more* than will dissolve.
7 Next day and daily thereafter remove scum and top up salt (always until a little remains undissolved at bottom).
8 Stir again after taking any out.
Less than ½ pint will do for 60 lb cheese.

7

Aroma and Flavour

Experienced cheese eaters have learned to expect broad characteristic flavours from some familiar types of cheese. In a more subtle way cheeses within one type may vary in character from area to area, farm to farm, field to field and, with weather and season, from day to day. These subtle variations, and even some of the broader ones, are often reduced or eliminated by modern farming methods, by bulking of milk, and by pasteurisation.

Through their effect on acidity and texture, cheesemaking methods influence basic character. Hygiene in milking parlour and dairy is also influential, because laxity can cause outside contamination which is irremediable, though not always disagreeable.

Food flavour research

By 1970 Professor E. L. Crossley's research team at Reading University had discovered fifty different compounds in cheese, none of which produced a 'cheese flavour'. This led him to suggest that cheese research had only reached 'the end of the beginning'. By 1980, he told me, another twenty compounds had turned up, without solving the problem, contributing only minute mineral traces. Dr Manning says that although the National Institute for Research in Dairying has now named over two hundred volatile compounds in Cheddar, 'little is known about their contribution to flavour' except that 'Cheddar flavour' has been identified as the product of sulphur compounds. Blue cheeses apart, though, Cheddar is not the only British cheese flavour, as any lover of Double Gloucester, Caerphilly, Leicester, Cheshire, Lancashire or Wensleydale will assert. Some basic differences stem from variations in method rather than in milk: thus slackness in the making or factory methods can produce Cheshire and Lancashire indistinguishable from one another, or Double Gloucester and Wensleydale which lapse into Cheddary consistency and flavour; but there are distinctions which cannot be so explained.

The most obvious example of regional character is the unmistakable overtone in Cheshire flavour, attributed for centuries, with good reason, to the area's marl arising from the subsoil salt-beds. Even an exiled Cheshire cheesemaker, who took topsoil as well as methods with him, could not sustain the illusion of counterfeiting his old cheese. Lancashire's distinctive tang owes much of its 'meatiness' to the prolonged, two-day, traditional operation of making and to its moist, open texture. The new 'single-acid' cheese, made in one day from pasteurised milk with artificial speeding up of acidity, is completely different in texture and, apart from the over-saltiness of the block version, completely lacking in flavour.

The natural sources of aroma and flavour

Excluding taint, much of the flavour of cheese remains unaccounted for, except by the constituents of the milk rather than the methods of making. These constituents and their proportions are the products of subsoil, soil, pasture and dairy breed. They explain more than just the regional differences; they account for those differences I have mentioned between the cheese of one farm and another, even between one day's cheese and another on the same farm.

I put it to Professor Crossley that the likeliest sources of these elements were aromatic esters of pasture species and mineral traces from the subsoil. He agreed that aromatic elements could be released during the breakdown of fat and protein by bacteria, and by rennet and mould enzymes during the making and maturing of the cheese. He also agreed that mineral traces could become attached, through fatty acids, to esters and casein. Jeffrey Harborne, another noted scientist in the area of food flavours, has found that numerous compounds, including toxic elements from sprays, have passed from flowers into honey. He has also traced taints in Australian cheese back to oil-rich umbelliferous plants of unpleasant odour. Wild garlic, a notoriously unwelcome species sometimes taken by cattle straying into woodland, is similarly oily; and Dr Harborne pointed out to me that artificial fertilisers and many weedkillers and pesticides are oil-based. At the opposite end of the flavour scale Dr Manning found skimmed-milk cheeses to be devoid of flavour, although the solids-not-fat in milk considerably outweigh the fats. Dr Harborne says that this lack of aroma and flavour in fat-free cheese is significant.

At one stage in Dr Manning's research he removed volatile fatty acids from the other compounds found in Cheddar without reducing aroma (which was traced primarily to sulphur compounds); but his cheeses were made from pasteurised milk where the ester aroma is likely to have been neutralised. In Dr Manning's words: 'Butyric acid contributes to taste, not aroma, in the young cheese. It acts further as a precursor to the esters. High level ethyl alcohol reacts with butyric acid chemically or enzymatically, with sweet-smelling results.'

The key to the transference into the milk and cheese of both desirable and undesirable influences on flavour is the way fats and oils attract and conduct aroma and flavour. Traditional butchers praise grass-fed beef, with its rich yellow fat, and look for old-fashioned marbling of fat in the lean meat. This is what gives beef flavour. Its absence explains the tastelessness of so much of today's excessively lean corn-stuffed beef. Indeed, tasters of de-fatted meat in a Unilever experiment some years ago could not distinguish beef from lamb. This is an interesting parallel to the dependence of so much of cheese flavour upon fat.

Scent distillers exploit the extraordinary aroma-conductivity of fat to extract the aromatic esters from certain plants, such as jasmine and violet, which do not yield to ordinary distillation. Leaves or flowers are laid daily on plates covered with fat. When the fat is saturated, it is melted and strained for its scent. Something of this sort goes on inside the pasture plants and the grazing animal. A number of grasses and other plant species which flourish in unpolluted permanent pastures are rich in aromatic esters, which may be fatty acids or glycerides (derived from naturally sweet glycerin). Together with mineral trace elements from the soil, these esters pass in some strength from the stems and leaves of the plants through the filter of the rumen into the digestive system and milk-forming process of the grazing animal. This is hospitably rich in fatty acids, and harbours a small amount of albumin, which also interacts with acid esters.

So it should not seem surprising if the fats in unpasteurised milk stemming from old pastures with richly variegated herbage prove receptive to and carry with them into cheese noticeable plant and mineral aromas and corresponding flavours.

Aroma and flavour are the most vital points on which cheese is graded, recognised and enjoyed. If they are lacking, however good its texture and appearance, the cheese is fit only for the dullest of palates; it is no better than a dummy to a discriminating connoisseur or any other lover of full-flavoured food. Yet, apart from the sulphides in Cheddar, sources of flavour and aroma in cheese derived from soil and pasture have remained beyond the reach of grassland, dairy and food science research. Plants such as garlic and oil-seed rape have long been known to cause taints, but sources of pleasanter flavours, logically just as attributable to soil or pasture, have eluded detection, or even attention. Nevertheless, the general principle that ester development enhances flavour now seems to be accepted. Potential flavour and speed of ripening of young cheese can even be estimated by measuring the level of ethyl alcohol and by gas chromatology of the volatile elements present. When this new discovery is fully exploited the grader will have an invaluable additional scientific aid to his judgement. It will save waste by indicating that some cheeses should be sold young before a taint gets out of hand; it should also lead to higher grading marks for cheeses of exceptional potential aroma and flavour, thus encouraging reward for interesting character over dull consistency.

Unfortunately, however, most of these natural sources of aroma and flavour are destroyed by pasteurisation, the subject of my next chapter.

8
Pasteurisation

Raw milk cheese nearly always has a fuller flavour than pasteurised milk cheese.... The farmhouse maker should normally not need to have recourse to pasteurisation. Such a need would indicate extremely careless methods of production for which there is no excuse.... The commonest danger in pasteurising milk for cheesemaking is the assumption by less well informed workers that pasteurisation will make dirty milk clean, and eliminate all troubles of bacterial origin.

Dr J. G. Davis

The purposes of pasteurisation of milk for cheesemaking are to kill pathogenic micro-organisms which might harm the eater or taint the cheese, and to improve the cheese's keeping quality. Pathogenic bacteria are not a serious problem in cheese, because its acidity is not only unfavourable to them but fatal within three months, beyond which time chemical and enzymal action takes over development of flavour. Few British cheeses should be sold before three months, but in many cheeses that are sold younger the exterior or interior moulds provide a natural prophylactic.

Only two outbreaks due to infection of unpasteurised cheese have been recorded in Britain since 1961, both affecting Italian families. They contracted brucellosis from Pecorino, a ewes' milk cheese, which had been bought in a part of Italy notorious for brucellosis in sheep and eaten too young. In one case the cheese was available for examination, but, because three months had passed before the diagnosis, no trace of infection remained. Pecorino should not be sold in mainland Italy at under three months. In the same period there have been many times that number of families infected by pasteurised cheese from such pioneers of modern dairy practices as Australia and New Zealand.

Dr Davis says that 'a well made cheese is virtually never the cause of food poisoning'; even in hot climates where cheese is made from new milk with a high bacterial count, quick starting and the rapid development of lactic organisms suppress the growth of any pathogens. I have corresponded on the subject with the Director of the Public Health Laboratory Service Board, Dr N. S. Galbraith, who wrote: 'I am inclined to agree with you that we can certainly interfere excessively with nature, but this is rarely in the cause of safety, and usually in the cause of mass production of foodstuffs, particularly convenience foods, and of commercial enterprise and profit.' (Dr Galbraith wishes me to say that he nevertheless supports pasteurisation of milk products.) One of Dr Galbraith's colleagues, N. D. Noah, Consultant Epidemiologist in the Communicable Diseases Surveillance Centre at Colindale, wrote in the *British Medical Journal* of 6 April 1974: 'Even those with palates for very ripe cheese do not apparently risk their health in eating it.'

Dr Davis describes pasteurisation as more for the purpose of killing fault-producing micro-organisms than for making the milk safe. In fact a number of taints are heat-resistant. These include bitterness from excessive dimethyl sulphoxide, which need not worry makers of otherwise agreeable cheese worth maturing because the taint dies away within eight months of making. *Escherichia coli*, an engaging bacterium helpful to medical research (for example in development of Interferon), is heat-resistant and harmless, but does give a controversial sharpness to Cheddar, and may attract mould. Some Cheddar lovers seek out cheese with this edge to its flavour, or that of *Streptococcus foecalis*, another tasty non-toxic intruder normally present in raw milk.

The effects of pasteurisation

Pasteurisation is convenient for the big cheesemakers because it enables them to neutralise many defects in bulked milk of varying quality and to produce a standard cheese. Dr Davis finds that this process 'kills about 99 per cent of the micro-organisms and destroys most of the enzymes in milk, some of which may be responsible for the development of flavour as the cheese ripens'. This has been proved by my own experience with one of the most individualistically aromatic and flavoursome of cheeses, Saint-Nectaire.

Saint-Nectaire, in farm and creamery, is made from the milk of Salers cows pastured on the flower-rich hillsides of the Puy-de-Dôme, in the Auvergne, and ripened in the mould-rich *caves* of local cheese factors. After selling it for fifteen years I suddenly met sales resistance: customers were not happy with their tasting and did not buy it. As I could confirm, the usual aroma and flavour were absent; despite its beautiful triple-mould coat, the cheese inside was dull. At first I blamed possible refrigeration at some point on its journey, and warned the supplier of my misgivings when re-ordering. My sales went down to half a cheese a month, the other half being trimmed away and discarded; and even a new batch, whose succulent-looking interiors proved that they had been perfectly looked after, had no smell or taste to match the texture.

There could be only one explanation, difficult to reconcile with life in the Auvergne: these cheeses were now being made from pasteurised milk. I ordered no more and myself went down to the Puy-de-Dôme. Sure enough, there outside the little creamery at Besse-en-Chandesse was the sinister steaming bulk of a pasteurisation plant. Happily, hundreds of farms were still making the old flowery cheese with milk straight from the cows, and plenty of their cheese was being bought in the market by factors with Paris connections. I came home laden with cheeses bought both from the factors and direct from farms, and armed with the right instructions for my importer and his shipper. Unpasteurised farmhouse Saint-Nectaire raised sales in my shop from half a cheese a month to between three and five cheeses a week. When one of my hotel customers complained of dull Saint-Nectaire recently, we discovered under the surface mould of the cheeses the tell-tale rectangular mark of the creamery instead of the oval mark of the farm. Our shipper had erred. Normally we should have detected this on their arrival, but as our customer had been waiting the cheeses were despatched unexamined. His guests noticed the difference at once. The milk for farm and creamery cheeses comes from the same cows on similar pastures, the methods of making do not vary significantly, and the finished cheeses are ripened side by side to achieve the same mould-encrusted appearance. This evidence of customers' ability to distinguish between farmhouse and creamery cheese can only be accounted for by the one difference: pasteurisation.

Until the 1950s many British dairies and creameries collected milk from farms they knew. Respect was mutual. Now milk is anonymously delivered by tanker. It may travel 300 miles and take up to three days to reach the creamery. Pasteurisation is convenient for the sort of dairy farmer who is ready to throw mastitis- and antibiotic-affected milk in with the rest; but it is not just these medical troubles which show up in milk. The head of a lively independent creamery told me in October 1980 that milk was dirtier than it had ever been. 'Farmers don't think they have to care any more, and there's plenty in the milk that pasteurisation won't kill.' He grumbled that the Board did not impose the penalties, and that he got no compensation for inferior cheese; the Board said he should have waited for test results, which would mean holding up the delivery vehicle and the cheesemaking for eight hours. One of the biggest butter buyers in the kingdom (herself qualified and practised in dairying) told me recently that she had found considerable deterioration in dairy practice since pasteurisation became general, and that this affected the end product. I hope that new finer sampling techniques and penalties will correct this because the milk of the 2 per cent of serious offenders contaminates much more than 2 per cent of all the milk collected. The Scottish Milk Boards have reduced the payment for third-time offenders to 1p a litre, an example followed since 1 October 1981 by the Milk Marketing Board for England and Wales.

The ultimate in unnecessary pasteurisation is that of his own milk by a farmhouse cheesemaker. The need to do so, as Dr Davis writes, 'would indicate extremely careless methods of production for which there is no excuse'. If the farmer pasteurises his co-operators' milk he implies that they are guilty of such carelessness. Unfortunately misguided advice and hard salesmanship have made most Cheddar farms buy pasteurisation plant. A moderate heat treatment was suggested in 1965 by Sharpe, Fewins, Reiter and Cuthbert. They confirmed earlier findings that for Cheddar cheese 15 seconds at 150°F (65.5°C) was adequate. The shocked cells of Staphylococcus failed to multiply in the unfavourable conditions of the curd. They considered that the 15 seconds at 154°F recommended by the Milk and Milk Products Technical Advisory Committee in 1964 destroyed these bacteria in the milk, but destroyed good with bad. Cannon, a century ago, would never let his scald exceed 130°F. As bacterial life ceases in cheese at three months, pasteurisation is a wasteful, expensive and inefficient substitute for clean milk. Some farmers were told that EEC regulations would require them to pasteurise, but this is a salesman's bluff, which no Lancashire or Cheshire farmer has taken any notice of; and in France more and more creamery as well as farm cheeses' labels are now proudly proclaiming with the words *non-pasteurisé* or *au lait cru* that they are made from raw milk.

The disadvantages of pasteurisation

Dr Davis mentions, among others, the following disadvantages of pasteurisation in his work *Cheese*: increased cost; encouragement to use low quality milk; no natural ripening in the event of starter failure; poor renneting (prolonged cheesemaking); weak curd; slow drainage; inferior body and texture of cheese; insipid taste – a too-clean milk (very low in bacteria) may give a slow-ripening, mild-flavoured cheese; bitter taste on ripening; longer ripening period (Dr Davis says twice as long as that needed for raw milk cheese); slower blueing (in Stilton, for example); increased tendency for 'bloated' cheese (cheese blown out by anaerobic spores); destruction of micro-organisms playing a leading role both in protein degradation and in flavour development (products essential for the proliferation of the desired Streptococci and Lactobacilli); destruction of enzymes: lipase, considered of prime importance in ripening, is largely destroyed; loss of vitamins: 25 per cent of vitamin C and 10 per cent of vitamin B_1; exacerbation of some faults (e.g. gas) which may be worse in pasteurised than in raw milk cheese; and, perhaps the most important factor, the tendency to a standardised flavour. 'Different localities can lose their character, and there is a temptation to replace lost elements. Nature is rarely imitable with accuracy, and side effects may be unpalatable, even poisonous.'

The dairy industry, leading or led by the Milk Marketing Boards, has tried to push the idea that standardisation is an advantage because the public wants milder cheese. My twenty-eight years of experience in selling and serving cheese have shown me that the opposite is true. Given the choice (a rare thing these days, but mercifully becoming less rare), a cross-section of the public will leave more dull cheese than strong cheese uneaten, and will respond to what real British traditional cheese has to offer in richness and variety of flavour and texture. Tests and market research confirm my view, as do reports of increased demand for traditional cheese from creameries. As the head cheese man in one of our biggest creamery concerns said to me in the summer of 1980: 'The customer is the last to be considered. Pasteurised, standardised block cheese severely curtails the consumers' choice by eliminating a broad spectrum of delectable natural flavours.' He drew a direct parallel between the cheese market now and the ale market before the Campaign for Real Ale triumphed. He knows what he is talking about; he worked then for one of the 'big bad brewers'.

Dr Davis would like to see this threatened monotony of British cheese averted by solving the problems arising from the use of raw milk for cheese manufacture in creameries. There is no greater service dairy· research could do for British food than to fulfil Dr Davis's wish. 'We have no understanding as to why certain bacterial faults "flare up" at certain times ... the wise cheesemaker can only minimise this by the most vigilant supervision of the quality of his milk.'

──── **9** ────

The Making of Milk for Cheese

Note: In considering the aspects of farming practice which affect the quality and character of cheese I have consulted a number of scientists. Some of these are listed on p. 121, together with my written sources, to avoid unnecessary interruption of the text by full references. I have also had personal contact with a large number of farmers, including many who make cheese themselves or employ cheesemakers.

Introduction

It may be helpful for the layman to have a brief introduction to the pasture side of dairy farming.

Species and varieties differ according to soil, elevation, climate and care, but simply speaking pastures contain grasses and legumes (vetches, clovers, etc.), and other plants, commonly thought of as wild flowers by nature lovers and as weeds by farmers. Sir George Stapledon (1882–1960), Britain's greatest name in grassland research, preferred to call them 'other species', and I follow him. Leys are fields sown with selected grasses and clovers, on ploughed-up arable or old pastureland. The product of grassland is as important as any arable crop in this country, so much of which is suited by soil and climate to dairy farming.

Like an arable crop, herbage for grazing or cutting needs a nutrient-rich soil. The three main fertilising elements are nitrogen (N), phosphates (P) and potassium (K), all of which can be applied to the soil either in chemical or in organic form. Leguminous crops can reduce the need for nitrogenous fertilisers by reason of their nitrogen-fixing ability. (The roots of legumes attract nitrogen-fixing bacteria, which increase the nitrogen available to the crop. These Rhizobium bacteria establish a symbiotic relationship with the plant and form nodules in the root system. This is nature's way of keeping up the nitrogen content of the soil and nourishing the grasses which are neighbours of the legumes.) Grazing animals naturally return much of the plant nutrient to the soil, including most of the potassium, but a good hay crop can take 168 lb of potassium from an acre of meadow, and this needs to be replaced. Lime is also of importance in a balanced soil to correct acidity. Soil analyses can guide farmers on the need of their land for phosphate, potassium or for lime. It is false economy not to have a soil analysis when you take over a farm, unless a recent one is available. Thereafter, subject to your remedying the deficiencies revealed, frequent analyses are unnecessary, particularly on fully exploited grazing land where phosphate and potassium wastage is very slow.

The use of chemical fertilisers and of pest- and weed-killing sprays can change the balance of plant species in pastures; and, because some sprays are oil-based (though not those usually used on grassland), taints may be picked up by plants and by the milk-forming system in the ruminant (see p. 108). Both these influences can affect the flavour of cheese, and it is for this reason that I dwell at some length on the farming side of cheese producing.

The influence of the soil

The strong affinities between cheese and wine are of much deeper origin than their final complementary relationship on the table. Both are fermented products which have their origins in soil and plant, susceptible to damage by cold, and both require patient care and a moderate temperature to mature naturally. The finest examples of wine and cheese are unblended products of a single vineyard or farm, where vines or herbage have been long and happily married to a well-cherished local soil. For both vines and the herbage producing cheesemakers' milk appreciate a good climate and plenty of organic manure and lime. The same species of grape produces completely different wines in different regions, and even in adjacent vineyards of different aspects. So it is with pastures and cheeses.

Broad influences of soil and altitude on cheese are illustrated by the character of marl-based Cheshire (see p. 55) and by the fact that the upland Lancashire farms, all permanent pastures on land with limestone outcrops, produced tastier cheese than the leys of the low-lying, high water-table farms near the coast, which have all now gone out of cheese production. S. D. O. Brown, who told me this in 1973, had tested the milk on every dairy farm in the County Palatine and tasted the cheese on every farm that made it in his time. Kit Calvert, the most notable veteran of Wensleydale cheesemaking, always found the cheese from the higher limestone pastures better than that from the sandier ground near the River Ure. In 1974 when I mentioned the chemists' theory that, given a satisfactory standard of milk, any type of cheese could be made anywhere, he commented, 'That is fast becoming an accepted lie'; and he uttered the warning which I thought premature at the time, but not for long: 'Within ten years we shall have forgotten our traditional skills.'

Local variations of cheese can depend on where cows grazed before milking. I have known two Cheddars made on the same day in separate vats on the same farm to mature with contrasting sweet and sharp characters. Camembert connoisseurs, according to the late Raoul de May of Louvis, could tell on tasting a farmhouse cheese which side of the hill the milk had come from. The same could be said of Swaledale today: on one small farm I know, sweet cheese comes from the limestone above Oxnop Ghyll, and slightly bitter cheese from the acid peat below.

Dr Davis has advised us to fight for our regional heritage against the danger of monotonous standardisation, for reasons succinctly summarised by Pierre Androuët, France's second great *maître fromager* of that name: 'Every region has its mysteries, over which no technology, no chemistry have yet prevailed ... vegetation, climate, rainfall, nature of the subsoil, breed of animal, all contribute towards making a cheese into a unique, inimitable product.'

I went to the Agricultural Research Council headquarters in July 1980 to consult Dr George Cooke on these aspects of the background to cheese. Above all that Dr Cooke had to tell me, this verdict on the force of fashion stood out starkly: 'Soils have an enormous influence on pastures, but it has been largely obliterated by modern grassland management.'

Confirmation of the relevance of Dr Cooke's message to cheesemakers was already in my hands in the form of a lament from a well-known Cheshire cheese farmer at Adderley Hall in north Shropshire. With thirty years of cheesemaking experience behind him, Mr Cope wrote: 'We are of the opinion that the current heavy use of fertiliser is having an effect on the making of the cheese. We no longer get the same mellowing effect in the three weeks' ripening period after manufacture that we used to get when the system was based on old permanent pastures and lower fertiliser usage.' Pasteurisation has not intruded into the dairies of Cheshire farms, and grading standards have not changed during the last thirty years; so changes in soil and grass alone must be held responsible for this deterioration.

Farmers who are interested in cheese must be pressed to preserve or restore the local character of their natural assets: their own soil and pastures. They can then exploit them by producing cheese of a character which cannot be imitated by any factory at home or abroad, to appeal to discriminating buyers. It is in farmers' own interests to make British cheeses more attractive to the ordinary cheese lover again and to break his addiction to imports.

The advantages of permanent pasture

In 1971 a joint group was set up by the Grassland Research Institute and the Agricultural Development and Advisory Service to study permanent pastures, a resource which was not only under-used but, in Frank Raymond's words, 'almost unnoticed', and becoming more important: temporary grassland decreased by 20 per cent between 1960 and 1977. He attributed any improvement in permanent pastures to economic pressure rather than research, which he thought should have top priority in the 1980s. It is to be hoped that once the rigid attitudes on so many aspects of grassland practice have softened, the prejudice against organic dairy farming will evaporate too. The fashion used to be for heavily fertilised leys, which obliterated the enormous influence of local soils on pastures and (with the help of pasteurisation) killed the characteristic flavours of so many British cheeses. None of the old Grassland Research Stations is in a traditional grassland area. This error has now been corrected; a report in the Reading *Mercury* of 5 August 1981 stated:

> Permanent grassland is the most important category of grassland in England and Wales – over half the farmland is permanent grassland. Yet up until now relatively little research (other than surveys) has been carried out on it. Professor Alec Lazenby, Director of the GRI, says: 'The establishment of the GRI Permanent Grassland Division in South Devon will enable the Institute to explore the problems associated with the improvement of permanent grassland and to demonstrate the potential of such land in achieving high levels of productivity of milk, beef and sheepmeat.'

Permanent pastures offer not only the types of herbage we seek (which could also be sown in herbal leys) but under good management a variety which broadens with the years. Philip Oyler wrote in *The Generous Earth* (1950): 'It is curious that grapes from old vines produce the best wine. Possibly the roots of young vines do not tap all the mineral resources of the soil.' Louis Latour found that 1979 Burgundies were light, except for the wines made from grapes of older vines. The great Bordeaux *vignerons* only apply their *Grand Cru Classé* labels to wines made from vines which have reached their twentieth year. It is logical that old pastures should have similar advantages over young grassland for cheese.

Animal behaviour certainly shows that old permanent pastures have a strong appeal because of their variety and richness of flavour, and probably for their medicinal value too. Charles Martell has had neighbours' cows breaking out of their lush home leys to gatecrash into the old permanent pastures already very closely grazed by his own Gloucester herd at Dymock. Richard Bishop keeps sheep on reseeded Berkshire downland above Streatley Farm; but they leave it for some hours every day to graze the steep slopes where the unploughable old pastures could not be interfered with. Sir George Stapledon spent many hours watching his cows behaving in the same way. They often left the good grass to wander off in search of what today's ley farmers would call weeds. Sir George's observations led him to respect these weeds so much that he not only insisted on terming them 'other species', but laid down the law to farmer friends who came to buy his new seed mixtures. One of them, Stanley Allwright, used to take along his son, now farm manager on the Mapledurham Estate, who remembers to this day Sir George's admonition to his father: 'When you plough up your old pasture leave a drill's width unploughed round the outside. It will attract the cows and stop them bloating themselves on the new clover. If you're starting a new pasture, sow a drill's width of yarrow, chicory and dandelion and so on round the edge.'

This was one of the aspects of pastures on which I consulted P. J. Boyle, director of the Commonwealth Bureau of Pastures and Fieldcrops in the

Grassland Research Institute at Hurley. Confirming the observation from Sir George, he said:

> Cows not only like but need many herbs in their pastures, including the minerals they contain. Grass is unbalanced by itself. The oriental fashion of small amounts of many different natural foods is correspondingly a much better régime for human beings. Very refined elemental human diets are rightly called 'junk foods'. Some of the single or two species pastures of today could be considered the junk food of the cow.

Mr Boyle also agreed that there were natural checks on pests in old mixed pastures; and variety itself makes it more difficult for plant diseases to spread, limiting damage to a small section of the sward if the disease gets any hold at all. In American experience organic farming shows up well in controls of weeds, pests and disease. In Britain, as part of the Butser Ancient Farm Project at East Meon in Hampshire, simple varieties of corn were sown, mixed with fifty varieties of weed commonly found in old cornfields. No fertilisers, weedkillers or pesticides were used. The crop was good and healthy, free of aphids and rust, demonstrating natural pest and disease control. The prehistoric Celtic type of cereal, Emmer, yielded 25.5 cwt per acre (seed ratio 1 to 51), while the modern wheat Sicco yielded only 13 cwt (seed ratio 1 to 26) in identical conditions.

A further advantage of variegated pasture plants is the spread of their individual period of climax, giving a longer and fuller grazing season. A. Hollins, who has been restoring his old Fordhall pastures near Market Drayton with well over twenty species, is able to keep his herd out all the year round, a practice once common in the Cheshire region and the South West.

The ability to stand up to close grazing in almost all conditions is of vital importance, because the newest growth, closest to the tiller (including the young stem which is even more digestible than the leaf), is the most palatable, nourishing and digestible part of the herbage for cows and sheep, and therefore the most efficient source of weight gain and milk yield. Cows and sheep have a built-in work-study element which gives them a positive relish for what is good for them and an appetite which grows with their enjoyment of it. (Goats, contrarily, appear to relish equally what we should regard as uneatable, let alone merely indigestible.) What is more, close grazing is the best stimulus for healthy regrowth and spread of pasture plants through tillering. Frequent harvesting, avoiding the flowering stage of at least the taller species, has long been known to encourage herbage, but Dr McMeekan has shown that continuous grazing yields as much as strip- or paddock-regulated rotational grazing, with the supreme advantage of simplicity. Furthermore, recent research by Dr Melvin Dyer at Colorado University has shown continuous grazing to have a vital additional advantage for grasses over the most frequent cutting and over controlled grazing. The saliva of grazing herbivores has a chemical which positively stimulates the growth of the new seedlings or shoots for the first three days during which leaf and root develop, with an advantage of 15 per cent over ungrazed plants. This initial advantage is held subsequently, but not increased, so it is only available to the youngest growth on continuously grazed grassland. These stimulating factors in plant growth help to explain why the optimum intensity of grazing for gross yield of milk (as opposed to record yield per cow), as Dr Raymond records, requires stocking beyond the point where yield from the individual cow begins to fall.

Milk for cheese

For cheesemaking of the quality and character required by the top of the market, milk should come from pastures which are naturally suited to the local soil and reflect its character without the artificial interference of chemical fertiliser, pesticide or fungicide. The milk target should be high fat and casein content with the appropriate balance between them, rather than record-breaking gallonage. The breed of animal should be selected accordingly (see p. 125–6).

The farmer whose first aim is good cheese will find that he is more in tune with accepted farming practice today than he would have been ten years ago. The gospel of the practical advantages of high-grade permanent pastures over leys was being preached then, but hard economies had not yet bitten the excessive users of artificial fertilisers. These continued to destroy the balance by encouraging rye-grass to such an extent that clovers died from lack of light. Aberystwyth has bred a new long-stemmed clover to surmount this problem, but with so much recently discovered or rediscovered about the importance of close grazing or frequent cutting it should not now be needed where grassland management is brought up to date. Clover, in particular, benefits from frequent grazing. Although Rothamsted Experimental Station does not include grazing in its Park Grass Experiment, since 1965 it has tested the effect of large amounts of nitrogen and more frequent cutting on a small plot. Yields have increased, and, no doubt because the frequent cutting preserved its access to light, clover has flourished. Dr Cooke told me in March 1981 that the average yield over the last few years of Park Grass areas given high-fertiliser nitrogen has been '12 tons per hectare of dry matter, better than Rothamsted usually gets from new leys treated with much nitrogen. The mineral composition of the herbage, cut at silage stage four times a year, was also satisfactory. This is a very good performance for an old grass sward that is at least 150 years old, and might be much older. One doesn't *have* to go to leys to get good yields from grass.'

We have enough nitrogen-fixing legumes available to do without nitrogenous fertilisers, but they have been under-used, partly because of bloat problems. These problems were understood by Sir George Stapledon, but the wisdom of preserving attractive mixed herbage was largely forgotten after his time. Lucerne has been most neglected. Grown on its own it is vulnerable to disease, but with its deep root penetration it is drought resistant and particularly good on chalk-lands. Other species, such as red clover and sainfoin, also regarded as forage legumes, could be used more both for soil fertility and, with lucerne, for their contribution to ruminant diet. Fenugreek, long known as a tonic food for cattle, is another nitrogen fixer which might be mixed in for pasture or fodder. White clover has been shown to give higher weight gain than rye-grass, but unbalanced though an all-grass diet is, it has still to be beaten for crude weight gain, despite the claim for clover.

Dr Cooke, hoping to see Britain self-sufficient in dairy produce by 2000, wrote in 1970 that yields might be increased 'by research on pests and diseases of grasses, of which little is known, and by breeding more productive strains. Species that are particularly suitable for local conditions need to be developed; for example species that survive by forming rhizomes may have advantages in light soils in dry areas.' Persistent local species will be found in surviving old pastures and in banks and hedgerows. Run-down old pastures can be built up by 'stitching-in' selected species without ploughing.

While it is true that the most intensive management of permanent pasture can equal leys in output, the fact must be faced that this involves using artificial fertilisers. Dr Cooke said that grass can yield 5 tons of dry matter per acre (the keep for one cow) with full artificial treatment, against $3\frac{1}{2}$ tons from an acre of grass-clover pasture appropriately treated with potassium, phosphorus and lime. This should not discourage the cheesemaker. Dr Davis has been astonished by the recorded keeping quality (implying cleanness) and yield of the cheese coming from the herds of the best nineteenth-century Cheddar makers. Their figures, like those of eighteenth-century Gloucestershire, suggest an average milk yield not reached again until well after the Second World War; Dr Davis thinks that the old pastures and the favoured breeds may have produced 'a better quality of milk from the cheesemaking point of view'. Other reasons suggested by Dr Davis for high standards are that there was almost no artificial feeding, that before milking machines there was far less mastitis, and that there were no antibiotics to get into the milk. Milking parlour and cheese dairy practices must also have been excellent, and we know that one important factor was the emphasis laid by leading cheese farms both on closeness of milking to cheese dairy, and on care in passing the milk without contamination from one to the other (although they had then no idea of the nature of most contaminants, their instincts were right).

Organic farming v. chemical farming

By an American study team's definition, organic farming avoids or largely excludes synthetically compounded fertilisers, pesticides, growth regulators and livestock feed additives. It relies as far as possible on crop rotations, crop residues, animal and green manures, legumes, off-farm organic waste, mechanical cultivation, mineral-bearing rocks and 'aspects of biological pest control' to maintain soil productivity and tilth, to supply plant nutrients and to control insects, weeds and other pests. The remarkably full historical records of a number of areas show a very high standard of milk production and cheesemaking in Britain, particularly in Ayrshire, Cheshire and (rather more patchily) in the Cheddar counties during the nineteenth century. The level of milk yield achieved when there was no alternative to organic farming methods was not equalled again until the second half of the twentieth century, by which time, from the cheesemaker's point of view, the standard of milk had generally deteriorated.

Many of our traditional cheesemaking farms have never abandoned the old methods and almost all the successful new cheesemaking farmers have adopted them with enthusiasm. The justification of organic farmers could be left to time and the virtues of their cheeses alone, if they were not so few in relation to demand and if modern methods were not so damaging to cheese standards.

The importance of this aspect of farming is that there is far too little British cheese of interesting flavour, good texture and good keeping quality to meet today's general demand. Nor, on a more limited scale, is there enough cheese of certified organic origin to meet the special demand served mainly by health food shops. Creameries can use non-animal renneting agents and sell 'vegetarian cheese', but the bulk milk supply has removed that degree of control over the provenance of their milk necessary to satisfy the growing demand for organic and Kosher cheese.

Farmers who make cheese from unpasteurised, organically produced milk therefore have an opportunity to enter a limited, but probably expanding high premium health food market, and to cater for a much wider public of ordinary yet critical lovers of British cheese. In many areas of Britain such customers have got into the habit of buying pleasant, but quite undistinguished, cheeses from abroad. When block and prepacked versions ousted the traditional in their local shops they were turned off British cheese altogether. They too are willing to pay more for the British cheese they like than is charged for the cheese they rejected, so it is economic madness that farmhouse traditions and skills should be diverted into making the wrong sort of cheese. When praising multi-species pastures organically managed as the best source of good milk for cheese I am often told (rightly) that high fertiliser usage produces more, and (wrongly) that the traditional way is uneconomic. Economics of production must stand or fall by market price. The higher reward to the maker for good cheese makes a paying proposition of his organic farming and his, perhaps, smaller-scale production.

Arguments in favour of the traditional methods of farming and cheesemaking are given added force by these figures from the United Kingdom Provision Trade Federation market prices to the wholesaler, published on 23 May 1981 (the farmer's or creamery's prices are lower than these by the cost of first-hand distribution; prices are per metric tonne): 60 lb traditional farmhouse Cheddar, £2005; 4 × 5 kilo block farmhouse Cheddar or Scottish creamery (mature), £1840.45; 4 × 5 kilo block English creamery ('selected', the minimum creamery selling grade) up to £1850. At the same time I was paying from £1.30 to £1.50 a pound (£2860 to £3300 a tonne) *on the farm* for cheeses made from the organically produced, unpasteurised milk of nine small-scale cheesemakers. Packing and carriage charges, paid by me, bring the retail price of these alongside those farmhouse Bries and other fine French cheeses, and the demand for this sort of cheese from retail customers and *Good Food Guide* restaurateurs shows that this is the class to which such cheeses properly belong. They can compete on equal terms with the best foreign cheeses on the market, a claim which could never be made for block Cheddar. Market research in spring 1981 showed that a considerable public will respond to this class of English cheese, not least because it is unpasteurised. A French importer serving English supermarkets has found that raw milk cheeses are a positive attraction to supermarket customers. Further proof of this came at the 1981 Royal Show. At the invitation of the Royal Agricultural Society of England, I was able to test the reaction of a wider public to ewes' milk cheeses from five British farms, selling at from £2 to £2.80 a pound. Tasting before buying, visitors bought 4½ cwt in four days, paying over £1200. The Baracs were selling in London for £3 a pound then.

Unfortunately most agricultural research and research in cheesemaking has hitherto been directed towards the over-simplified goals of 'trouble' saving and higher production. This has benefited factory farmer and factory cheesemaker at the expense of the state of soil and countryside, standards of dairy practice, and quality of the final product, the cheese we eat. Let us hope that the recent encouraging demand for traditionally made cheese will soon alter this short-sighted attitude.

Sources for Chapter 9

P. J. Boyle, MA   Director, Commonwealth Bureau of Pastures and Field Crops, Grassland Research Institute.

Dr G. W. Cooke, FRS   Formerly Chief Scientific Officer, Agricultural Research Council. 1. _Fertilising for Maximum Yield_, 2nd ed. (Crosby Lockwood Staples, London 1975). 2. 'The role of organic manures and organic matter in managing soils for high crop yields. A review of the experimental evidence', Proceedings of the International Seminar on Soil Environment and Fertility Management in Intensive Agriculture, Tokyo (Agricultural Research Council, London 1977).

Dr Melvin Dyer   Proceedings of the US National Academy of Science, August 1980.

Sir William Henderson, FRS   Formerly Director of the Institute for Research in Animal Diseases, Compton, and formerly Secretary to the Agricultural Research Council.

Ministry of Agriculture, Fisheries and Food   _Modern Farming and the Soil_ (HMSO 1970).

Frank Raymond   Deputy Chief Scientist, Ministry of Agriculture, Fisheries and Food, 'Grassland' section of the Agricultural Research Council's Jubilee Publication (1981).

United States Department of Agriculture   Study Team on Organic Farming (USDA, July 1980). Apart from first-hand investigation in the USA, Europe and Japan, the team consulted the Report and Recommendations on Organic Farming, and numerous written sources (including several of Dr G. W. Cooke's English publications) which are listed in the report section by section. Copies of the report can be ordered through the Agricultural Counsellor, the American Embassy, Grosvenor Square, London W.1. The team made special acknowledgements to: 1. The International Federation of Organic Agricultural Movements (with 80 groups and 40,000 individual members) which publishes an informative quarterly bulletin from IFAOM, the Coolidge Center, Topsfield, Massachusetts. 2. _The New Farm Magazine_, the Organic Gardening and Farming Research Center, Rodale Press Inc., Emmaus, Pennsylvania (estimated to have 24,000 organic farmers in its readership).

10
Stockmanship and the Dairy Animal

The dairy cow

Milk production is naturally affected not only by grassland management and grazing practice, but by other elements of stockmanship. On this big subject I will only mention points which have been brought to my personal attention by living authorities, or which stand out in the writings of experts who were concerned with dairy farming and cheesemaking when British farmhouse cheeses were at their peak. Few dairy farmers today neglect them, but it is well to record them for newcomers.

Having emphasised the economic and qualitative value of a prolonged grazing season in producing the sort of milk required for cheese, I would remind farmers of the need for constant access to water, shade and windbreak. Sir William Henderson points out that because cows, like us, are social drinkers the conventional piped trough gauge can be too quickly exhausted when a herd joins its leaders for a drink. Salt licks should be freely accessible.

'It is essential for cows to have shade and water in every field', in the words of Mr Hayward, whose Frocester Court herd produced milk for the most highly regarded of Gloucester cheeses in the mid-nineteenth century. Generally speaking our cheese dairy regions have preserved their trees, hedges and walls for shade and shelter better than most; but the fashion for hedge-grubbing (abetted by grants for some years), elm disease and other tree troubles have left many pastures without shade or shelter. Wire is a poor substitute for tree, hedge or wall in high summer, high wind or unseasonable blizzard. Unfortunately for cows, more research seems to have gone into proving their hardiness than into studying how more considerate treatment can increase milk yield. Val Cheke found weather and treatment of animals to have a marked effect, and as Sir William Henderson said in his 1978 Golden Jubilee lecture to the Hannah Research Institute: 'My veterinary training has always made me very conscious of the importance of the animal's response to its environment, and the essence of good stockmanship can perhaps be defined as the continuous provision of the least stressful environment.'

Research by Lawrence and Gilles at the New Zealand Dairy Research Institute has shown that milk from cows under stress (e.g. very dry or very wet weather) although normal in chemical composition often produces cheese of inexplicably abnormal textures and uncharacteristic flavours in their ripening period, not detected at grading time.

Cows demonstrate their appreciation of trees and hedgerows against extremes of weather. I have even seen them, contrary to their normal habit of almost continuous grazing, leave pasture in search of shade which they could only find by standing on the tree-shaded tarmacadam of an abandoned stretch of road.

Indeed, if cows did not care about cold and wet they would not give us the familiar warning of rain by lying down to reserve a dry, warm patch of grass before a storm. I have seen encouraging evidence of a revival of cut and laid and stake and bound hedging skills. I hope that dairy and stock farmers will recognise the virtues of this practice, and will abhor the often unseasonal flailing of hedges with the accompanying loss of young trees.

Barbara Woodhouse is famous for her mastery of dogs and dog owners, but in earlier years she looked after cows and spent more time with them than most stockmen. Not being able to afford a horse she even schooled and jumped cows, and would have ridden them to hounds, but for an uncharacteristic outbreak of stuffiness on her mother's part. She found that rugging up cows in winter greatly increased their milk yield, provided they were left uncovered long enough in the day to wash themselves. Failure to allow for this godly habit appears to cause such irritation that the extra milk is withheld. Sir William confirms the advantage of rugging: 'Because of the energy used in maintaining body temperature, it's correct, it's logical; though it's not terribly conventional as far as cattle are concerned.' It is difficult to conceive of rugging up very large herds, but many cheese farms are small and may like to try it. The same logic applies to the provision of wind shields and other shelter against cold.

As so many cheesemaking farmers feed their whey to pigs, I add Sir William's further comment: 'Warmth is very significant, indeed vital in pig production. Inadequate insulation of pig houses is very wasteful.'

Mr Hayward, whom I have already quoted, advocated the siting of milking parlour and dairy close together in the centre of the farm, to minimise the strain on the cows of being driven in for milking. On the other hand deprivation of exercise is equally harmful: Dr Robert Lamb of the US Department of Agriculture has shown that cows will produce more milk and have fewer calving problems if they walk at least two miles every day.

The milk of newly calved animals is adapted to the needs of the calf and is not suitable for use in cheesemaking. It should be excluded from the milk for the cheese dairy for at least a week, according to Val Cheke, by which time its composition has again become normal. Other opinions are less strict, but it is better to be safe, especially if a number of cows in the herd have calved close together. About eight months after calving, 'late lactation', milk again becomes abnormal, low in casein, lactose and calcium and high in chloride and albumin, which gives it an alkaline tendency. It is similar to mastitis milk, and late lactation mastitis tests are so uncertain as to be untrustworthy; so, although mastitis-causing organisms are not in themselves harmful to cheese, both milks should be excluded because they can slow up, or even stop, coagulation and will reduce flavour. Unfortunately clinical mastitis tests are only 10 per cent reliable, and other tests only 30-50 per cent effective, so great watchfulness is needed. The disease is much more common than before the days of machine milking, which is a pointer to the need for the strictest standards of hygiene in the milking parlour. Many forms of mastitis are commoner now than before the use of penicillin became widespread.

This must call in question the wisdom of giving blanket treatments to herds. Understandable though this practice is while detection of mastitis is so chancy, resistant strains develop, and penicillin itself renders milk unsuitable for cheesemaking as it inhibits essential bacteria including many starter Streptococci. It also encourages Betacocci which are heat resistant and gassy, and can make milk in a Stilton dairy vat froth over. At least four clear milkings should be discarded after the final veterinary treatment.

The American report of 1980 (see p. 121) showed that almost no organic farmers used hormones or growth stimulants, or antibiotics other than for strictly necessary healing purposes, although they are widely used as prophylactics in England. A number of herds on American organic farms showed lower birth mortality, higher reproductive efficiency, fewer respiratory ailments, and in consequence lower veterinary costs compared with herds on conventional farms. The report asked for speeding up of research on organic farming which had already been recommended, and added its own recommendation for research into problems arising from mastitis and antibiotic residues in milk and the development of resistant micro-organisms. US Department of Agriculture scientists put a high priority on 'utilizing and enhancing animals' natural defense mechanisms to prevent infections from becoming established'.

For cheese of good flavour, hay and silage should be made from grass and legumes with the characteristics already recommended. With the exception of the regeneration advantage in the cow's saliva, the factors making close grazing best for pasture regrowth and for palatability, digestibility and nutritive value also apply to cutting for hay, silage or any other form of preserved grass. The more often, thus the shorter, it is cut, the better the product. It was until quite recently supposed that a cow could obtain no more than 35 per cent of her nourishment from silage on account of its being less easily digested, but a re-reading of the century-old definition has shown that properly made silage is grass stored free of air. This and the virtues of the youngest pasture growth mean that silage can be as digestible as any other forage.

Among the newer grass preservation methods 'hay-flaking' proved popular with cows: 35 lb a day over a 305-day lactation yielded 1150 gallons of milk, this feed being preferred even to spring grass, according to one report. The Ministry's Experimental Husbandry Farm at Boxworth in Cambridgeshire did a five-year test, but I was told in 1980 that rising fuel costs had made hay-flaking less economical.

One of nature's shortcomings is that while cows drop their manure in the right place and save carting, they do not spread it. Ideally they should share the grazing with sheep, a requirement which some of our cheese farms can meet; left to herself the cow will neither spread her own manure, nor graze in its vicinity. If it is not spread for her by sheep or farmworker, she will avoid the affected ground, which consequently develops a lush growth. This looks attractive to anyone other than a cow or a sheep, but it is waste; even if cut for silage it is of poor palatability and digestibility. So the muck must be spread with hand-labour or during cutting with forage harvester or mower before the excess growth appears. I have recently heard of an ingenious method of overcoming the difficulty without extra fieldwork: while the cows are in for the winter and have no freedom of choice, their hay is treated with diluted faeces, and they then get so used to the flavour that they will graze right up to the turds when they are out again.

Cows fed for a prolonged period on roots and cereals without any grass-based fodder can give milk which has a conflicting relationship with rennet. This leads to poor clotting of curd, or even no clotting at all. Strong winter feeds, as compared with good silage, hay and winter grass, can come through in rough cheese flavours. While not necessarily disagreeable they tend to please only the minority of cheese lovers looking for very sharp cheese. Poor silage and linseed, or sunflower-seed cake in quantity, can also affect cheese flavour and quality. Groundnuts have been found to build up not only the protein element in feedstuffs but also Aflatoxin B1, which can cause deterioration in animal health and milk yield and can be passed on through milk to human beings.

Breeds of cattle for cheese

After the decline in the South West of the renowned Gloucester breed during the late eighteenth and early nineteenth centuries, first the Longhorn and then the Shorthorn predominated in all the cheesemaking regions of England, while the Ayrshire ruled in Scotland. During and after the Second World War emphasis on quantity rather than quality of milk and a catastrophic drop in the number of farmhouse cheesemakers brought new waves of fashion, first for the Ayrshire (still a good cheesemakers' cow) and then for the Friesian, which is now predominant in the dairy.

The distinguishing factor not disclosed by milk analysis is the size of the fat globules. High-fat Channel Island milk has large globules, which can more readily resist coagulation and be lost in the whey. This was why Jerseys and Guernseys were not used traditionally for hard cheesemaking in the British Isles. New Zealand has long been successful with them, as have some recent

Three stalwarts of the dairy world. The old Gloucester breed (top), recently restored in its county of origin at Dymock (see p. 31); the Shorthorn (below), one of the most popular dairy cows for cheesemaking today; and the Jersey (right), renowned for her rich, yellow milk, not ideal for cheesemaking, however, on account of the size of the fat globules.

recruits to British cheese farming. Shorthorn, Ayrshire and Gloucester cows have small globules well suited to cheesemaking. Friesians are not outstanding for anything but quantity of yield. This sufficed to bring them into fashion, even on many cheese farms, but breeding has since greatly improved the quality of their milk.

Readers interested in particular breeds for cheesemaking can consult farmers who are using them. They will find the breed of cattle given in the particulars of most of the farms listed in Part One of this book.

Dairy goats

Goats are being more widely milked in Britain for cheesemaking than ever before. Their milk is rich, its average fat content (6 per cent) being half as much again as that of cows, and its solids-not-fat being higher, with an advantage in casein.

There are special health advantages in goats' milk: for instance, children with allergies and migraine sufferers who cannot tolerate cows' milk cheese can usually enjoy goat cheese without any ill-effects.

Olivia Mills offers the following basic points for consideration by potential goatkeepers.

1 Because goats are primarily browsers, not grazers, grass alone is not enough for them.
2 They must have shelter from rain and cold.
3 They do not have to kid every year and will go on milking for long periods in certain circumstances.
4 They are more difficult than sheep to fence in and may require tethering.

Popular breeds of goat for the cheesemaker are the Toggenburg (above left), British Alpine (above right) and British Saanen.

Most established goatkeepers belong to the British Goat Society, which has affiliated goatkeepers' federations all over the UK and in the Channel Islands. Many who make cheese and other dairy products also value the National Dairy Goat Produce Association for its practical advice on standards and marketing of goat produce. Both societies publish a monthly journal. The BGS has produced a book on dairy work, _Dairy Work for Goatkeepers_, which is recommended for goat or cows' milk cheesemakers working on a small scale, with one reservation: p. 7 suggests cutting builders' heavyweight plastic pipe for moulds, but toxic matters used in its manufacture make it unsuitable for cheesemaking. The best British goat cream cheese I have ever tasted was made from a recipe in this book by Mrs C. W. Hawley at Upper Basildon in Berkshire. Mr and Mrs Hawley have regrettably now retired from goatkeeping. These two organisations, both of which have helped me, do not appear to be on very friendly terms. You can take your choice, or risk using both (their addresses can be found on p. 165).

Sheep dairying in Britain

Note: I am indebted to Olivia Mills for the information contained in this section, much of which is quoted from a paper she wrote in connection with the demonstration of sheep dairying and ewes' milk cheeses at the Royal Show in 1981.

Sheep have been milked since the dawn of agriculture and in Britain were milked in large numbers until the Middle Ages. Much of all the butter and cheese was made from the milk of ewes, which were often rented out to cheesemakers after their lambs had been weaned.

Sheep continued to be milked in Scotland until this century. Meg Dodds, Sir Walter Scott's character, who kept an inn at Howgate in Midlothian, remarked that 'the old ewe's milk cheese of the Scottish Border we have found an excellent substitute for Gruyère'. Scott himself was painted with his daughters dressed to go sheep milking. A retired shepherd of Annan in Dumfriesshire can remember his father and grandfather milking ewes in the Cheviots. This led him to encourage the making of an excellent ewes' milk cheese at Annan (see Barac, p. 96).

Two farms in the North of England made ewes' milk cheese into the 1900s. In the Eppynt area of South Wales ewes were milked for mixed-milk cheese-making until 1939 (see p. 22), and on the Wales–Herefordshire border ewes' milk was used for cheese at least until 1977.

In marginal areas with small profit from fat lamb production an added bonus may be found in milking a selection of the best ewes in the flock. This 'third profit' can equally apply to owners of small flocks or of sheep kept in places frequented by large numbers of tourists where there will be a seasonal demand for the milk. Pure dairying with exotic, high-yielding sheep can be profitable, but demands very special management

A dairy ewe gives a sustained yield of milk over and above her lambs' needs. She must have a placid temperament, a well-shaped udder and good teat placement, and is likely to be found in a flock with high lambing percentages. In Britain she is likely to have some Friesland blood.

Ewes' milk cheese has seen a recent revival in Britain, though it was known to have been exported as long ago as the eighth century. Frieslands, shown here, have a very high milk yield.

The pure East Friesland gives the highest yield, but unless her progeny are crossbred they will be unsuitable for the fat lamb trade. The East Friesland crossed on to almost any breed greatly increases milk yield in the half-bred daughters. Better ewes from the ordinary flock can be selected and milked as it suits the owner. 'The choice will be based on the number of lambs reared, weaning weights, her inherent character as a dairy animal and her general suitability to the disciplines of the parlour.' The animals must be kept healthy and the milk flow maintained. Dairy ewes quickly respond to parlour training so that the use of dogs should be kept to a minimum.

Milking can be by hand or machine. For a large herd, rotaries or other parlours are needed. With numbers under a hundred, two-point bucket plants are quite adequate. A ewe with a well-shaped udder should milk out fast and not require stripping, although older ewes with a good yield can be slow and may need hand-milking.

Ewes selected must be put on a high plane of nutrition, with the best grazing which should be kept at optimum grazing length. For this a gang mower may be more useful than a conventional one. Dependent on quantity and quality of grazing forage, crops may have to be grown and concentrates fed, as for dairy cows. A small 'come-on' feed is usually necessary at milking time, to maintain discipline. Clean water must be available at all times.

Dairy ewes are subject to stress and to certain diseases specific to milk production. Mastitis is a constant risk particularly with machine milking. Orf, a form of dermatitis which may affect the teats, may present special problems, especially where hand milking is practised. Hypomagnesaemia can be a problem for the dairy ewe if her lambs are removed early.

Sheep's milk has more than twice as much fat and albumin as cows' milk, and more than half as much again of casein. Dr Davis gives the following figures: 9 per cent fat, 4.7 per cent lactose, 4.6 per cent casein, 1.1 per cent 'albumin etc.' and 1 per cent ash, a total of 20.4 per cent solids, but up to 25 per cent solids in ewes' milk can be attained. The milk is without taint and very white in colour. It will freeze like goats' milk, and also shares its health advantages (see p. 126). The fat globules are tiny, and do not form a head of cream.

Ewes from which lambs have been removed at 40 days or so may be expected to yield a further 100-150 litres before tupping. Better ewes may give a further 100 litres. Pure Frieslands yield much higher.

Sheep's milk has been used to make hard and soft cheeses and excellent yoghurt. Because of the problem of a limited seasonal supply summer tourist areas and other seasonal markets should be considered. The difficulty about extending the season is that little is yet known about how to provide milk-producing feed other than grass for the lactating ewe. If this obstacle can be overcome, both Frieslands and Dorset Horns could be used for staggered lambing.

Ewes' milk cheese is growing rapidly in popularity, and an exhibition of milking ewes at the Royal Show in 1981 provoked great interest and huge sales of cheese. Two or three enquiries a week on sheep dairying were still coming to the Royal Agricultural Society over two months after the show.

A list of farms keeping dairy flocks may be found on p. 165.

11

The History of British Cheese

English cheese from the eighteenth century

The stories of individual English cheeses are related in the chapters dealing with them and their regions by name. My concern here is to give a brief account of the way cheesemaking developed in England in modern times until the drastic changes imposed on farms and dairies with the outbreak of war in 1939.

By the 1720s, although cheesemaking was still spread over most of the country, the types of English cheese were broadly established as they exist today. Those cheeses I have listed as extinct were no longer of distinctive character and national importance in relation to their bigger and better neighbours. The newcomer, Quenby cheese, was already widely known by the name of the town on the Great North Road where it was sold to travellers: Stilton. It was highly priced, at 2s 6d a pound, compared with 6d to 8d for esteemed, scarce Cheddar, and 2½d a pound for Cheshire. Cheshire was cheap because the mild climate and fine pastures of the area enabled a great quantity of cheese to be produced. It was handled by a highly organised wholesale trade: one syndicate had sixteen ships carrying cheese from Liverpool to London. Gloucester cheeses were on their way up to the peak they reached in the 1780s. Cheddar production was less advanced and less organised, but there were some village co-operative dairies which had existed since Elizabethan times. In Scotland Dunlop was becoming nationally known and marketed. The remaining British cheeses were produced for comparatively local consumption.

Changes in the nineteenth century

The first event that began to undermine Britain's self-sufficiency in cheese and the general prevalence of farmhouse cheesemaking was the mushroom-like growth of railways all over the country. Suddenly liquid milk could be transported from farm to city, and the seven-day labour of cheesemaking was no longer necessary to make safe the dairy farmers' product for future, perhaps uncertain sale. This change had reduced Gloucestershire cheese to less than a quarter of its 1780s production by the 1850s, a tribute to the efficiency of Brunel's Great Western Railway. Less affected were the more remote Dales, unpenetrated by the railways even at their zenith.

In the latter part of the eighteenth century the Board of Agriculture's reports and the activities of the Agricultural Societies stimulated interest in cheesemaking methods in various counties, but it was in the making of Cheddar and Dunlop that the greatest changes took place. Many Cheddar makers had emigrated to Canada and the United States, and cheesemakers in Scotland turned first to Somerset and then to Canada for advice on improving their methods. In Somerset the old wisdom and methodical approach of the notable families (Harding, Candy and Cannon) was being recorded and studied, achieving standards of herdsmanship, dairy practice and cheesemaking which were to astonish Dr Davis a century later. Lloyd was the man who collated this knowledge at the end of the nineteenth century and tied it in with new discoveries, such as the use of starter. The term Cheddar was now used internationally to describe the method of making cheese, and was sadly beyond retrieval as a protected trade name for England's greatest cheese gift to the world.

In the 1870s Derbyshire started the first large-scale cheese dairy, and led the way with five of the first twelve factories established in England by 1876. Here was another secure outlet for farm milk, relieving many more farms of anxiety. Factories were often opened in the countryside where the milk was produced.

In the last decade of the century the annual United Kingdom cheese production averaged 141,396 tons, showing a slight downward trend. Foreign imports (of which, surprisingly, the United States supplied more than half) stood at 52,299 tons, with a downward trend. The growing share of this expanding market went to imported Colonial cheeses, consumption of which rose steadily from 43,228 tons in 1891 to 74,702 tons in 1900. Of this Canada sent the lion's share, over 70,000 tons. New Zealand was just beginning to make herself felt with 4000 tons in 1900. Most other imports came from Holland, leaving only about 1500 tons (0.6 per cent of consumption) to the softer cheeses of France.

The First World War

The 1914-18 war was the next dire influence on farmhouse cheesemaking.

The revival of interest in Real Cheese over the past few years has encouraged small farmers to make on a moderate scale by traditional methods, selling locally and experimenting with new cheeses.

Much of it ceased, never to resume. In the farming conditions of the immediate post-war period cheese prices were quite uneconomic; on the other hand retail dairies in the cities were liable to reduce prices at will, or return whole consignments of milk unsold, thus forcing cheesemaking on even unwilling farmers, unless or until they had an expanding creamery in the neighbourhood.

The Milk Marketing Boards

This state of uncertainty was not conducive to a recovery of pre-war quantities and standards of farmhouse cheesemaking. The formation of the Milk Marketing Boards in 1933 as statutory controllers of milk sales brought security and order out of anxiety and chaos. All dairy farmers had to sell their milk to the Boards, but the purchase and resale of the milk was done on a co-operative basis, the ultimate payment to the members having had marketing expenses deducted and profits added.

Where cheese was made, the milk bought by the Board at liquid milk price stayed on the farm, being sold back to the farmers at the lower price paid by industry for manufacturing-milk (milk used in the making of creamery butter and cheese, milk powder and so on). The difference, originally considerable, helped to finance the extra investment in equipment and the cost of maintenance and labour incurred by cheesemakers (the difference in 1978 9 was only 0.75p a litre or 3.3p a gallon). In return for this the farmer had to account to the Board for every gallon of milk with a pound of cheese.

Traditional bonds between farms and cheese factors continued, but the Boards took over some of these wholesale concerns and marketed cheese themselves. The Boards could require farms to sell them cheese to meet Board commitments to the wholesale and retail market, a power which sometimes sacrificed old private channels of trade. The great benefit was felt by dairy farmers whose outlets had been precarious; at last they knew whence and when their milk cheque was coming, and that their cheese would gain them further profit later.

In the twentieth century Stilton production began to move from the farm to the dairy, and methods were modified for the first time in two hundred years. The change was so complete that the last farmer (probably the fourth-generation Watson of that Stilton making family) ceased making in the early 1930s.

By 1939 the only considerable areas of English farmhouse cheesemaking were the South West (514 Cheddar and Caerphilly farms in Devon, Dorset, Somerset and Wiltshire), the North West (405 farms making Cheshire in Cheshire, Shropshire and Flint, and 202 Lancashire farms), and the Dales (176 in Wensleydale and 257 in Swaledale and Teesdale). These were individual farms making cheese in traditional form from their own unpasteurised milk. They had survived against factory competition and against the desperately discouraging conditions of the 1930s. It is safe to say that without the advent of the Milk Marketing Board during this period, with its organisation and guarantee of a market, many more dairy farms would have been unable to sell their produce and forced to sell up.

The Second World War

There must have been about 1600 cheese farms in the United Kingdom at the outbreak of the Second World War, producing nearly a quarter of all the cheese then made in Britain. All this cheese was what today has to be qualified as traditional, to distinguish it from the then unheard-of block.

The creation of the Ministry of Food in 1939, and its implementation of forward planning to preserve the nation's diet and share it equitably, could scarcely be faulted. All comparisons with what happened in the First World War favour the achievements of Lord Woolton and his Ministry in the Second War.

There is, however, one blot on the Ministry's escutcheon. Professor Capstick advised that, to make the most of national resources, all milk available for cheese should be brought to the factories and made into the hard cheeses: Cheddar, Cheshire, Dunlop and Scottish Cheddar, Leicester (unrecognisable without its characteristic annatto colouring), and, with the help of Kit Calvert's determined advocacy, a hard, creamery version of Wensleydale. Stilton, the Gloucesters, Lancashire, Caerphilly, the succulent cheeses of the Dales and all the soft cheeses were written off, as was farmhouse cheesemaking everywhere in the country. The most ancient and distinguished branches of Britain's richest food tradition were cut off, badly stunting the tree.

In wartime much capital does have to be squandered as income, but in this case the sacrifice was extravagant and unnecessary. First of all, the labour, almost entirely female, was trained, and was in the best possible place for making good cheese: close to the milk. Secondly, much of the cheesemaking met local demand and was therefore economical in distribution costs. Thirdly, the collection of milk from all farms, however remote and roughly reached, was a ridiculous waste of precious petrol, tyre rubber, vehicles and drivers. Milk had to be collected daily; cheese could wait a fortnight, or even a month, if not already distributed in the course of necessary market journeys without extra transport cost at all. Finally, for every gallon of milk collected daily only one pound of finished cheese needed to be carried monthly.

So the Second World War saw the untimely dispersal of many hundreds of cheesemakers from the farms where they were serving Britain so economically and so well. They left, most of them never to return. The 'Utility' standards imposed on wartime cheese production, and the rationing and price control that went with them, prevailed into the 1950s. Cheese finally came off the ration only in 1954. Farm production was minute, but many small creameries were turning out unpasteurised, clothbound, traditional products, of good flavour, texture and maturing potential.

The death of farmhouse cheese

At this point the Ministry of Agriculture and the Milk Marketing Board tried to revive cheesemaking on farms. Officials armed with the 1939 registers of cheesemakers set out to resurrect the tradition they had killed in 1940.

In 1948, 44 farms in Cheshire produced their own cheese, compared with 405 in 1939; 29 against 202 in Lancashire, and 61 against 514 in the South West. Wensleydale had only 9 farms making cheese compared with 176 before the war. Kit Calvert warned the revivalist officials that they were wasting their time, but he had to conduct them round the Wensleydale farms to prove his point. (The last of his nine cheesemakers retired in 1957.)

Some reasons for this irreversible loss were common to all regions: war work had scattered many cheesemakers and death had taken its inevitable toll. After the long break in continuity only a small minority of those left on the farms felt the pull of family tradition and personal vocation strongly enough to go back to all-day and everyday cheesemaking. They had savoured for too long the comparative freedom of just milking the cows and selling the result without further ado.

The reason that registered cheesemaking in Wensleydale, Swaledale and Teesdale ceased altogether was the Board's failure to adopt relevant standards of farmhouse cheese grading. The wartime standard for hard dairy cheese was imposed on the semi-soft cheese artists of the farms, a fatally unimaginative blunder.

There was some wastage of cheesemakers from farms in other regions for related reasons. The difference between their pre-war and post-war cheeses was less obvious; but makers of the moister cheeses, which if allowed to do so would often mature beautifully, were liable to find them roughly graded, at a few weeks old, in a world increasingly dominated by the less risky, quicker selling hard cheeses.

The supermarket era

In the sixties a tidal wave of concrete swept over the life, charm and traditional trades of many town centres: the old provision merchants, who knew and respected their cheese, were swept away. If they were tenants, the new rents and rates were beyond them; if they were freeholders, they either retired on their compensation or caught the supermarket fever. Many of the earliest supermarkets made a feature of their delicatessen counters, but staff training often lagged behind their pretensions. Unfortunately the supermarket multiples found investment in equipment more economical than investment in staff training. Once they decided that it was cheaper to cut and wrap cheese by machine and leave customers to help themselves, the rot had set in. Cheeses had to be tough enough in texture and angular enough in shape to cause no problems requiring human understanding to solve them. They must submit, uncrumbling, to the violation of automated cutting and prepacking.

Traditional cheesemakers at this difficult time were inadequately guided and supported by the Board. Farmhouse price premiums over creamery cheeses were small and the sales pattern was erratic. There were occasions when the farm I bought from could not meet my advance orders because it had been forced to deliver cheeses to the Board for their multiple customers, who would chop them up and prepack them. At other times a frustrated public could not obtain traditional cheese properly matured and presented, while traditional producers were loaded with unsold cheeses.

In 1974 I went on a tour of all the cheesemaking areas of England. Since 1948 the numbers of registered cheese farms had dropped from 44 to 22 in the Cheshire cheese territory, from 29 to 7 in Lancashire and from 61 to 33 in the South West. The Board's divorce from reality in the farmhouse cheese world can be judged by comparing these figures (checked by me on the ground) with figures similar to some the Board gave me before I set out, which were accepted by Stanley Baker for his official history of the English Milk Marketing Board (*Milk to Market*, 1973). 'There are currently some 240 farmhouse cheesemakers in England and Wales, just about double the number of twenty years ago.' The real number was 62 (the figure given to me was 263); the number of cheesemaking farms was less than half the number in 1949. The explanation was probably that co-operator farms had been lumped in with cheesemaking farms in the figures given to Stanley Baker in 1973 and to me early in 1974. These farms only supply milk for the cheesemaking farms, some of which now work on a factory scale.

Rebellion against prepack

At this time the demand for Real Ale had already started to make the brewers repent their gaseous sins; and the end of 1973 brought a spontaneous supplication from supermarket customers for 'more fresh cheese (NOT prepack)'. In the market survey concerned, commissioned by un-cheesey, disinterested Birds Eye, cheese was not even the subject of a question, but Derek Bayliss, head of grocery services STATS (MR) who analysed the results, was convinced that this was the call of the silent majority.

'Each man kills the thing he loves', wrote Oscar Wilde. So, by penny-pinching and neglect, the post-war Englishman had almost killed good ale, good bread and good cheese; until at last their absence made his heart grow fonder.

Just in time, the wrath of discriminating beer lovers frothed over into the Campaign for Real Ale. The resulting boom among surviving small brewers so dented the profits of the mass carbon dioxide manufacturers as to shock them into making and serving some drinkable brews again. It was the same with bread. Traditional bakers, undermined by the cut-price 'slice-wrapped' trade, had been dying off for years. Then strikes acquainted the public once more with the products of the remaining small bakeries, and crusty loaves and brown bread began to win back the allegiance of consumers all over Britain. Now most of us can find Real Ale and Real Bread; but fortunate and few are those within reach of Real Cheese to go with it.

Some supermarkets reacted to the Birds Eye report and similar signs of public unease by instituting or resuming counter service for cheese. They won considerable extra trade but found it increasingly difficult to get real traditional cheese to put on their counters.

The reaction of the Milk Marketing Board, our biggest mass cheesemakers and the controllers of almost all farmhouse cheesemaking in England and Wales, was perverse. At the Board's launching of a booklet called _Farmhouse English Cheese_ in 1978 at the Farmers' Club more than fifty guests were asked to taste two apparently identical cubes of nine-month-old farmhouse Cheddar. The one they unanimously preferred proved to have been cut from a clothbound cylindrical cheese; its rejected rival had been Cryovac-sealed block cheese from birth. Despite this incontrovertible proof of consumer discrimination and preference, the handout claimed that 'the test demonstrated the identical flavour' of the two types of cheese; and the booklet revealed that things had got worse, not better, in the farm world since 1973: '70 per cent of Farmhouse Cheddars are provided in rindless blocks to meet the demands of the supermarket cutting machinery. Do not let this bother you – it makes no difference to the cheese', the book claimed; 'the flavour is just the same.'

Discouragement of small cheesemakers

Perhaps the Board was catching the Scottish attitude towards anyone producing or encouraging cylindrical as opposed to block cheese. The Scottish cheese authorities squeezed the last farmhouse Dunlop maker out in 1974 because, to use his own words, he was 'a bit of a nuisance'. These exact words were used to me by an official of the Milk Marketing Board's South East regional office at Reading about a keen cheesemaker and several organic farmers who were willing to supply milk for her to start cheesemaking in Sussex. With the co-operation and approval of the cheese department at Thames Ditton and of the local Board representative, Inez Vermaas had gone through all the formalities needed and was all set to start making cheese. Then the Reading office stepped in to raise the price she must pay for her milk by 2p a litre (equivalent to nearly 9p a pound on her cheese) with no provision for milk disposal in an emergency. This made the whole enterprise uneconomic and all the preparatory work abortive. The Reading official adamantly refused to discuss or justify this last-minute interference, about which he knew. He revealed himself adequately in his unguarded comments, however: 'This is not a cheesemaking region; the Board would have to replace the milk used from elsewhere for liquid sales', and 'these keen organic types can be a bit of a nuisance'. I must add that I have found other Reading staff both keen about cheese and most helpful, but theirs is not the power.

In the South West Chloë Cox wanted to use her Devonshire farmhouse dairy to make cheese from milk produced in the adjoining pastures, which were formerly farmed from her house. The farmer was willing and the milk was on her doorstep, eliminating transport costs, but the Board said she was too small to get milk at manufacturing rates and must pay the full liquid milk price. The South West is a cheese area producing surplus milk which sometimes goes as far afield as Lancashire; consistency is not a feature of Board attitudes.

Other discouraging cases have come my way, despite my getting from Roy Cornwell of the English Country Cheese Council both heartfelt sympathy and this declaration: 'The Milk Marketing Board will do nothing to interfere with (even) unlicensed cheesemakers. It loses nothing by their activities, and will give advice and help to those who ask.'

'You mention your friend at the MMB', one of them in County Durham wrote to me. 'I only wish I had your confidence in them.' At least her cheeses do get to the public, but another Dales cheesemaker insisted: 'We are not allowed to make cheese and sell it, so we do not want *any* publicity.' Indeed, looking for a mythical source of farmhouse Wensleydale, I approached a village shopkeeper who said: 'I wouldn't be allowed to sell the cheese anyway.' His source of intimidation was the Middlesbrough local authority inspectorate; and the National Farmers' Union secretary for one of the Dales areas told me that the only potential farm cheesemakers he knew of had been put off by the red tape.

Restrictions on licensed cheesemaking

The Board's policy on licensed cheesemaking is that new farms should only take on cheesemaking if other makers retire. This is deplorably negative policy, but the facts are even worse. Potential newcomers have been held off in recent years despite retirements. Expansion has only come from higher production on existing farms, which has taken some of them right out of the genuine farmhouse category. The Board seems to resent extra milk demands from small cheese-makers, so the big two in the Cheshire region produce two-fifths of all the cheese made on twenty farms. As the MMB booklet pointed out, the position as far as Cheddar is concerned is far worse: 70 per cent of farm Cheddar was made in block in 1978, and there are eight times as many co-operator farms supplying milk for farmhouse Cheddar as there are farms making it. Few of the traditional makers use the milk of more than a handful of co-operators, so the bigger block farms are really making a creamery product on creamery scale. Dr Davis wrote in 1976 that 'farmhouse cheesemakers are only such in name today'.

Yet the Board appeared in 1980 to have arrogated to itself the sole right to use the words 'Farmhouse Cheese', enveloping even these creamery-scale enterprises within the description, provided their cheeses were marketed through the Board's agents. The aim had been to protect farmers; but farmers who had built their own cheese stores because they were not satisfied with those agents, such as Lord Chewton at Priory Farm, Chewton Mendip, and the Quicke Partners at Newton St Cyres, were told not to use the term Farmhouse Cheese, but to call their products 'Traditional'. Two other farmers who discussed this with Mr M. E. Bessey at the Board's headquarters got the impression that the Board was confident of winning a test case. Unable to believe that any court would forbid use of plain English to describe genuine farmhouse cheese, I took the matter up with Mr Bessey, now Managing Director of Dairy Crest, the

Board's newly formed manufacturing and marketing company. He wrote to me on 28 August 1981:

> We certainly did take the precaution, many years ago, of registering the name 'FARMHOUSE CHEESE' in association with the three cheese symbol . . . to protect the substantial advertising investment made in this mark jointly by the Board and the makers. As the holder of the mark, its main use is in relation to the Farmhouse Cheese sold by Dairy Crest. Arrangements have been made, however, for its use on sales made by individual makers where these are in accordance with the Farmhouse cheesemakers' contract. . . . the registered mark is quite clearly applied both to block and traditional cheese where they are covered by the contract arrangements.

By return I told Mr Bessey that I took this to mean that registration was attached to the symbol, and that it was a misunderstanding to suppose that farmers could not call their product what it was: farmhouse cheese. Having heard no more I must take it that my inference was correct. However, Lord Chewton, looking at what passes as farmhouse cheese, now feels that 'Traditional' is more accurate and select.

European Community regulations have now brought a new factor into play, which prohibits the Board's former monopolistic control of milk; but the Board has obviously hoped that no one would hear about it. When Elliot Hulme recently went independent in Cheshire he had to quote EEC regulations to the Board to force them into letting him buy his neighbour's milk for cheesemaking. Indeed, milk for anything but block cheesemaking seems to be grudged by some of the Board's employees. Singleton's Dairy in Lancashire managed to get extra milk for some export orders for traditional cheese, but some bureaucrat in the Board tried to cut their later allocations to make up for it, as though milk were on ration and exporters of cheese must be penalised by cutting their production for home consumption. This comparatively small creamery has blazoned the way for makers and marketers of traditional cheese. In 1980 it sold nearly four times as much traditional Lancashire as it did the previous year, and sales of its block production (down to 25 per cent of its total output) actually dropped.

As a result of the Board's generally discouraging attitude and considerable red tape, almost all new farmhouse cheesemakers of the last few years have sacrificed possible financial advantages over milk pricing and sold their cheese and other dairy products under licence from the Ministry of Agriculture. Two farmers known to me adopted this course after severe obstruction on the Board's part.

This negative attitude towards traditional cheeses has brought Britain to a humiliating state. Cheese calling itself Cheddar formed 68 per cent of our total consumption in 1978. Of this category a quarter was imported block cheese (for which the Danes regularly win prizes): less than one-hundredth was 'Real' Cheddar from the traditional farmhouse production of 7000 cheeses a month. Dairy cylindrical waxed Cheddar is made, but only to be sold mild, not for keeping. Keymarkets, when they could no longer get mature traditionals, substituted polythene-sealed quarters of this dairy cheese and suffered a severe loss of Cheddar sales. Their contrasting growth in turnover of Stilton and other dearer English cheeses showed that lower prices are no compensation for lower quality in a significant section of the market.

In the face of such demands, ten fewer Cheddar farms were registered in 1980 than in 1974, and most of the survivors make only plastic-sealed blocks which, despite the advertisements, cannot honestly be classed as 'Real' traditional cheese. The Milk Marketing Board justifies this misdescription of block cheeses by saying that they come from the same curd as the cylindrical cheeses. Even this is no longer true, as automated factory machinery has now invaded the farm world. In any case, curd (the concentration of solids from milk) is not finished cheese; it still needs moulding, pressing and maturing.

Curd moulded into plastic-sealed blocks, even if initially hand-made, turns out very differently from the same curd cylindrically moulded and clothbound: it is stodgier and slower ripening, and therefore duller in texture and flavour. Furthermore it can be imitated by makers all over the world, whereas traditional cheeses cannot.

The loss of character in cheese

One of the effects of the emphasis on block cheese is to blur the differences between one cheese and another. Joyce Ward, who lectures for the English Country Cheese Council, tells me that the only recognisable unblue cheese of the nine that she lectures on is Cheddar; she lives in Somerset. The others she can buy locally only in block or prepack, and although she is a trained cheesemaker she has to label quickly the cheeses she buys for demonstration and tasting, because she would otherwise be unable to tell them apart.

In the North many lovers of Lancashire cheese have been put off by the block and other tasteless, poor-textured 'single-acid' substitutes devised for quick sale. The ordinary customer has no way of knowing that real old Lancashire still exists, and often condemns it all on tasting the new, so-called 'Lancashire'. Cheshire sales have also dropped in proportion to general British sales since so much block cheese came on the market. Stilton has been the biggest success on the home market and in exports; and the new Farmhouse Blue Cheshire, invented by Mrs Hutchinson Smith (see p. 65), has taken on so well that two more farms have tried to follow her lead.

Other new cheeses have been developed since the war, mainly by the use of flavours introduced into the broken curds of creamery cheeses, which are then re-moulded into rindless drums. They have added ten or so varieties to the English list and undoubtedly helped to divert some customers from buying foreign cheeses. Scotland has revived its old Crowdie and its very old Caboc, and produced a number of variations in soft cheeses by the use of herbs and smoking, and by the production of crusted cheeses in the French style.

In general, the trend has been towards making block cheeses almost universal in order to make life easier for the multiple traders. It is true that total home production has increased and meets a larger proportion of Britain's total cheese consumption than ever before; but our average consumption is lower than in 1900, and has fallen a long way behind that of our neighbours, and this has happened in a period when the EEC has been virtually excluding Canadian, New Zealand and Australian cheese from the British market. New Zealand alone sent over 68,000 tons to Britain in the first year of EEC membership. In

1980 6500 tons of New Zealand cheese and over 5000 tons of Canadian and Australian cheese were on their way back to the British table.

If Britain's cheese is to have a future, we must pay more attention to the cheeses our competitors cannot begin to imitate, old cheeses made and finished in the traditional way.

12

The Future of British Cheese

Dairy research and investment by government and industry since the war appear to have concentrated on making the life of big cheesemakers and big cheese sellers as trouble free as possible. With tiny honorable exceptions, no research has been applied to the discovery of what we British liked about our traditional cheese and to the understanding, preservation and propagation of this knowledge so that more of it could be made and enjoyed. The customer has been the last person to be thought of while the old-time virtues of his favourites were being ruthlessly eliminated for the convenience of manufacturer and multiple. The first results, a few years ago, were cheap and nasty. Now they are still nasty and no longer cheap.

The results of market research should be enough to persuade the controllers of cheesemaking that a significant section of the public would like a reversal of present policy. A number of multiples who responded by instituting or reviving counter service for cheese alongside their cold cabinets of prepacked portions have already acknowledged that this is only half enough. Many of their customers (Keymarkets say 30 per cent) prefer to have old-fashioned 'cheese-shaped' cheese cut for them on these counters, rather than just another block cheese that happens not to have been prepacked and therefore needs a little less sweaty thawing out.

The difficulties which the multiples and the Board must overcome are these. The present supply of traditional cheeses is only 3.7 per cent of the current consumption, and a much smaller percentage of potential demand. The waxed dairy Cheddars the Board have produced to sell at two months are no substitute. Traditional Cheddar production is 0.66 per cent of our so-called 'Cheddar' consumption. A number of the bigger farms which have turned over to block cheesemaking will have to change back and the production of smaller farms must be increased. Strong encouragement must be given to the resumption or to a new start of traditional cheesemaking at other farms and small creameries, not least in the counties whose cheeses are not recognisable in the forms in which they are usually available today. My own selling and catering experiences have taught me that, although over 90 per cent of the general public eats cheese, many people are astonished and delighted by the taste of properly matured traditional English cheese (farm and dairy), compared with their usual supermarket fare. They are also amazed at the number of British cheeses they have never heard of.

Roger Davenport of Unigate pointed out in *The Grocer* (8 September 1980) how far behind Europe we were in cheese consumption, and maintained that it would not be raised by protectionism and higher production. He said, 'There is a lot going for English pedigree, and markets such as our territorial (county) cheeses are grossly under-exploited.'

The French example

French exporters traditionally have a foot in the British market which is being fully exploited by their newer large-scale cheese producers. They give prizes to shopkeepers, their cheeses are beautifully presented, and some of their post-war inventions make pleasant additions to the range of French cheeses; but their inroads into our market are also attributable to the coincidence of this selling expertise with the diminishing supply of real British cheeses to compete with them as dinner-party fare. Food from France publicity, now reckoned to have taken Brie and Camembert to every quarter of Britain, is turning its attention to less common French cheeses. As a seller of over a hundred French cheeses I must stress that the general run of French soft cheeses sold outside specialist shops is of indifferent standard, yet they have made a significant impact on our dully provided home market. Discriminating cheese buyers do not regard block cheese as acceptable fare to put before guests, particularly not before foreign guests. The result is a significant loss to the British cheese trade in areas where block cheese rules. The French exploit this vulnerable spot in our market. They are spreading their sales to many customers who just find the French creamery cheeses more palatable and succulent than the sort of British cheeses they are offered. Continental cheese bought by the British increased in weight from 730 grams per person per year in 1978 to 795 grams, about 13 per cent of our total cheese consumption, in 1979.

French exports to Britain went up by 20 per cent in volume between 1976 and 1978 according to Unigate figures, and are now growing by 13 per cent per annum. Unigate's own share of French sales is increasing at the annual rate of 25 per cent. Unigate, who sold all their English cheesemaking creameries except their Stilton factory to the MMB in 1979, retained their sales force. They find it more profitable to use it to sell cheese bought abroad, competing with what they used to make. The lesson to the Board should be clear. The mass of what is now made and sold under old English names, however efficient and hygienic the creamery and machinery, is not representative of the name it is sold under and not worthy of respect as cheese for the dinner table. Even our remaining traditional cheese sales are ill-served by the claim that there is no difference between them and the block cheese made in the big farm dairies. The Board itself has proved the contrary, so it is dishonest and self-defeating to continue the 'tastes just the same' campaign. The results have angered cheese lovers and put many people off buying English cheeses at all. We are losing that section of our market, estimated by one supermarket cheesebuyer as 30 per cent of his custom, to foreign cheeses.

Most of my customers, including notable _Good Food Guide_ restaurants on the Distinction list, regard British cheese as a vital part of their cheese course. They make a particular point of offering it to foreign visitors, many of whom come to me afterwards to buy British cheese to take home. This should be happening all over the country; and we should be looking to the future of our traditional cheeses on foreign markets, with the strength of follow-through demonstrated by the French in their sales to us.

In 1977 the United Kingdom was third in the European league in total milk production with over 15,000,000 tons, just over half that of the leader, France. France retains more milk on her farms for cheesemaking than any other country, and still has a very large number of independent cheesemaking dairies. French annual cheese consumption, then 35 lb a head, nearly three times the British, had grown to well over three times our figure by 1981.

British cheese today

The bulk of cheesemaking in Britain is done by the Milk Marketing Boards and Express Dairies. In the late 1970s traditional farmhouse cheese provided about one-thirtieth of our national production, which in its turn met 70 per cent of our cheese consumption. Our average annual consumption at $12\frac{1}{2}$ lb a head is 16 per cent lower than it was in the 1890s when 80 per cent of our cheese was 'home and colonial'. European community policy over the last few years has virtually excluded Commonwealth cheeses, which should have helped home producers to take more than 70 per cent of our market; but Europe has shown itself able to compete with block Cheddar in a way which it could never do with the farmhouse product. Austrian, Belgian, Danish, Dutch, French and even Rumanian Cheddar have come in, and now Canadian and New Zealand cheeses are back again. French Cheddar won favourable comment, but the French have sensibly decided that their own native types are more profitable: their expansion of trade is in soft cheeses. Our emphasis on bulk and neglect of quality has been misguided.

Dr Davis foresaw years ago the danger of reducing cheese to a few common types, and of standardisation within those types: 'The biggest problem of the food industry in the year 2000 AD may well be not quantity but monotony. Each county should fight to maintain the integrity of its indigenous cheese varieties.' Dr Davis followed this up by reminding us that the best cheese is farm made from raw milk, and that it is on this factor that the individuality of all regional cheeses depends: 'If science can solve the problems of using raw milk we may see the elimination of heat-treatment and the restoration of the traditional flavours of raw milk cheese in factories.' We should stop the disproved, and therefore dishonest, pretence that people want dull cheese, and concentrate research resources in the direction Dr Davis has pinpointed as vital.

The Milk Marketing Board proved in their impeccable blind test in June 1978 that people could tell the difference between farmhouse block and traditional farm Cheddar of identical age, and acknowledged at the time that everyone taking part preferred the fuller flavoured cylindrical cheese. This should have put a stop once and for all to the Board's propaganda, conforming to that of the biggest supermarket companies, that block cheese is the same as round, and that they make cheese this way and sell it young because the public prefer it mild;

but, for all the notice the Milk Marketing Board and its offshoots took, the 1978 test might never have happened. The Country Cheese Council was represented when that test was made, yet when its Director, George Holmes, was interviewed for Radio 4's *Food Programme* in September 1980 he rolled out all the old exploded myths: 'Our cheeses were too strong ... now we are taking cheeses out of store earlier and selling them young ... there is no difference between block and round; the cheese is the same, the flavour is the same ... if it was possible to have a test it would prove me right.' Derek Cooper tested: two-thirds of his sample recognised cheese from the cylindrical Cheddar for what it was; only half knew what the Cryovac-packed Cheddar block was supposed to be. The greatest indifference was shown towards the plastic-wrapped cheeses, and the most appreciation for the twelfth-month matured traditional Cheddar. This was enjoyed by the majority. With people in charge of British cheese who do not know what it really tastes like, the way is open for foreign cheeses of even moderate interest to mop up the considerable section of the market which the Board ignores. I sent the letter of complaint about indistinguishable British cheeses by one of his lecturers to the Chairman of the Milk Marketing Board, Steve Roberts, on 5 September 1980, but the vast resources of his organisation have not conjured up a reply.

On 21 August 1981 cheese farms were told of the transformation of their relationship with the Board. Monthly milk cheques would stop. Farms selling all their cheese through Dairy Crest would get 'favourable' financing from the Board, but others would have to finance their ripening cheese themselves until it was ready to sell. One Cheddar farmer told me this would mean a gap of four months at least, amounting to £160,000 in extra overdraft.

On 25 August the new chairman of Dairy Crest, Michael Bessey, told me that it was too early for details of the financing, but that Dairy Crest was prepared to buy cheese at two months and mature it. He said he would be happy to discuss with farmers who sold their own cheese terms for the disposal of any surplus they could not clear themselves, and would encourage them to sell substandard cheeses to Dairy Crest for processing. He valued the local market for its tapping of the tourist trade and of local loyalties, and for its economy in transport and administration. He was open-minded about serving small shops, and about handling the comparatively few surplus cheeses from small farms flourishing on tourist trade in summer, but capable if given an outlet of extending their cheesemaking season through most of the winter. He seemed well aware of the public demand for more interesting cheese, and of the part that these small cheese producers can play in meeting it. He was also sympathetic towards my view that present grading times and standards tend to under-rate some of the most interesting farm cheese.

Mr Bessey's aim is flexibility, and his warmth of feeling about traditional cheese made me more optimistic than I had been about the breadth of service Dairy Crest might perform for cheesemakers, cheese sellers and cheese lovers in England and Wales. However, a few days later two Cheshire farmers grumbled to me about 'apathetic' marketing of their cheese. They said that early in 1981 the minimum delivery by Embertons of Crewe had jumped from 'one or two cheeses' to twenty-five, cutting out small shops. Mr Bessey told me that this was the result of higher distribution costs, but promised to see what could be done for smaller customers; they, after all, sell a great deal of traditional cheese which multiples spurn.

It is to be hoped that at least some of the multiples will face up to the crisis they have created and earn the right to call themselves 'provision merchants' again by treating cheese and cheese customers properly. To do this they will need to train their staff to understand and look after cheese, and to provide cellars or other suitable un-cold stores for the cheeses to mature in. The determination of firms such as Marks and Spencer not to employ counter staff makes repentance on a large scale seem unlikely. Yet a good cheese counter with one or two trained assistants is one of the most concentrated profit earners available. If the big shops refuse to see this, the way is open for many more independent shopkeepers to profit from their omission. Unfortunately, however many better cheesemongers are recruited to serve the public with the British cheese it wants, it will take years to restore adequate bases of manufacture and to organise effective maturing and retail marketing of traditional cheese. Meanwhile we should mobilise the Boards' and the Ministry's Advisory Services on both cleaning up delinquent dairy practices, and encouraging newcomers into the farm cheese world. These are the most urgent, practical and profitable investments for the future of British cheese.

Further evidence was supplied, just as this book was going to press, in a _Guardian_ article dated 27 January 1982. A report commissioned by the Agriculture Minister to investigate the working of the Milk Marketing Scheme included among its findings the disturbing information that British milk contains a higher level of antibiotics than that of any other European country. The report recommends that farmers should be required to take more rigorous precautions against contamination, that tests for pesticides should be initiated, and that the MMB should reject contaminated milk outright rather than imposing fines. The committee chairman, Dr Janet Cockcroft, said that the incidence of mastitis was very high in Britain, and that higher standards of hygiene in the dairy industry would reduce the need to use antibiotics.

Part Three
PRACTICAL
ADVICE

——— 13 ———
Finding and Choosing
Cheese

There is an irresistible charm about the waxed and clothbound wheels and cylinders in a proper cheese shop or cellar. The satisfaction to the eye given by the time-honoured shapes and sizes and their natural patina is akin to what a lover of architecture feels for ancient buildings in their unspoiled state. To the true gourmet rectangular shapes and polythene coats are as repellent as flat-roofed extensions, pebbledash and Snowcem.

It is true that even mature waxed and clothbound cheeses can look deceptively neat and new when perfectly looked after; but clothbound cheeses matured in normal cellar conditions collect a fair coating of mould between brushings and are neither less beautiful nor less healthy for that. Colours, too, enrich the scene. The deep internal annatto red of the great Leicester wheel is only veiled by the cheesecloth. Some Double Gloucester millstones are red with external annatto staining, Sage Derby shows greenly through its thin muslin, and coloured Cheshires shine pinkish through their wax. These shades are set off by the glossy white wax of wide Derby wheels, and of Lancashires and Cheshires in their large and middling drums. It is a pity that the jet glory of the black-waxed Cheddars and Black Diamond is now so rare.

None of these external coats and colours is unnatural or harmful. Pure paraffin wax is tasteless and edible (after all, liquid paraffin is prescribed medicinally), annatto and charcoal are both used internally in cheesemaking in Britain and abroad, and mould is benignly prophylactic inside or out. Anyway, the coats come off before the feast, and the residual rind of the old cheese provides a protection against deterioration that is denied the bare flesh of upstart block.

Finding the right shop

So look for a shop where openly displayed traditional cheese is cut for each customer from mature cylindrical cheeses, which only emerge from their protective cheesecloth binding for final sale. The only traditional cheeses without this binding are Stilton, Cotherstone, some Swaledale, some of the Gloucesters from Laurel Farm, and most Caerphilly (a few of the farm cheeses are bound). The newer cheeses with chives, onion, beer, wine and pickle flavourings are unbound. Only fresh cream and 'cottage' cheeses should be under refrigeration. If you do not know of a shop within your maximum travelling radius which presents at least some good mature cheese in this manner, look at Useful Addresses on p. 162 or consult the *Guide to Good Food Shops* (2nd ed. 1981). You can also write to Farmhouse English Cheese Information Service, Hesketh House, Portman Square, London W.1, to find out where you can buy (or order by post) clothbound traditional English cheeses.

Once inside the chosen shop, let your nose and eye take you exploring until you have decided on your probable choices for the day. If an unaccustomed, dazzling range of cheeses, or sheer mental exhaustion, has enveloped you in that embarrassing fog of indecision which affects us all at times, just plead for helpful suggestions. Ask what cheeses the counter hand feels most tempted by today. In the right shop you will then be offered tastes until you are suited. In such a shop you need to be patient and interested while others are tasting. Cheese buying cannot be hurried.

When tasting, proceed from mild to strong, leaving blues and most cheeses with added flavours until last. It is important to remember that cheeses of the same name vary greatly in flavour and strength according to the maker, the seasons of making and of selling, and the method and length of keeping. Never delude yourself that you know what some favourite cheese of yours is like without tasting the particular example in front of you. You will save yourself disappointment and money by testing it every time.

The cut face of the cheese from which you are being served should have a fresh look. It should not be hardened, cracked or sweaty, nor harbour surface mould, faults which betray a surface left uncut for a day or so. If necessary, ask for it to be trimmed before your piece is cut, or for your piece to be cut from another more acceptable face of the cheese.

Mould in itself is harmless, and internal mould in a cheese not normally blue is often a sign of richness; indeed it can be a bonus, but only for those who like blue cheese.

Unless you are going to work on a whole small cheese, buy only what you can eat in a day or two. Cheese is always at its best when fresh cut and pieces never improve with keeping. You can no more mature a slice of cheese than you can age a glass of wine. 'Little and often' is the best guide for cheese buying.

When you are given your taste take it between finger and thumb, or on the palm of the hand, if the cheese is crumbly. You may have caught the aroma as the cheese is cut; if not, put the piece first to your nose, then on the tip of the tongue, and finally press it up on the palate to test the consistency and the after-taste. If you find the consistency disagreeable, despite pleasant flavour, or have any other doubts, do not buy.

Cheese for cooking

It is as important to taste cheese you buy for cooking as to taste any other. The better the cheese, the more economical it proves in flavour and consistency. The only recipe poor cheese is good for is disaster: the result will be either insipid or plain nasty. Four ounces of a good cheese will do more for flavour and consistency than four pounds of an inferior one.

A harder cheese may grate well, but make sure it has not lost its savour. Do not buy more than you can use quickly and do not buy ready-grated cheese, which soon goes dull (if it is not so already).

Cooking cheese should also be of appropriate flavour for the dish. I do not advise using substitutes where classic recipes specify Gruyère or Parmesan, for instance. However, if the real thing is not available think again. You may do better by deliberately amending the flavour, using good, sweet old Cheddar. Beware particularly of cheese that looks like Parmesan but is second rate, immature Grano, or a substitute Parmesan from Argentina. Either of these can completely miss real Parmesan characteristics and so prove inferior to, but far more expensive than mature farm Cheddar. Genuine Parmesan carries the legend 'PARMIGIANO REGGIANO' repeated all round the cheese, so never pay Parmesan price for a bare-crusted or differently marked cheese. As always, taste first and judge by flavour. Strength, however, is not all; character is what matters most. The subtle delicacy of a sauce made with Cheshire can be a joy with fish, scallops, cauliflower, mushrooms and other dishes where the underlying flavour should never be overwhelmed by the sauce. Christian Plume wrote of Cheshire in *Le Livre du Fromage* that 'it is probably the only English cheese worthy of use in *grande cuisine*'.

When buying cheese for toasting you will save on quantity (and on mustard and other hotting-up ingredients) by keeping to full-flavoured cheese of good consistency. After all, whether it is called simply toasted cheese or Welsh Rarebit, it should taste more of cheese than of anything else. No amount of hotting-up will rescue cheap watery block or that abysmal white or bright pink soap which seems to have strayed from second-rate chemists on to many a so-called cheese counter. Traditional Cheddar, Leicester and Cheshire are all agreeable toasters, but Lancashire, for those who love her, is queen of them all.

For cheese straws, buy the strongest old Parmesan or good old Cheddar you can find, and do not stint on quantity. Nothing is sadder than the perfect-looking cheese straw which melts in the mouth and tastes of nothing.

Cheddar and Cheshire offer two equally rich centres for cheese omelettes, completely different in flavour and consistency.

14
Serving and Keeping Cheese

Selecting and arranging cheese for the table

Selection of cheese for a meal naturally depends on the number of guests and on what you know of their tastes and appetite. If you are serving an informal meal or a buffet where cheese is the bulk of the food, allow 4 ounces a head. Towards the end of a well-balanced and leisurely meal 2 ounces of cheese a head is normally an ample allowance. However, there are some enthusiasts whose appetite is rejuvenated by the sight and smell of good cheese; they (I should say 'we'; not surprisingly, I confess myself to be one of them) will compulsively nibble away as long as cheese stays on the table. This can upset calculations, so get to know your friends' addictions.

With this warning in mind, do not buy more cheese than will provide decently for your guests and leave a surplus which your household can eat in two or three days. The quantity thus calculated controls the number of different cheeses you can serve, because the pieces should be large enough to give the last to be served as much choice as the first and allow a second bite for all.

A limited choice of good, honest cheese in superb condition is better than a startling array of sorry bits. If there are only four people at table, three cheeses will do: say, a soft, a semi-soft and a hard, of which one may be a blue. However, should you have some particularly fine and delectable cheese to offer, such as soft summer Cotherstone, serve just the one small whole cheese in all its beauty. Never be diffident about serving British cheese to guests from abroad, provided you can buy good examples. If you can only get second-rate cheese do without and save your country's reputation and your own.

Whatever you do, avoid flavours which will clash with your chosen drink, or be unsuitable to follow the previous course. For instance, I recommend a 'sorbet' of a cheese to clean the palate after curry or other highly spiced or peppery dishes: Cotherstone, a fine farmhouse Cheshire (not fully mature and not blue), Caerphilly, Llangloffan, or a White Stilton. These cheeses have plenty of character but are young and refreshing in flavour and gentle in texture, rather than sharp and hard. They caress and soothe the palate, and set off any good wine, ale or cider. After a more neutral main course you can serve richer cheese. If the wine will take it you can serve strong cheese, and then have a sorbet type of pudding to follow.

Inspect the cheese you plan to eat within an hour of the meal for traces of hardening or discoloration. Surface mould can be scraped off with the blunt edge of a straight-bladed knife. If necessary, use a very sharp, clean-edge knife to trim a sliver off the surface as well. Remove superficial hardening in the same way.

Now arrange your cheeses. You need one or more boards, dishes or trays, allowing enough room for each cheese to keep the flavours and crumbs apart. A blue merits its own dish with a very keen fine knife, better not serrated. Serrated knives are unsuitable for any sticky or crumbly cheese, though ideal for the harder cheeses.

Do not have a board that is too large or too heavy to pass round the table. Flat basket-work trays are attractive for serving cheese, or you can lay it direct on straw or rush mats for a buffet, which dispenses with trays and dishes and shows off cheese admirably.

When cutting from a whole cheese, especially Stilton, take a horizontal slice, leaving the top surface as even as possible. Scooping or gouging messes up the interior and leaves a deep, rough wasteland of cheese to dry up near the crust. Shallow rings of cheese should be cut from the centre to the rind. Wedges should be cut lengthways from nose to crust. Always cut so as to take your full share of crust, and leave the next comer with a neat, attractive surface to cut from. Never cut across the nose of a wedge.

Follow your own inclination as to whether to eat crust or rind. Taste a small piece first to guide you, unless it appears powdery (probably from cheese mite) or soggy (probably from over-wrapping or refrigeration, but occasionally from a heatwave). Mite tastes a little like curry, and soggy crust is usually bitter. Cracked rind on an old cheese may be spoiled by one of the less palatable moulds, for example a black one which sometimes penetrates the crevices of old Derby.

Cheese for parties

With large numbers of cheeses it is of interest to label them, and perhaps group them geographically by regions of origin, or by types. For instance when I am laying out cheeses for a big party, I put Scottish, Durham and Yorkshire cheeses at the northern end of the table, Lancashire and Cheshire on the west, and Derby and Vale of Belvoir cheeses across from them. The rest I group round the southern end of the table.

With a smaller number I arrange them in alternating types and colours. If your cheeses have dates you can add these to the labels; if not, put on a guide to strength. This is important to ensure that guests eat them in the right order: mildest first, strongest last. It also avoids the devastation which occurs when people help themselves indiscriminately, and then leave on the plates good cheese which happens to prove too mild or too strong for their particular palates.

Make sure that there is plenty of space round the tables, so that guests can circulate freely without queuing or scrambling.

Use only unsalted butter; salt cuts across the flavour of a good cheese. Bread should be well crusted, and at least half of it should be granary or other good wholemeal. Rye bread is delicious, particularly with the lighter, younger cheese. Poppy-seed coated plaits complement stronger cheeses well. Always support a good local baker, and help him and avoid disappointment by ordering for a party a few days ahead. You need one French loaf or small loaf for every five people. Unless your bread is of a late baking, bought warm in the afternoon, restore the crust by placing the loaves in a very hot oven for a few minutes shortly before they are needed.

As guests arrive, encourage them to taste around, not just to tuck into their accustomed daily fare. Without this prompting, the unadventurous may sate themselves with one large chunk of one kind of cheese on one large hunk of bread: appropriate for a ploughman's lunch, but sad waste of a good party.

Where to keep cheese

Cheese needs a moderately humid atmosphere and, like wine, a temperature in the fifties Fahrenheit. This is easy for innkeepers, publicans and the fortunate minority of restaurateurs and householders with undisturbed cellars or old-fashioned larders. Unfortunately central heating plant has not only expelled wine and provisions from numerous cellars but destroyed the cool humidity of many an old larder. Modern premises frequently lack either of these civilised amenities.

Wine and provisions need a better resting place than a warm cupboard or a cold refrigerator. Refrigerators, as well as being too cold, are too airless for cheese. Like plastic boxes, and even old-fashioned covered cheese-dishes, they tend to make cheeses sweaty and stodgy and to spoil their flavours. (There is one gleam of hope for modern houses, however: in late 1979 Zanussi brought out a refrigerator with a new type of storage. Capacious not cramped, cool not cold, it is called 'the cellar compartment'. If this lives up to its name, staying generally towards 60°F and never dropping below 50°, it should do tolerably well for wine and cheese.)

So keep your cheese in the nearest thing to a cellar that you can find or devise. Cool garages and outhouses sometimes have a safe corner or a high shelf where you can put an airy wooden cupboard or a mesh-sided box of the old meat-safe type. Hanging is even better for circulation of air and for security against rodents. In winter you must guard against unkind cold, remembering that 40°F is the lowest temperature for cheese life and 50° is a healthier minimum. If you have to choose between too low a temperature and too high a one, be humane; cold kills.

Wrapping and handling cheese

The *cut* surfaces of the cheese only should be sealed with cling-film, foil or some other smooth, close-fitting material. The crust should not be sealed in, but allowed to breathe, or you will make your cheese as stodgy and dull as a prepack. If the atmosphere is rather dry or cold, or if flies are in season, add a loose outer wrap, which must be flyproof but never airtight. Muslin, a thin old tea cloth or greaseproof paper will give extra insulation against extremes of temperature, humidity or dryness without inhibiting the necessary breathing.

Unless the piece is so soft that it would collapse, rest the cheese on its longest cut surface. Soft cheeses, having to lie flat, need to have their cut surfaces kept in place by a separate wrap for each side, tucked in tightly, with generous overlap at the two outer corners. This overlap should be folded and tucked under in two stages to hold securely (like the corners at the foot of a hospital bed). The wrapping on the cut surfaces of a very soft cheese must be reinforced by strips of marble, or by pieces of wood held firmly in place by something heavy. The cut face of a half cheese, or one of the cut faces of less than half a cheese, can be pushed against the wall. An extremely volatile cheese will still need something weighty against its outer edge to prevent its spreading backwards.

Whole small cheeses can also be given greaseproof protection outside their own cheesecloth coat, just as Stiltons are sent out by their makers with a greaseproof wrap to guard the crust against cracking. Until they are cut whole cheeses should be turned twice a week in the house, or once a week at cellar temperature. This prevents one end from becoming moist and soggy, and the other from drying out, cracking internally and 'doming'. If doming does occur gently press the cheese down on the domed end to expel air and gas, and leave it that way down for a week or two until it appears to have firmed up again. The cheese will be crumbly in that quarter when you open it, but it will not have deteriorated seriously. It may not be tidy enough for the table, but it will be useful in the kitchen if used quickly.

When you open a whole cheese, peel down the cheesecloth only as deep as you propose to make the first cut, and remove the muslin cap on the exposed end. Only skin the whole cheese if you expect to use it quickly, as the cloth helps to keep the cheese moist and happy. Cut it in rings, the outer rings deep enough not to leave a disproportionate amount of crust to cheese. Before you put the part-cheese away, seal the cut surface, and then rest it face downwards on the sheet of greaseproof paper. Draw up the two ends of this sheet round the cheese and double-fold them together in a French seam over the top. Then fold in the sides, adding just enough Sellotape to hold them in place. You can normally use the same piece of greaseproof again, only replacing it when it is torn or worn, or if the cheese has cheese mite or unwelcome mould.

Cheese mite and natural blueing

Mite is a harmless but pervasive nuisance; its minuscule yet hungry multitude looks and smells like curry powder. Try to eliminate it by removing any affected cheese, mite and all, carefully from the shelf. Take it to a place out of doors where you have a lined bin into which you can drop the greaseproof and other wraps while holding on to the cheese. Knock and brush the cheese over the bin until no more powder flies off, then wrap it in fresh greaseproof paper. Do not put it back near other cheeses in the cellar or store, unless you have no alternative. In any case you must clean the shelf thoroughly, holding some impervious container below, to avoid spreading mite on to lower shelves or floor. You should nevertheless clean the nearby shelves and the floor as a precaution. Once you have detected a mite-infested cheese, keep it elsewhere, or at least low down and clear of other cheeses. Clean it and its surroundings regularly. Some old Stilton dairies used to regard mite as an essential feature in the crust of a good mature cheese, and their floors were carpeted with it.

Segregate blue cheeses, whose spores, less visible than mite, fly around seeking what innocent moist virgin cheese they can enter and devour. If the mould appears to be penetrating your White Wensleydale, Cheshire, Leicester, Double Gloucester, or any other attractive target, wrap the cheese up and leave it for a week or two: you may have a delectable bonus of natural blue. Even if you are not a blue cheese lover remember that mould is medically speaking benign and, as grocers used to say when more of them understood their provision trade, 'it's a poor cheese that attracts no mould'. You can experiment with a good mould naturally present in your cellar or outbuildings by pricking cheeses you would like to blue, so making it easier for the mould to penetrate. Pricks at one-inch intervals with a skewer, or other fine straight implement long enough to reach the middle of the cheese, should be enough to blue a good moist cheese. Leave it for at least a month (turning it weekly of course) before testing progress. Unwanted superficial mould should be scraped off crust and cut faces in the same way that mite is dealt with.

Keeping cheese for cooking

Excessively hardened cheese may be softened, at least enough to use for cooking, by wrapping and keeping it in cloth soaked with white wine.

Do not grate cheese in advance unless you can only rarely get good grating cheese, and wish to lay up store for barren weeks ahead. In the latter case apportion the grated cheese into bags, each containing enough for one occasion. Expel the air and seal and freeze the bags. Defrost cheese only a few hours before using it and always use it quickly once it has been defrosted. Always taste cheese again before you use it for cooking. If it has lost its savour do not use it.

The cheese iron

A cheese iron is an expensive but essential instrument for anyone buying whole cheeses where they are not ironed for you, and for anyone intending to mature whole cheeses. Ask your cheesemonger to order one for you. It is a metal scoop, like half a tube with cutting front and side edges and a transverse wooden handle. Insert it with a corkscrew action firmly into the side of the cheese, not too near either end. Withdraw it carefully with a slight twist, producing a cylindrical core of cheese. This you smell, and taste too, if the smell has not satisfied you. Then take a crumb to test the consistency, rubbing between thumb and forefinger. Remove as little as possible cheese from the core for the test, and leave the core on the iron. When you replace it in the cheese it must fill the hole or the cheese will deteriorate. With thumb or finger against the rind or crust end of the core, gently withdraw the iron and smooth over the wound, using any cheese on the surface to seal it up; put the cheesecloth back over the scar. The iron should show a film of fat when withdrawn. A dry iron is the sign of an underfat cheese.

Clean the iron thoroughly, immediately after use. Acid from the cheese can quickly spoil an iron by pitting the metal, and this in its turn spoils the clean flavour of future tastings.

15
For Restaurateurs and Caterers

The professional attitude towards cheese

The average British restaurant 'cheeseboard' is a disgrace. 'The cheeseboard' as a description sets my teeth on edge. For me it has too often proved a pretentious cloak for an untoothsome collection of sweaty Edam and other forms of indigestible refrigerated hardware. It is an ironically appropriate term for what is, indeed, often more like board than cheese. The constant miracle of a French meal, however good the earlier courses, is the pleasurable reawakening of hunger at the sight and smell of the cheese. Sadly, in Britain, the second greatest cheese country in the world, the cheese course often proves more an unappetising irritant than a pleasure to sample or behold. There are reasons for the contrast between French and British performance in this rich area of gastronomy; but let no British caterer try to fool himself with any excuses into viewing the contrast with anything but shame.

Most French and some of the best British restaurateurs offer at least one set menu including a cheese course. Regional menus are particularly amenable to enrichment by appropriate cheese. This practice establishes the rightful importance of cheese as an essential part of the complete meal, introduces it to some of the less experienced guests and makes sure that the cheeses turn over at a reasonable rate.

A distinguished cheese-loving restaurateur visiting a highly regarded rival was met near the door by 'three sad-looking cheeses on a trolley' and asked the proprietors why they did not offer a better selection. 'They replied that nobody ever ordered cheeses. Nor did I, having seen what was offered,' wrote my friend. 'In France I would opt for cheese in a restaurant as often as not; in England I would studiously avoid it. The biggest problem with cheese in most restaurants is simply poor quality. Secondly the choice is very limited, and everywhere the same: an English lump, a supermarket Camembert, often packed in little triangles, and a blue of some sort.' So it is no wonder that some caterers gain the impression that 'people do not want cheese'. Diners-out would not eat their sort of cheese as a penance, let alone pay for it as a pleasure.

There are honourable exceptions among the restaurateurs of Britain, a number of whom helped to keep my feet on the restaurant and kitchen floor while I was writing this. These believers in the importance of cheese include four who have earned *Good Food Guide* distinctions and are financially successful. Their backing should surely help me persuade their less-instructed and less-interested brethren that cheese is a good thing, a necessary thing, and, when properly chosen and cherished, a beautiful and a profitable thing.

Airlines

One of the murkiest areas of catering is that of airline food. Of fourteen airlines flying out of London whose food was reviewed in the 1980 Egon Ronay _Lucas Guide_, none had praiseworthy cheese, and I cannot myself remember ever eating anything in an aircraft meal which deserved even the name of cheese. Biscuits and cheese would make such an acceptable alternative to the unspeakable concoctions of tasteless flab usually cluttering up the little tray. The cheese should be good, plain English, cut from the whole cheese; the saving in cost would compensate for actually having to employ someone to cut up real food.

To the restaurateur

If your cheeses are well chosen they will bear their names and places of origin, which cannot but add to the character of the menu and the confidence of the customer; English farmhouse cheeses and many traditional English dairy cheeses also start life with their dates of birth on them. These are as useful and interesting to the keeper and eater of the cheeses as vintage dates are to the user of a wine list. If you do not handle whole cheeses ask your supplier before he skins his cheeses to note the dates on the cloth and the dairy or farm number, which will enable him to trace the origin. If you are in a cheesemaking region this will be of extra interest. Where cheeses are not identifiable by this means their origins can be discovered through the factor or the Marketing Board Depot which supplied him. A restaurateur pioneering in Northern Ireland wrote to me: 'We took the trouble to list our cheeses on the menu with a short description of where they came from and what we thought of them, and invited people to comment, thereby creating general interest.'

So, whenever possible, give the name, source and birthday of your cheese on the menu and alongside the cheeses themselves. Do not stick pointed markers into them: apart from being cruel this leaves unsightly wounds.

Experiment on yourself, not on your customers. Learn all you can from eating cheese at home and abroad, and encourage your staff to do the same. Books give background information and encourage exploration, but reading is no substitute for first-hand experience of how different makes of the same cheese vary, and how cheeses behave under different conditions and at different stages of ripening.

In a small establishment, or in any restaurant when you are starting off without any guidance on customers' tastes, keep the cheese good and simple. Some fine restaurants are content to serve a good Stilton and a mature farmhouse Cheddar. One soft, one semi-soft, one or two hard (British) cheeses, and perhaps a blue will certainly be enough until you have the demand and the experience to justify a change. Remember that cheese does not sell itself to the ignorant or the diffident, and that those who do not know about cheese cannot sell it to anybody. Choose cheeses you and your staff know and enjoy, and which you can be enthusiastic about when suggesting them to customers.

Cheeses should be ripe enough to offer distinctive textures and flavours, but not so sharp as to kill the wine and the dessert. Avoid coarse flavours, such as Danish Blue, but do not be afraid of a mellow blue, nor of a rich mature Cheddar. Good Cheddar often has a certain sweetness in its strength, and is the best cheese in the world to set off good wine of any kind.

Having studied the advice given in Chapter 13, find the nearest seller of traditional cheese or, if you are surrounded by a cheese desert, write to a shop which will send you good cheese. One notable restaurateur recommends visiting the chosen cheesemonger, even travelling a hundred miles to do so, 'and spending one or two hours talking and tasting'. You may find the right kind of shop, but not all the cheeses you want. The right shopkeeper will be able and willing to order them for you. Indeed one restaurant owner I know has stirred a neighbouring kitchen shop into starting a cheese counter, where Stilton and mature farmhouse Cheddar are available to his town in their proper state for the first time since block and prepack took over in the grocers' shops. If your needs are still small, it may be sensible to make your grocer's trouble more worth while by getting some friendly competitors in your trade to join with you in giving cheese orders.

'I always try to have a few "interesting" cheeses which our customers won't have encountered elsewhere,' says Paul Henderson of Gidleigh Park in Devon; but he insists on keeping his local traditional farmhouse Cheddar from Newton St Cyres. If you too live in a cheesemaking region, you should above all take pride in presenting your local cheeses. Failing a local shop where cheese is matured, find a farm or small dairy which matures and sells its own, and feature on your menu the fact that it comes direct from the maker.

When you have brought your cheese home follow the advice on storage in Chapter 14. In choosing cheeses for the day's menu, balance textures and flavours, having some thought for variety of colour (although this consideration must come last). Cheeses already open should look freshly cut when the guests first see them. 'Trim daily if necessary, and don't worry about waste' is another tip from Paul Henderson, who keeps up to twenty different cheeses at Gidleigh Park. Any old trimmings or substantial crumbs left over should be sent to the kitchen, as should any pieces no longer in prime condition; all these will be good for grating or toasting.

Cheese should have the same mark-up as any other raw material you are pricing as part of a dish. If you include cheese in *table d'hôte* meals (not just as an option) and still have waste you cannot usefully absorb in prepared dishes, consider whether the cause is too many kinds of cheese, poor or dull cheese, poor condition of the cheese or poor presentation and waiting, and act accordingly. In my twenty-eight years of selling cheese I have found that no real cheese lover regards a fine cheese as too expensive if it is in the right state and the right place at the right time.

———— 16 ————

For Shopkeepers

A good name for cheese will bring customers long distances whatever the cost, but a good name has to be earned with knowledge, skill and devotion. That is why I have left till last my address to shopkeepers. You should not start to make up your mind about cheese until you have read everything that has gone before.

Good cheese has been almost killed by lack of understanding and care among politicians, bureaucrats, dairymen and retailers. It can only be raised back to health by a professional, indeed a vocational, attitude in those who wish to put things to rights and make their living by doing so.

Since the 1960s the smaller grocer has had unenviable problems in reconciling public relations with the need to survive. Recently I congratulated a well-sited grocer of my acquaintance on his hard work and prosperous business. Far from thanking me he looked and sounded sour. His seven-day week of hard slogging achieves a volume of turnover his predecessor would have thought astronomical; but, sadly, much of this does not earn enough to meet its share of overheads. His battery of cold counters and deep freezes costs more to finance and maintain than the profit margin on the contents warrants.

My own solution owed nothing to business acumen. I just happened to loathe electrical appliances and love cheese. When I started in 1954 uninteresting cheese was 4 per cent of total turnover and tobacco (profit 5 per cent or so) was 20 per cent. Now tobacco is 1 per cent and cheese 75 per cent. As my happy exploration of the cheese market progressed in the 1950s I discarded my inherited New Zealand Cheddar, Danish Blue and Edam, replaced them with cheeses of character and learned how to mature traditional English cheeses. Within a few years I was being asked to cater for large parties and give lectures and demonstrations. This was timely compensation for the seepage of grocery trade caused by the advent of supermarkets and the increase in public mobility during the flourishing sixties.

Stocking and storing cheese

Any shopkeeper seriously interested in cheese should have tasted as many as possible in as many conditions as possible before starting to look after his customers' needs. Bear in mind the sizes of the different cheeses and what the surface can tell you. Graders' marks on clothbound farmhouse cheeses read 'Superfine' or 'Fine', on dairy cheeses 'Extra selected' or 'Selected'. Lower grade plain cheeses are not circulated, but second-grade Stiltons are unwisely let loose on the market with the sole provision that they must not be sold as Stilton. The Farmhouse English Cheese Publicity Office (Hesketh House, Portman Square, London W.1) has a list of farmhouse cheese factors most of whom handle all the traditional English dairy cheeses as well. Provide yourself with a cheese iron and explore possible factors until you find extensive, good-looking stock combined with a positive attitude towards your needs.

If you are assured of steady supplies of mature cheeses you need not keep a heavy stock yourself. However, traditional Cheddar is so scarce that you will do well to stock up. In any case your customers' views of maturity may not coincide with your factor's and you will probably need to keep your cheeses for a further three months or so to meet the demand for full flavour. Remember that Cheshires and Lancashires not bearing farm numbers are dairy cheeses and likely to be pasteurised, which delays their maturity and reduces their potential flavour.

Go gently into your stocking up until you get a clear indication of demand and of how much cheese you need to have maturing in store. Chapter 13 contains advice on storage. If you have no cellar, a north-facing room or outhouse is the next best store for your reserve cheeses. If the temperature is between 50 and 60°F and fairly even (or can be made so by insulation), do not invest vast sums in air-conditioning. Weight loss during storage is inevitable. A lower temperature and the optimum humidity reduce the rate of loss; but cold also slows the rate of maturing. To begin with keep records of cheese weights and dates as you receive them into store and note the weight loss and length of keeping when you put the mature cheese on sale. It is important to allow for this in your pricing. In optimum conditions Dr Davis expects a Lancashire to lose 10 per cent in its first three weeks (before it would normally reach you) and a further 5 per cent of its original weight between the ages of three weeks and three months (equal to $5\frac{1}{2}$ per cent of its three-week-old weight). Stilton will lose easily 15 per cent of its weight in two months. The harder cheeses evaporate more slowly, especially the larger ones, but a 9 lb truckle Cheddar may lose over 10 per cent in nine months.

If the flavour and consistency of the mature cheese is good, my own advice is to leave well alone and charge the right price. If you invest in expensive (and noisy) plant you may reduce weight loss, but this advantage can be wiped out by the cost, together with the need to keep the cheese longer or to sell it less mature at a lower price. If your cheeses are seriously drying out, however, you obviously need humidity control and possibly temperature control as well.

Your store should have slatted wooden shelving strong enough to carry half-hundredweight cheeses and deep enough to allow of their being turned with ease. Narrower, closer shelves for smaller cheeses may also be fitted in alcoves and odd corners, but keep flexible by having most shelves of the first kind: you can keep truckles two deep on the larger shelves, but you cannot put large cheeses on the smaller ones. It is prudent to partition off the blue cheeses, or put them in a separate store, so that their moulds are kept from undesirable exploration of more innocent cheese.

Most farmhouse and some dairy cheeses are dated, which makes it easy to keep them in order in the cellar, the oldest nearest the door. Arrange undated cheeses in their order of receipt, the dates of which you should attach to the side of the cheeses. My practice with Stilton is to iron every cheese as it comes in. I send back the over-salt, the under-fat, and also the chalkily immature, unless they show promise of fine flavour. Each acceptable cheese is then dated and given a character on its greaseproof coat (or box, for a small Stilton).

Clothbound cheeses need to be partially or wholly skinned before they are divided, but while the skin is still complete note any useful facts stamped on the cloth or wax, or on labels attached to the cheese. When you put part of a newly opened cheese on show be sure that its price label includes all these facts. Cheddars and Somerset-made Double Gloucesters from the farm have tie-on labels with dates of making and the vat numbers (the latter are only of significance if you need to complain about faulty cheese). If you buy through a factor and the cheeses are unmarked, ask him to trace the farm for you and give you at least the month of making. Farmhouse Cheshires and Lancashires have a number representing the farm (which you will find in the list of farms) and the date of making. Wensleydales and some Derbys are usually stamped on the side with the date and vat number (for instance, 0406,1 meaning 4 June, first vat) and the dairy number (now changing to initials). Regrettably, some dairies do not conform, and all you can do in such cases is to keep the cheeses in batches marked with your date of receipt and arrive at a suitable time of opening by ironing the oldest looking cheese of a batch when its turn comes. If it is not ready, put an estimate on the batch label of the date on which it will be worth ironing the cheese again. Too much ironing is damaging to cheese, so if maturing is going along smoothly only iron to satisfy a customer requiring a whole cheese, or to check after a gap in deliveries.

Cutting the cheese

Once the cheese has been skinned (or partially skinned, if a slow seller) by unrolling the bandage or splitting and peeling off the waxed cloth and then removing the caps, it is ready for cutting. For this you need 36-inch cheese wires with metal handles. The only satisfactory ones I have met are made and sold through the post by The Reynolds Patent Cheesecutters (32 Gloucester Road, Teddington, Middlesex) in sets of twelve and the handles in pairs. Have plenty of them and do not bother with shorter wires, which are no good for large cheeses. Hang them on rounded pegs, not on hooks or rails, and never handle them roughly or they will kink and cause inaccurate and untidy cheese cutting. Renew wires as soon as they start to look irregular.

Before using the wire on a cheese make sure the last threads of cheesecloth have been removed from the cutting area. Then make an incision on any hard-ringed cheese with a sharp, but not too fine knife, to help the wire to bite. The incision on a full-size Cheddar needs to be up to 10 inches across. It is also wise to make cuts in Stilton, Blue Wensleydale, Blue Cheshire and any other cheese with a crust firmer than its interior, otherwise the first pull may buckle the cheese before the wire penetrates the crust, spoiling its interior. Having made the incision, ease the middle of the wire into it. Draw the ends round the cheese, hold both handles together in the master hand with the wires between the middle fingers, place the thumb of the other hand where the wire should come through on the near side of the cheese, and pull firmly. Keep that thumb in place until it stops the wire and then steadies its withdrawal. This prevents the wire from kinking and from cutting your hand between thumb and first finger.

Lancashire should be skinned whole too, very gently, or you will lose a lot through crumbling. When you have cut the top third with the wire slide it delicately on to a board, or direct on to the counter, and do all further cutting with a fine sharp knife. Use the same technique for any other exceptionally fragile, crumbly cheese.

Other large cheeses, such as Cheshires, Leicesters and Derbys, can be partially skinned to the depth at which you want to cut for the counter. The cut face on the reserve part should be sealed, but not the crust. If the paper you use does not cling well, lard the cut surface lightly before pressing on the wrap. The spare skin can be folded across this sealed face to give extra insulation against too dry an atmosphere or too extreme a temperature and protection against mould penetration. This must be very neatly done, because the cheese is now turned to rest on the cut face and needs a smooth, steady base.

Cheese and the customer

Tasting is a pleasing and practical ritual and should always be encouraged, for it saves the customer from wasting money on cheese which disappoints, and saves the shopkeeper from the consequences of such disappointment. You are seldom faced with disgruntled faces and unsaleable returns, nor are you likely to suffer that damage which you can do nothing to repair because it is inflicted by the public grumbles of dissatisfied customers out of sight or hearing.

Not all shoppers are clearheaded and decisive. Some are too nervous or too dull of palate to register a first taste, others are too diffident to say what they think. Watch the customer's face during the tasting, and, if you sense doubt rather than joy, either give a second, more generous taste or offer another cheese. The tasting should never be skimped, let alone skipped.

Envoi

In earlier chapters I have recorded evidence of growing demand for more natural and more interesting food. Brewers' company reports continue to be cheerful from real ale producers but gloomy from those who brew the beer equivalent of block cheese. The latest government figures reveal continued demand for brown, whole-wheat and wholemeal bread. Christopher Nelson of Express Dairies has spoken of equivalent revulsion against 'soap' in the cheese trade. Bernard Dove of Booker McConnell has told the Wholesale Grocers' Federation that people are buying more semi-prepared meals and more interesting food, whether they eat out or at home. He thinks public houses, restaurants and industrial canteens will benefit from offering more variety and higher standards.

In March 1981 the eminent management consultants, Halliday Associates, severely criticised the food trade for ignoring the general change to more sophisticated tastes. They deplored 'bleak and unimaginative' packaged food displays, when customers should be being coaxed by 'the appetising appeal of foods' to try 'new, more varied and better-tasting menus'. No class of food could benefit more than cheese from this change in attitude. The Milk Marketing Boards and the multiples should ask themselves why, with traditional British cheeses so rare that they are not even quoted on the weekly provision trade price-list, stocks consisting almost entirely of block stood at 117,337 tons on 31 December 1981, a rise of nearly 15 per cent since January 1980.

All these authoritative statements and figures confirm the economic good sense of my views on the future of British cheese. There should be energetic encouragement, instead of the Boards' perverse discouragement, for high-quality traditional cheesemaking on our farms. Indeed, there should be more encouragement for all kinds of premium-standard agricultural products, especially on smaller farms. This is the sort of agriculture which has already made many small farms economic without subsidy and without adding to Europe's farm surpluses. This is the sort of production to whet British and foreign appetites and reduce still further our dependence on imported food.

The United Kingdom Provision Trade Federation, with a membership of over 400, includes almost all importers and distributors of provisions. The Federation pointed out in March 1981 that European Economic Community farm pricing policy overpays industrial-scale enterprise and under-rewards traditional farmers. They suggested pricing at industrial-scale levels, and compensating the traditional farmer openly, with due precautions against dumping, by subsidies. If the Federation and the Milk Marketing Board paid more attention to the growing demand for higher quality food, which the small traditional farmer is best equipped to meet, at least some of this need for subsidy could be eliminated.

There is another aspect of traditional farming, moreover, of separate but equal importance to the country: the conservation of Britain's most priceless national asset, a countryside worth living in, which attracts visitors from all over the world for our biggest foreign currency earner, tourism. The aesthetic, ecological and economic benefit to the whole community of non-industrial farming deserves a reward for conscientious maintenance of the landscape, which should never be confused with agricultural or food subsidies. In the earlier days of the European Economic Community this conservation role of small-scale and marginal-land farming was a recognised and declared factor in moulding European agricultural policy. It is urgent that it should be so considered once more, before sad dereliction of the landscape in marginal farming areas and sheer destruction of it in the more profitable regions make town or desert dwellers of us all. Lack of constructive policy now can destroy in a few reckless years all that remains of the beauty built up by centuries of conscience, care and love.

Let Sir George Stapledon have the last word: 'The spirit of a country, if it is to be true to itself, needs continually to draw great breaths of inspiration from the simple realities of the country; from the smell of its soil, the pattern of its fields, the beauty of its scenery and from the men and women who dwell and toil in the rural areas.'

Glossary

Abomasum   Fourth, true stomach of the ruminant (q.v.).

Annatto   Natural vegetable colouring for cheese.

Ash   Mineral constituents of milk.

Bulk milk   Milk from numerous farms collected in one tanker for delivery to dairy or creamery.

Buttermilk   What is left after cream has been churned into butter.

Carotene   Yellow to red pigment from vegetation converted through the liver into Vitamin A. Fat soluble, natural colorant.

Casein   Milk's chief and particular protein, precipitated in cheesemaking by acid development and by rennin enzyme, becoming curd.

Chesset   Old word for mould or hoop.

Coagulation   Casein's insoluble curd state (see above) caused by acid and enzyme precipitation of other protein in milk to form curd through heat.

Colostrum   First milk for new-born calf, unsuitable for cheese.

Enzymes   Part of make-up of living cells, causing chemical change when associated with particular substances (e.g. rennin enzyme causing coagulation of casein protein in milk).

Esters   Fatty acids and glycerides in plants. Aromatic esters give aroma and flavour.

Follower   Circular wooden or metal piece used to fit closely in the hoop or mould over the curd before the cheese is pressed.

Globules   Form in which fat is present in milk, varying in size with breed of animal.

Globulin   Some of the albuminous proteins present in plants and in animals (including their milk).

Green   I have only used this of mould or vegetable colouring of cheese, but it is also applied to young cheese.

Hoop   Cylindrical open-ended cheese mould.

Hoven   Split or blown by gas from unsolicited fermentation.

Hydrolysis   Decomposition by dissolution of a substance with water.

Lactation   Milk production, often used of the period covered by a cow's milk season from calving to drying out.

Lactic acid   Formed from the bacterial action on lactose in milk. Within three months the natural acidity of the cheese will paradoxically have killed off the remaining bacteria, leaving the enzymes to continue the ripening (q.v.).

Legumes   Class of plants including lucerne and the clovers, particularly valuable for their fixing of nitrogen in the soil.

Mastitis   Infection of udders which changes the make-up of milk, rendering it unsuitable for cheesemaking.

Meal   Old term for a single milking.

Milking   The yield of the cow at morning or evening.

Mould   1. The shape of the cheese into which the milled curd is packed after salting (usually now called a hoop when open-ended, a mould when end is fixed; formerly vat or chesset). 2. The source of blueing (or green fade in Cheshire); common natural coat acquired by cheese during ripening.

Pasteurisation   Heat treatment to destroy harmful micro-organisms in milk, which also destroys many flavour-enriching micro-organisms.

Pepsin   Digestive enzyme present in rennet which breaks down milk protein in acid state into peptones.

Pitching   Settling of curd at the bottom of the vat.

Pricking   Needling of a cheese to facilitate the entry and development of mould spores.

Processed cheese   Cheese (usually broken or substandard) virtually cooked and melted down, and moulded and packed while still hot.

Proteolysis   Breakdown of proteins by enzymes, acids, alkalis or heat.

Raw   Term used of milk, in its natural state, not subjected to heat treatment.

Rennet   The distilled extract of the

abomasum (q.v.) containing enzymes which break down the solids in milk into digestible form, helping coagulation.

Rennin The main coagulating agent in rennet; an enzyme.

Rhizome Plant stem under soil.

Ripening 1. (of milk): natural maturing of milk through rising acidity before renneting, without addition of starter (q.v.). 2. (of cheese): continuing enzyme action of rennet and completion of bacterial action on curd, and consequent enzyme action.

Rumen The outer part of the ruminant animal's digestive system which filters the product of its food, expelling some elements before they can enter the main system.

Ruminant Animal chewing the cud of the herbage or other fodder it eats.

Scalding The heating of the curd during cheesemaking to make it contract and expel more whey.

Serum In dairying, the residue of the milk (the whey) after most of the solids, including the fats, have been coagulated into the curd.

Silage Preservation of grasses and legumes by air-free storage, with limited fermentation.

Sinker Old word for follower (q.v.).

Spore The seed of mould which is airborne, particularly in moist conditions.

Starter Lactic bacterial culture used to start transformation of solids in milk to cheese.

Tub *See* Vat.

Turning The turning over of cheeses during ripening to ensure that moisture remains evenly distributed.

Vat Container in which the milk is put for cheesemaking (formerly, and still in the Dales, called a tub). The word vat was formerly used for the mould, hoop or chesset which shapes the cheese.

Vell The skin of the abomasum from which rennet (q.v.) is distilled.

Whey *See* Serum.

Select Bibliography

The following are some of the works I have referred to in the course of writing this book. There is an additional list of sources on p. 121.

British Goat Society, *Dairy Work for Goatkeepers*, revised ed. (1981).

Burdett, Osbert, *Book of Cheese* (Gerald Howe, 1935).

Campbell, Susan (ed.), *Guide to Good Food Shops*, 2nd ed. (Macmillan, 1981).

Cheke, Val, *The Story of Cheesemaking in Britain* (Routledge and Kegan Paul, 1959).

—— and A. Sheppard, *Butter and Cheesemaking*, revised ed. (Alpha Books, 1980).

Davis, John Gilbert, *Cheese*, 4 vols (Churchill Livingstone, 1965–76).

Defoe, Daniel, *Tour Through the Whole Island of Great Britain* (1724–6).

Hartley, Marie and Joan Ingilby, *Life and Tradition in the Yorkshire Dales* (Dent, 1968).

Manning, Donald J., 'Cheddar Cheese Flavour Studies', 1 and 11, *Journal of Dairy Research* 45 (1978) 479; 46 (1979) 523.

—— with Heather Robinson, 'The Analysis of Volatile Substances Associated with Cheddar Cheese Aroma', *JDR* 40 (1973) 63.

—— with Helen Chapman and Zena Hosking, 'The Production of Sulphur Compounds in Cheddar Cheese', *JDR* 43 (1976) 313.

—— with J. C. Price, 'Cheddar Cheese Aroma', *JDR* 44 (1977) 357.

—— with Carolyn Moore, 'Headspace Analysis of Hard Cheese', *JDR* 46 (1979) 539.

Marshall, William, *Rural Economy of Gloucestershire* (1796).

—— *Review and Abstract of the County Reports of 1809*, vol. 1.

Mason, Kate, 'Yorkshire Cheesemaking', *Folk Life* 6 (1968) 7.

Morris, Christopher (ed.), *The Journeys of Celia Fiennes* (Cresset, 1947).

National Institute for Research in Dairying, Biennial Reviews 1972, 1974 (University of Reading).

Plume, Christian, *Le Livre du Fromage* (Flammarion, 1968).

Raymond, Frank, 'Grassland Research', in Agricultural Research Council's Jubilee Publication (1981).

Reiter, Fryer, Sharpe and Lawrence, 'Symposium on the Microbiology of Desirable Food Flavours, Studies on Cheddar', *Journal of Applied Bacteriology* 29, no. 2 (1966).

Scott, R., *Cheesemaking Practice* (Applied Science, 1981).

Stout, Adam, *The Old Gloucester* (Alan Sutton, 1980).

Note: The Gloucester Library, Brunswick Road, Gloucester, has a particularly good collection of leaflets and articles on cheesemaking from earliest times.

The City of Edinburgh Central Library, George IV Bridge, has the valuable First Statistical Account of Scotland, prepared in the 1790s.

Useful Addresses

Shops

The following shops were selling at least some British traditional cheese or local farm cheese in 1981.

England

ALFRISTON, East Sussex: The Village Store, Waterloo Square

ALTRINCHAM, Cheshire: The Cheesery, 1 Regent Road

ANDOVER, Hampshire: Shaw and Son, 9 High Street

BARNARD CASTLE, Co. Durham: Eggleston Hall, Romaldkirk; W. Kidd (Butcher), 13 Market Street; Morrell's, Galgate; P. A. and D. O'Brien, Galgate; Partners, Horsemarket; V.G. Stores, near church

BATH, Avon: Cater, Stoffell and Fortt, 23 High Street; Harvest Wholefoods, 9 New Bond Street and 37 Belvedere; The Butter Pat, Upper Burgh Walls

BERKHAMSTED, Hertfordshire: L. Cook (Butcher), Northchurch

BINGHAM, Nottinghamshire: The Cheese Shop, 14 Market Street

BOVEY TRACEY, Devon: W. Mann and Sons, 43 Fore Street

BRIDGE, Kent: Golds, 73 High Street

BRIGHTON, East Sussex: The Cheese Shop, 17 Kensington Gardens

BROCKENHURST, Hampshire: Purkess, 31 Brookley Road

BUNGAY, Suffolk: M. Ramm, 29 Earsham Street

BURY, Lancashire: Market (daily), Mrs M. Smith

BUSHEY HEATH, Hertfordshire: L. J. Cook (Butcher), 14 High Road

CASTLE CARY, Somerset: Castle Cary Dairy Products, High Street

CHESTER: E. Ruscoe, 131 Christleton Road

CHEWTON MENDIP, Somerset: Chewton Cheese Dairy, Priory Farm

CHICHESTER, West Sussex: Say Cheese, East Street Arcade

CHORLEYWOOD, Hertfordshire: La Source, 9 New Parade

CIRENCESTER, Gloucestershire: Market (Monday, Friday), Charles Martell

COTHERSTONE, Co. Durham: Post Office Stores

COWES, Isle of Wight: Curds and Whey, Dottens Farm, Baring Way

CRANLEIGH, Surrey: Tyler and Co., High Street

DARLINGTON, Co. Durham: G. Wildsmith, 12 Skinnergate; Market (daily), David Wilson

DULVERTON, Somerset: Dulverton Fruit and Vegetables, 1 Fore Street

EXETER, Devon: Waites, Cathedral Close

FARNLEY, West Yorkshire: Farnley Shop, The Square
FELIXSTOWE, Suffolk: E. E. Burt, 64 Hamilton Road
FLEET, Hampshire: Mr Woodman, 150-156 Aldershot Road
FOREST ROW, East Sussex: Redmile-Gordon, The Square
FROME, Somerset: J. Harding (Spar), Vallis Way; Lawrence Waite, Palmer Street
GLASTONBURY, Somerset: Mulberry Farm Dairy Sales, West Pennard
GLOUCESTER: Cattle Market (Saturday), Charles Martell
GODALMING, Surrey: De Courcy's, 44 High Street; Sayers, Brighton Road
GUILDFORD, Surrey: Loseley House Farm Shop
HARTPURY, Gloucestershire: St George's Bakery
HAYWARDS HEATH, West Sussex: Clough and Sons, 27-31 Surte Avenue, Lindfield
HEADINGTON, Oxford: Nason's, 3 Osler Road
HEMEL HEMPSTEAD, Hertfordshire: R. Bird, The Marlows
HENLEY-ON-THAMES, Oxfordshire: Jennings, 3 Reading Road; Le Gourmet, 3 Market Place
HEREFORD: Fodder, 27 Church Street
HOLMES CHAPEL, Cheshire: M. G. Williams and Son, Cambrian Stores
HOLT, Norfolk: Meadow Dairies, 37 Bull Street
HUNGERFORD, Berkshire: E. P. Spackman, 25 High Street
ILKLEY, West Yorkshire: T. A. and G. Wood, 52 Cleasby Road, Menston
LAUNCESTON, Cornwall: Folley and Sons, Castle Stores, High Street
LEDBURY, Herefordshire: Market (Saturday), Charles Martell; Oaklands Country Kitchen, Lower Eggleton
LEICESTER: Market (daily), Burroughs
LEISTON, Suffolk: Baker Bros, 3-5 High Street
LEWES, East Sussex: Middle Farm Shop, Firle
LEYBURN, North Yorkshire: Market (Friday), The Cheese Man (D. Morrison)

LONDON: *See end of list*
LYME REGIS, Dorset: The Little Dairy, 4 Broad Street
MARKET HARBOROUGH, Leicestershire: The Cheese Shop, 17 Church Street
MATLOCK, Derbyshire: The Coach House, Lea
NAILSWORTH, Gloucestershire: William's Kitchen, 3 Fountain Street
NANTWICH, Cheshire: A. T. Welch, 45 Hospital Street
NEWPORT, Isle of Wight: The Cheeseboard, 88 Pyle Street
NEWCASTLE UPON TYNE: Grainger Market (daily), J. H. Matthews
NORTHALLERTON, North Yorkshire: Lewis and Cooper, Market Place
NORWICH: The Mousetrap, 2 St Gregorys Alley
OAKHAM, Leicestershire: Murray's (Butcher), 26 Melton Road
OSWESTRY, Shropshire: R. W. Gilham, 27 Church Street
OTFORD, Kent: Annie's Delicatessen, 6 High Street
OULTON BROAD, Norfolk: The Cheese Shop, 74 Beccles Road
OXFORD: Palms, 84 Covered Market
PENRITH, Cumbria: Cumbrian Kitchen, 11 Market Square
PILSLEY, Derbyshire: Chatsworth Estate Shop, Stud Farm
READING, Berkshire: County Delicacies, 14 King's Road
RINGWOOD, Hampshire: G. H. Atyeo and Partners, Farm Shop, Three Legged Cross
SEDLESCOMBE, East Sussex: Burspin's, Great Buckhurst Farm
SHEFFIELD: Reginald Bush, 495 Glossop Road, Broom Hill; General Stores, 569 Abbeydale Road
SHERBORNE, Dorset: Mould and Edwards, 19 Cheap Street
SIDMOUTH, Devon: Trumps, Fore Street
STAINDROP, Co. Durham: V.G.Stores
STREATLEY-ON-THAMES, Berkshire: Wells Stores
TADLEY, Hampshire: Safeway Food Store, Bishopswood Road

TAVISTOCK, Devon: N. H. Creber,
48 Brooke Street
TIVERTON, Devon: Wychware,
Newport Street
TORQUAY, Devon: Crabb's of
Wellswood
TOTNES, Devon: Dartington Farm
Foods, Cider Press Centre, Shinners
Bridge
TRURO, Cornwall: The Real Ale and
Cheese Shop, 9 New Bridge Street
WHALLEY, Lancashire: J. G. and S. A.
Farnsworth, 103a King Street
WHITCHURCH, Shropshire: Alkington
Cheese Supplies, 10 Chester Avenue

London

E.4.: C. Chasney, 134-138 Station Road,
Chingford
E.C.3.: Leadenhall Market (Monday to
Friday), Mr Marsh
N.W.3.: Cavaciuti Delicatessen, 23 South
End Road; Rosslyn Delicatessen,
56 Rosslyn Hill
S.W.1.: Justin de Blank, 42 Elizabeth
Street and 136 Brompton Road; Harrods
Food Hall, Knightsbridge; Paxton and
Whitfield, 93 Jermyn Street
S.W.1.: The Common Wine,
14 Bellevue Road
W.1.: Fortnum and Mason, 181
Piccadilly; Fratelli Camisa, 1a Berwick
Street; Justin de Blank, 54 Duke Street;
Selfridges, Oxford Street; Wholefood,
112 Baker Street
W.11.: Mr Christian's, 11 Elgin Crescent;
Stout's, 144 Portobello Road
W.C.1: Wheeler's, 59 Red Lion Street
W.C.2.: Mace and Potts (Daly's Wine
Bar), 210 The Strand; Neal's Yard Dairy,
Covent Garden

Scotland

ABERDEEN: Farmhouse, 11 Chapel
Street
COMRIE, Tayside: Comrie Cheese Shop
(Minty), Drummond Street
CUMNOCK, Strathclyde: Stevenson's
Bakery (own dairy cheese products)
DALBEATTIE, Dumfries and
Galloway: Hodgson's Home Bakery and
Grocery

EDINBURGH: Valvona and Crolla,
19 Elm Row; Victor Hugo, 26-27 Melville
Terrace
HAWICK, Borders: Easter Weens
Enterprises, Bonchester Bridge
INVERNESS: Tarragon, 75 Castle
Street
KIRKCALDY, Fife: Fife Creamery,
Randolph Place (wholesale only)
NAIRN, Highlands: Rose Brothers and
Co., 24-30 High Street
PENICUIK. Lothian: Marwick,
Langskaill, Howgate
ST ANDREWS, Fife: Geddes,
100 Market Street
TAIN, Highland: The Cheese Shop,
17 Market Street
WESTFIELDS OF RATTRAY,
Tayside: The Swiss Cheese Shop,
Westfields Post Office

Wholesalers

The following are known to me as
suppliers of traditional English cheese to
the trade:
John Adamson and Son, 25 Short Street,
London S.E.1, tel. 01-928 6108/9
C. Chasney, 134-138 Station Road,
London E.4, tel. 01-329 1310, 8204
County Delicacies, 14 King's Road,
Reading, tel. Reading (0734) 54653
Eggleston Hall, Barnard Castle, Co.
Durham, tel. Teesdale (0833) 50378
Longman's Farmhouse Fare, North
Leaze Farm, North Cadbury, Somerset,
tel. North Cadbury (0963) 40285
Auguste Noel, 37 Britton Street, London
E.C.1, tel. 01-253 4893, 5011
A. Rowcliffe and Son, 4c Tyrrell Road,
London S.E.22, tel. 01-693 1529, 7896

The Milk Marketing Board

In April 1981 the Product Marketing
Section of the MMB was hived off to
operate under the name of Dairy Crest.
This has long been the trade name for
dairy products of the Board's creameries.
It will now be the title of an organisation
with a separate board, controlling
production and sales of creamery
products, and sales of butter and cheese
from farms operating under the Board's

scheme. The Board's four depots will continue to distribute to factors and wholesalers, and to retail provision merchants giving fairly large orders.

The depots are:
CRUMP WAY, Glastonbury Road, Wells, Somerset, tel. Wells (0749) 78755
EMBERTON BROTHERS, Weston Road, Crewe, Cheshire, tel. Crewe (0270) 582331
WHITELOCK'S, 24 Tynedale Street, Stockton-on-Tees, Cleveland, tel. Stockton-on-Tees (0642) 64120
WENSLEYDALE CREAMERIES, Gayle Lane, Hawes, North Yorkshire, tel. Hawes (096 97) 286

Note: There is a Freephone service for shopkeepers wanting advice on sources of supply (Freephone no. 2376). For publicity and point of sale material write to The National Dairy Council, 5 John Princes Street, London W.1.

Goat societies

The British Goat Society (Secretary Mrs S. May): Rougham, Bury St Edmunds, Suffolk IP30 9LJ, tel. Beyton (0359) 70351; British Goat Society Journal (Hon. Editor Miss E. Rockford): Green End House, Little Staughton, Bedford MK44 2BS
The National Dairy Goat Produce Association, Golden Grove, Llysty, Bishops Castle, Shropshire, tel. Linley (058 861) 323

Farms with dairy flocks

The farms listed below milk ewes for cheesemaking or keep potential dairy flocks. Those actually making cheese are marked with an asterisk

*BEENLEIGH MANOR FARM, Harbertonford, Totnes, Devon, tel. Harbertonford (080 423) 361
Robin Congdon   _East Frieslands_
GREEN COTTAGE, Newnham, Daventry, Northamptonshire, tel. Daventry (032 72) 4221
Joy Williams   _Dorset Horn (with Friesland ram planned)_
*HARTSLOCK FARM, Whitchurch,

Oxfordshire, tel. Pangbourne (073 57) 2254
Julian George   _Frieslands_
Julian George is moving to North Hoggs Park Farm, near Holsworthy, North Devon, in 1982 and hopes to be making ewes' milk cheese there by spring 1983
HOME FARM, Newton House, Newton St Cyres, Devon, tel. Newton St Cyres (039 285) 222
The Quicke family and partners; J. W. Endicott manages the sheep   _Friesland/ Dorset cross_
SHARPHAM FARM, Ashprington, Totnes, Devon, tel. Harbertonford (080 423) 216
Maurice Ash; Garth Bromley (manager)   _Mules and Border Leicesters_
*SLEIGHT FARM, Timsbury, Avon, tel. Timsbury (0761) 70620
Mary Holbrook   _Dorset Horns_
*VOCOT, Bigwood, Battle, Sussex, tel. Battle (042 46) 3827
Sarah Warren   _East Frieslands_
*WIELD WOOD FARM, Alresford, Hampshire, tel. Alton (0420) 63151
Olivia Mills   _Frieslands_
*WINDERMERE FARM, Annan, Dumfriesshire, tel. Annan (046 12) 4691
Michael and Carol Neilson   _Frieslands_

For cheesemakers

Training
The Agricultural Development Advisory Service, Great Westminster House, Horseferry Road, London S.W.1, has local officers who can advise and help you to sell your dairy products legally.
The Agricultural College, Cannington, Somerset, runs a valuable cheesemaking course.
Mrs May Priestlands, Claygate, near Marden, Kent, lectures, demonstrates, gives tuition and one-day courses (she is particularly noted for goat cheese).

Equipment
W. H. Boddington and Co. Ltd, Horsmonden, Kent (cheese moulds)
Clares Carlton Ltd, Townhall Buildings, Wells, Somerset (large-scale equipment, clothing and cleaning gear)
Dartington Cider Press Centre, Shinners

Bridge, Totnes, Devon (small-scale equipment, including moulds made to order)
Hansens (Chr) Laboratory Ltd, 476 Basingstoke Road, Reading, and Thornbury Trading Estate, Gloucester (rennet, colouring and starters)
P. D. R. Hutchings, The Hollies, Weston-under-Redcastle, Shrewsbury, Shropshire (cheese moulds made to order and repaired)
Mrs David Hutchinson Smith, Hinton Bank, Whitchurch, Shropshire, is a pioneer in blue cheesemaking and accompanying equipment
Samuel Jackson, Sandbach, Cheshire (presses and pneumatic prickers)
Landkey-Newland, Seven Brethren

Bank, Barnstaple, Devon (small-scale dairy machines)
Pourprix, éts, 15 rue de Gerland, 69007 Lyon, France (wide range of moulds, including goat cheese)
Self-Sufficiency and Smallholding Supplies, The Old Palace, Wells, Somerset
Silkeborg Ltd, 225 Walton Summit Centre, Bamber Bridge, Preston, Lancashire (perforated moulds)
Smallscale Supplies, Widdington, Saffron Walden, Essex (draining mats, etc.)
R. and G. Wheeler, Hoppins, Dunchideock, Exeter, Devon (small wooden cheese presses and stainless steel moulds; rennet, starter, thermometers, etc.)

Index of Cheeses and Cheesemaking

Names of cheeses are in *italics*